COMPUTING
FOR LOWER SECONDARY

Margaret Debbadi
Siobhan Matthewson
Series editor:
Peter Marshman

International COMPUTING
FOR LOWER SECONDARY

STAGE 7

COMPUTER SCIENCE

DIGITAL LITERACY

INFORMATION TECHNOLOGY

HODDER EDUCATION
AN HACHETTE UK COMPANY

The Publishers would like to thank the following for permission to reproduce copyright material.

Photo credits

p.4 *l* © antoniodiaz/Shutterstock, *rt* © nd3000/Shutterstock, *rc* © BEST-BACKGROUNDS/Shutterstock, *rb* © Besjunior/Shutterstock; **p.8** *t* © Carballo/stock.adobe.com, **p.9** *tl* © Annawin/stock.adobe.com, *tr* © Thananit/stock.adobe.com, *b* © Kekyalyaynen/stock.adobe.com; **p.10** *t* © Tierney/stock.adobe.com, *c* © Sementsova321/stock.adobe.com, *b* © Ingo Bartussek/stock.adobe.com; **p.12** © Kinwun/stock.adobe.com; **p.13** © Nirutft/stock.adobe.com; **p.14** © Jane Kelly/Shutterstock.com; **p.16** *t* © Susan sheldon/Alamy Stock Photo, *c* © Fizkes/stock.adobe.com, *b* © TheVisualsYouNeed/stock.adobe.com; **p.17** © Lalalululala/stock.adobe.com; **p.18** *t* © Leungchopan/stock.adobe.com, *tc* © Mrgarry/stock.adobe.com, *c* © Okinawakasawa/stock.adobe.com, *cb* © Belekekin/Shutterstock.com, *b* © Beeboys/stock.adobe.com; **p.19** © Dario Lo Presti/stock.adobe.com; **p.22** *t* © DragonImages/stock.adobe.com, *c* © DragonImages/stock.adobe.com, *b* © Zhu difeng/stock.adobe.com, *b* © Kaspars Grinvalds/stock.adobe.com; **p.23** *t* © Chesky/stock.adobe.com, *c* © Harry Scott/Redferns/Getty Images, *b* © Khaligo/stock.adobe.com; **p.25** *t* © Arfa Griffiths/West Ham United FC/Getty Images, *b* © Mark Lennihan/AP/Shutterstock; **p.26** © Monopoly919/stock.adobe.com; **p.27** *t* © Hanoi Photography/stock.adobe.com, *b* © ITAR-TASS News Agency/Alamy Stock Photo; **p.28** © Kirill Nikitin/Alamy Stock Photo; **p.32** © Nuamfolio/stock.adobe.com; **p.33** © Sorapop/stock.adobe.com; **p.40** © Ra2 studio/stock.adobe.com; **p.52** © Artinspiring/stock.adobe.com; **p.55** *t* © V.R.Murralinath/stock.adobe.com, *c* © Pixdeluxe/E+/Getty Images, *b* © Stígur Már Karlsson/Heimsmyndir/E+/Getty Images; **p.56** © Terovesalainen/stock.adobe.com; **p.58** © Antonioguillem/stock.adobe.com; **p.65** *t* © Pixel-Shot/stock.adobe.com, *b* © GaudiLab/stock.adobe.com; **p.66** © Nils Jorgensen/Shutterstock; **p.71** © Kampwit/stock.adobe.com; **p.74** *tr* © Soponyono/stock.adobe.com, *bc* © Arif/stock.adobe.com, *tl* © Elizaliv/stock.adobe.com, *bl* © Matkovci/stock.adobe.com, *tc* © Adisa/stock.adobe.com, *br* © Rawpixel.com/stock.adobe.com; **p.75** © Hor/stock.adobe.com; **p.83** © WavebreakMediaMicro/stock.adobe.com; **p.85** © Monkey Business/stock.adobe.com; **p.86** © WavebreakMediaMicro/stock.adobe.com; **p.88** *l* © Shutterstock / Yeko Photo Studio, *r* © Rabbit75_fot/stock.adobe.com; **p.89** *t* © Highwaystarz/stock.adobe.com, *b* © Silverkblack/stock.adobe.com; **p.98** © The History Collection/Alamy Stock Photo; **p.100** © DragonImages/stock.adobe.com; **p.111** © Zephyr_p/stock.adobe.com; **p.113** © Cegli/stock.adobe.com; **p.114** © Fizkes/stock.adobe.com; **p.116** *t* © Busakorn Pongparnit/Moment/Getty Images, *c* © Oneinchpunch/stock.adobe.com, *b* © Alex Segre/Alamy Stock Photo; **p.117** © PR Image Factory/stock.adobe.com; **p.118** © Adiruch na chiangmai/stock.adobe.com; **p.120** © Daniel Ernst/stock.adobe.com; **p.128** © FSEID/stock.adobe.com; **p.134** © Chokniti/stock.adobe.com; **p.136** © Rawpixel.com/stock.adobe.com; **p.140** © Burak/stock.adobe.com; **p.148** © motortion/stock.adobe.com; **p.149** © SDI Productions/E+/Getty Images; **p.166** © Metamorworks/stock.adobe.com; **p.167** © Isaiah Love/stock.adobe.com; **p.168** *t* © Tal Revivo/Alamy Stock Vector, *b* © Benny/stock.adobe.com; **p.182** © Vita Vanaga/stock.adobe.com

b = bottom, *c* = centre, *l* = left, *r* = right, *t* = top

Every effort has been made to trace all copyright holders, but if any have been inadvertently overlooked, the Publishers will be pleased to make the necessary arrangements at the first opportunity.

Although every effort has been made to ensure that website addresses are correct at time of going to press, Hodder Education cannot be held responsible for the content of any website mentioned in this book. It is sometimes possible to find a relocated web page by typing in the address of the home page for a website in the URL window of your browser.

Hachette UK's policy is to use papers that are natural, renewable and recyclable products and made from wood grown in well-managed forests and other controlled sources. The logging and manufacturing processes are expected to conform to the environmental regulations of the country of origin.

Orders: please contact Bookpoint Ltd, 130 Park Drive, Milton Park, Abingdon, Oxon OX14 4SE. Telephone: +44 (0)1235 827827. Fax: +44 (0)1235 400401. Email education@bookpoint.co.uk Lines are open from 9 a.m. to 5 p.m., Monday to Saturday, with a 24-hour message answering service. You can also order through our website: www.hoddereducation.com

ISBN: 9781510481985

© Margaret Debbadi and Siobhan Matthewson 2020

First published in 2020

This edition published in 2020 by
Hodder Education,
An Hachette UK Company
Carmelite House
50 Victoria Embankment
London EC4Y 0DZ

www.hoddereducation.com

Impression number   10 9 8 7 6 5 4 3 2 1

Year   2024 2023 2022 2021 2020

All rights reserved. Apart from any use permitted under UK copyright law, no part of this publication may be reproduced or transmitted in any form or by any means, electronic or mechanical, including photocopying and recording, or held within any information storage and retrieval system, without permission in writing from the publisher or under licence from the Copyright Licensing Agency Limited. Further details of such licences (for reprographic reproduction) may be obtained from the Copyright Licensing Agency Limited, www.cla.co.uk

Cover photo Jesus Sanz/Shutterstock.com

Illustrations by Aptara, Inc.

Typeset in FS Albert Regular 12/14pt by Aptara, Inc.

Printed in Slovenia

A catalogue record for this title is available from the British Library.

Contents

7.1	The Internet of Things: Merging the physical and digital world	8
7.2	Decomposing problems: Designing an app	34
7.3	HTML: It's all news to me	56
7.4	Block it out: Creating a game	87
7.5	Show and tell: Cloud based presentations	115
7.6	Data mining: Using spreadsheets and databases	148
	Glossary	186
	Index	193

Introduction

About this book

Today's technological society has changed the way you learn, problem solve and communicate. Advances in **big data**, **artificial intelligence (AI)** and **machine learning** are changing how we use computing in new and exciting ways. Computing of the future will require the development of a whole new skillset to support the use of these continually evolving technologies.

big data: extremely large amounts of data that are analysed to show patterns in things such as human behaviour and use of technology

artificial intelligence (AI): an area of computing which focuses on creating intelligent computers which can mimic the way humans think and make decisions; a computer system able to perform tasks normally done using human intelligence, such as understanding speech

machine learning: software that enables AI systems to automatically learn and improve from past experiences without being programmed to do so; the computer programs access data and then use it to learn things for themselves

This book will help you to develop your cross-curricular computing skills. It will provide you with the technical skills needed to engage effectively in the digital world of today. It supports the curriculum areas of digital literacy, computer science and information technology:

- **Digital literacy** focuses on the impact of digital technology in today's society. It promotes understanding of the impact of the digital world with an emphasis on maintaining safety and well-being online.
- **Computer science** is the study of computational thinking (see page 6) and the creation of computer programs to solve problems. It also explores how a computer interprets and carries out instructions.
- **Information technology** looks at how to use computer programs to solve problems. It takes into consideration both usability (how well a program works) and accessibility needs (whether or not everybody is able to use the program effectively).

4

Introduction

Units

This Student Book has six units:

7.1 The Internet of Things: Merging the physical and digital world introduces the concept of the Internet of Things and the impact it has on our lives. It looks at the technologies which support the Internet of Things and encourages forward-thinking in the design of future technologies.

7.2 Decomposing problems: Designing an app encourages problem solving skills through the development of a new mobile phone application while also encouraging consideration of a range of user interface types and accessibility.

7.3 HTML: It's all news to me focuses on the impact of online news and fake news on society and the work of journalists. It explores production of online news websites and supports the development of web pages through the exploration of HTML.

7.4 Block it out: Creating a game provides an introduction to programming through the development of a single player interactive game using the block programming language Scratch through the design and development of algorithms.

7.5 Show and tell: Cloud based presentations explores the use of cloud based applications through the development of a presentation. The information within the presentation will be organised using a logical structured approach to create a kiosk presentation.

7.6 Data mining: Using spreadsheets and databases looks at database and spreadsheet applications in problem solving. It focuses on the concept of data mining and extraction of useful information and investigates how organisations can use these applications to extract useful data.

Introduction

How to use this book

In each unit you will learn new skills by completing a series of tasks. Each unit starts with some information followed by a list of the learning objectives that you will cover. These features also appear in each unit:

Learning Outcomes

This panel lists the things you will learn about in each unit.

SCENARIO
This panel contains a scenario which puts the tasks into a real-world context.

Do you remember?

This panel lists the skills you should already be able to do before starting the unit.

Learn

This panel introduces new concepts and skills.

Practice

This panel contains tasks with step-by-step instructions to apply the new skills and or knowledge from the 'Learn' panel.

KEYWORDS
Important words are emboldened the first time they appear in a unit and are defined in this panel. They also appear in the glossary.

This panel suggests a simple task to check your understanding.

These speech bubbles provide hints and tips as you complete the tasks.

DID YOU KNOW?
This panel provides an interesting or important fact about the task or theme.

Computational Thinking

This panel highlights tasks in the unit which involve one of the key areas of computational thinking:

Pattern recognition: the identification of repeating tasks or features in a larger problem to help solve more complex problems more easily.

Decomposition: breaking larger problems down into smaller more manageable tasks. Each smaller task is examined and solved more easily than a larger more complex problem.

Abstraction: ignoring details or elements of a problem which are not needed when trying to solve a problem.

Algorithmic development: providing a series of instructions which include details on how to solve an identified problem.

Generalisation: the process of creating solutions to new problems using past knowledge and experience to adapt existing algorithms.

Evaluation: the process of ensuring that an algorithmic solution is an effective and efficient one – that it is fit for purpose.

Introduction

Go further

This panel contains tasks to enhance and develop the skills previously learnt in the unit.

Challenge yourself

This panel provides challenging tasks with additional instructions to support new skills.

Final project

This panel contains the final tasks of the unit which encompass all the skills developed. This panel can be used to support self/peer assessment and teacher assessment.

Evaluation

This panel provides guidance on how to evaluate and, if necessary, test the final project tasks.

Student resources are available at www.hoddereducation.com/student-resources

Unit 7.1 The Internet of Things: Merging the physical and digital world

About the Internet of Things

Advances in *internet* speed and connectivity have changed the way we do things. For example, we can use video streams and encrypted instant messaging to communicate, we can use the internet to obtain information or to entertain us, and we can go online to book concert tickets and flights. Artificially intelligent chat bots can even 'talk' to us online.

These tasks are completed using digital technology systems. The digital world includes all electronic devices and the *digital data* that is created by using the devices. Most of these devices can connect to the internet and can communicate in some way to provide data. Devices like this are called *smart devices*.

We use smart devices in many ways during our everyday lives. For example:

We use smart phones to communicate, stream videos and music, browse the internet, and use apps.

Smart smoke detectors can sound an alarm at home *and* send an alarm to your smart phone.

We can make use of artificial intelligence (AI) to speak to a virtual doctor and gain instant access to medical advice.

Most homes have a range of smart devices designed to help manage our daily lives.

There are billions of smart devices across the world connected to the internet. This network of devices is called the *Internet of Things (IoT)*. Each device collects and processes data and sends alerts and messages based on the data collected across the internet.

Can you imagine how much data is generated everyday by all of the devices connected to the IoT? There are more devices connected to the IoT than there are people on the planet. Through this data collection and processing, our physical world is merging with the digital world.

KEYWORDS

internet: an interconnected network or networks with a global reach

digital data: computers can only understand digital data; any data to be processed has to be turned into digital data so that the device can understand it; this data can be one of two values, '1' or '0'

smart devices: an electronic device that is able to connect, communicate and share data with other devices via a network

Internet of Things (IoT): a network of smart devices connected to the internet

smart devices: What smart devices do you own?

▲ Smart smoke detectors can send an alarm to your smart phone

8

Unit 7.1 The Internet of Things: Merging the physical and digital world

Learning Outcomes

In this unit you will learn about:
- your place in the IoT
- how the IoT connects devices
- input, output, processing and storage on smart devices
- how we use the IoT at home
- commercial uses of the IoT.

SCENARIO

MyBigCity has two million citizens. The city's mayor wants to make sure that all citizens can make use of the most modern smart devices to make their life as enjoyable and productive as possible. The mayor would like the city to hold the title 'Smart City of The Year'. The competition will take place in six months' time. A lot of research must be done to show what MyBigCity has achieved to date. Some citizens need to understand the IoT and learn to make use of it. Your challenge as an experienced user of the IoT is to help MyBigCity to win the title.

school network: What do you know about your school network? What components does it have?

KEYWORDS

school network: computers linked together through a main computer using cables or Wi-Fi; computers can share printers and the main computer will store users' data

cloud storage: a network of remote servers on the internet used to store and process data transmitted from IoT devices

cloud storage: Do you use any cloud storage facilities? Which ones?

Do you remember?

Before starting this unit, you should be able to:
- ✔ use the internet to do research
- ✔ use email to communicate
- ✔ use apps on a smart phone
- ✔ use a word processor to create a document, including pictures and tables
- ✔ upload or share a document with other students
- ✔ use a simple graphics editing package, such as *Microsoft Paint* or *Adobe Photoshop*
- ✔ use a presentation package, such as *Microsoft PowerPoint*, to create a presentation.

Uploading or sharing can be done using your **school network**, e-mail or a **cloud storage** area such as *Google Drive*.

9

International Computing for Lower Secondary

Your place in the IoT

> **Learn**
>
> Look at the **infographic** below. This shows a person and the different ways in which they are connected to the IoT.
>
>
>
> If you use smart phones, smart watches, computers or tablets you could be connected to the IoT. Each device that you use will connect to the internet and data can be collected. For example, a smart watch can transmit data about your daily exercise pattern, your health or about where you have been. Data generated from these devices contributes to a person's **digital footprint**.
>
>
>
> Smart phones can transmit a lot more data about you, especially if they are used to browse the internet or buy things online.
>
>

KEYWORDS

infographic: a visual representation of information or data

digital footprint: the data that exist about you as a result of online interactions and activities

digital footprint: Go on Google and Google yourself. What information did you find?

Unit 7.1 The Internet of Things: Merging the physical and digital world

Practice

- Create your own infographic showing how you are connected to the IoT.
- Add graphics to represent each of the devices you use at school and at home.
- Use arrows to link the devices to you and the other devices on your infographic.
- Complete the section on the infographic about your data. Use the picture on page 10 to help you.
- In a team of four, discuss each of your infographics. After discussion, create a table which lists all of the differences and similarities between each person's infographic. You could do this by using a table structure like the one below:

> Create the infographic using a word processor, graphics package, presentation software or a large sheet of paper and some markers.

We all use the following devices	Only some of us use the following devices

- Create a single infographic that shows the devices that you **all** use to connect to the IoT.

Evaluation and generalisation

Compare infographics for different teams and suggest which team is generating the most data.

Describe how your team infographic could be used to help the citizens of MyBigCity.

You could think about:
- when using the devices you have identified in your infographic, what personal data might be collected?
- if all the personal data was recorded, what sort of a picture, or profile, of you could somebody create?

Reflect on the data that may be being collected about you. Should you be able to prevent this happening?

How could the data help identify you online?

International Computing for Lower Secondary

How the IoT connects devices

> **Learn**

In order to make best use of the IoT, devices should:
- be able to access the internet wirelessly
- be able to send information easily
- have **sensors** to sense information in the physical environment; for example, the temperature in a room
- have their own power source; for example, a battery.

The devices can connect to the internet or to each other using a wireless network. The main wireless technologies are listed below.

Mobile Technology	Download speed	Latency time	Disadvantage
4G is fourth generation mobile phone technology. It supports services such as video streaming and mapping services which use a lot of data and require fast downloading speeds.	60 Mbps	60 milliseconds	4G networks use many antennae and transmitters making devices larger and prone to damage. Also, some users experience poor battery life on devices

Wireless Technology	Range	Use	Disadvantage
Wi-Fi uses radio waves to connect devices to a wireless network. Wi-Fi is used in most buildings to deliver internet access to people.	90 metres	Provides a wireless connection to the internet in hotels and airports for customer use.	Performance can be affected by physical barriers such as thick walls, and Wi-Fi can be prone to 'black spots' because of distance from the WAP.
Radio Frequency Identification (RFID) uses radio waves to identify an object. Objects are tagged and the tag contains data about the object. When the object is passed through an RFID reader it broadcasts data via a radio wave.	10–300 feet	Tagging products in a supermarket.	RFID tags can be costly.
Near-field Communication (NFC) is compatible with RFID systems. It is a very short-range wireless technology.	4–5 cm	Used in mobile payment technology such as *Google Wallet*. It allows two devices like a phone and a payment device to exchange data when they are close together.	Security concerns due to mobile phone hacking.
Bluetooth is a short range technology.	10–100 metres	Allows devices to connect directly to each other, for example, PCs and printers or phones, without the need for cables.	Security concerns if Bluetooth is constantly switched on.

Unit 7.1 The Internet of Things: Merging the physical and digital world

KEYWORDS

range: the distance within which a device must be to send and receive data

download speed: the speed at which data is downloaded from the internet usually measured in bits per second

latency: the delay between a request being sent and the request being processed

Mbps: megabits per second; a unit of measurement for transmitting data

mapping services: a feature on the web which allows you to develop an online map

sensor: a device which detects and measures a physical property, for example, the temperature in a room, sound intensity or motion activity

Practice

- On your infographic, can you identify what wireless or mobile technologies are used when you connect your device to the internet?
- Yan has got a motion gaming system which connects to the IoT. She was top of the high score board for the online game, but her position is slipping. She has had a number of problems with her system including:
  - the character in the game is slow to react when she moves in front of the screen, so she is losing games online
  - the game frequently freezes whilst she is using it
  - updates to the game have provided more detailed graphics but she is not able to use these as her system becomes slow.
- Yan's mum loves to listen to music in the evening. Yan's brother also plays games and frequently watches videos online. Yan's dad is a university professor and he makes use of video calling to talk to students and other professors.
- Yan's family all make use of 4G technology to do these things. In a group, discuss why Yan may be having the problems she has with her game. You could think about the technology she uses (4G) and the latency time, download speed and disadvantages of this technology.
- Now prepare a report which explains to Yan why she is having these problems. Your report should include:
  - an explanation of 4G
  - how latency might affect her game's performance
  - how the download time might affect her game's performance
  - an explanation about how her experience will improve if she changes to 5G.

> Motion gaming has changed the way we play online games. Every movement and body gesture is detected by motion sensors and the in-game character mirrors your actions.

DID YOU KNOW?

5G is fifth generation super-fast mobile technology and is becoming the new standard. It is designed to serve industry and consumers. Download times could be as fast as 1 Gbps and latency times as low as 1 millisecond.

13

International Computing for Lower Secondary

Using sensors

Learn

Sensors have the ability to detect or measure and report a physical quality that is changing in the physical environment. Sensors can communicate with electronic devices to allow data to be read. There are many different types of sensors. This table outlines some of the most common sensors.

Sensor name	What does it measure and report?	Example of where it is used
temperature sensor	temperature in a given space	central heating systems in buildings to maintain a constant temperature
light sensor	intensity or brightness of light	automated lighting systems which turn on at dusk and turn off at dawn
pressure sensor	pressure measurement of gases or liquids	monitoring oxygen levels in pressure tanks in hospitals to ensure patient health
humidity sensor (also called hygrometers)	moisture in the air and the air temperature	monitoring the air quality in museums to prevent artefacts from moisture damage
motion sensor	movement and body heat	burglar alarms; when an alarm system is armed, motion sensors are activated; the sensor can detect heat and movement in the immediate area, which creates a protective grid; a moving object can cause rapid changes in the temperature and trigger the alarm

IoT devices need a **gateway** to manage the two-way data flow between the devices and the internet. The gateway ensures that devices with different **protocols** can communicate with each other.

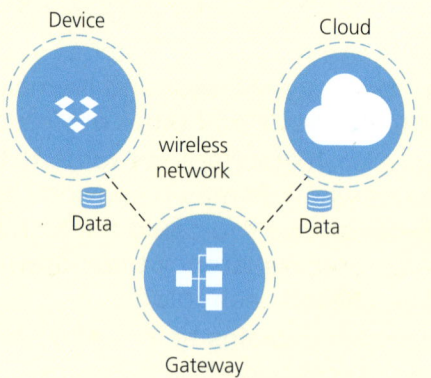

DID YOU KNOW?

Sensors and other devices can be used to send data to control robots. The robots can carry out particular tasks. For example, oil and gas companies are experimenting with pressure and temperature sensors which alert robots to visit hazardous areas and check equipment. This saves manpower and means that human beings do not have to work in dangerous areas.

DID YOU KNOW?

The IoT creates a massive amount of data which needs to be stored. The data can be stored on the cloud. Businesses and individuals can access this data, analyse it and make decisions based on the data. Some of these decisions are made automatically without human intervention.

KEYWORDS

gateway: a physical device or software program that is the connection for the cloud, sensors and intelligent devices

protocol: a set of rules which govern the way in which data is transferred around a network

cloud: a network of remote servers on the internet used to store and process data transmitted from IoT devices

Unit 7.1 The Internet of Things: Merging the physical and digital world

Pattern recognition and analysis

Analytics is the process of converting the data collected into meaningful information so that it can be interpreted.

Consider the data that may be generated about you. Review your infographic.

In groups of four, discuss how the data collected about your class could be used to provide information about their patterns of behaviour.

For example, location information could be used to determine the average distance people need to travel to school.

Make a list of five patterns, about the class, that could be identified through analysis of the data collected by your IoT devices.

Practice

- Open the file **IoT Technologies.docx** provided by your teacher. Complete the table about wireless technologies.
- With a partner, use the internet to research two additional uses for each of the sensors in the table above.
- Pair up with two other students and share how you think those sensors might also be used in the future.
- Use and adapt the **templatesensors.ppt** provided by your teacher to prepare a presentation for the mayor of MyBigCity about the new uses for each sensor. You could think about transport, making citizens' lives more enjoyable, or helping the environment, and so on.
  Your presentation should include five slides, one for each sensor.
  Each slide or page should include:
  o the sensor name
  o the two new uses for the sensor, with a picture of each
  o an explanation of how MyBigCity could benefit from using the sensor in these two ways.
- Select one of your slides and prepare a presentation (no more than two minutes long) in which you describe how the sensor will make a positive impact on the citizens in MyBigCity.

Abstraction

As you will be presenting some of your work, make sure that you include the key points about how the sensor might be used and its impact on the citizens.

During your presentation, explain how the sensor works by breaking your explanation into small steps.

Deliver your presentation to your whole class or a small group.

15

International Computing for Lower Secondary

Functions of an IoT device

Learn

IoT devices are basically input and output devices which connect to the internet.

The **user interface** allows the user to interact with the IoT. For example, simple touch panels and multicolour touch panels have replaced hard switches on many household appliances. These act as input devices.

Device	Advantage	Disadvantage
Touch screens work as input and output devices. They are used on many smart phones and on control panels.	Do not require a lot of training to use and they can be used without adding a keyboard or mouse to a device. The screen allows the user to zoom in and rotate images very easily.	Expensive and can be easily damaged. Also touch screens are not always suitable for inputting a large amount of data at one time.
Voice recognition software takes in voice commands through a microphone. These are processed and converted to commands which are executed on the device.	Provides a means of data entry which does not require typing. This could be suitable for individuals with limited mobility.	Can be affected by background noise and the system must be trained to recognise your voice.
A keyboard is the main input device used to input text and character data into computers.	Keyboards are widely available and relatively cheap. Most people have some keyboard skills so should be able to make use of them.	If you do not have a good level of keyboard skills data input can be very slow. Typing errors are common and keyboards are unsuitable for creating pictures or graphics.

> **KEYWORDS**
>
> **user interface:** sometimes called the UI; it is every part of the system with which the user can interact
>
> **voice recognition software:** software which can process voice commands and execute them on a device or computer

Unit 7.1 The Internet of Things: Merging the physical and digital world

DID YOU KNOW?

There are two different types of touch screen. A resistive touch screen is made up of two flexible plastic sheets, with a gap between them. If you press on the top sheet, it comes into contact with the bottom sheet and completes an electrical circuit. The screen is pressure-sensitive. If you did not apply pressure, the touch would not be detected.

A capacitive touch screen works by using the electrical properties of the human body to change an electrostatic field on the screen. That means you can't select options if you are wearing gloves or using a pencil. However, you can buy special styluses to control the screen.

Most smart phones use capacitive touch screens.

KEYWORD

resistive (touch screen): is made of two transparent layers of glass or plastic; when pressure is applied the top layer bends and touches the bottom layer and a current flows between the layers

Which type of touch screen is used on your phone?

Practice

- Open your presentation, sensors.ppt.
- On each slide add:
  o an input device for the sensor use
  o an explanation, stating why you selected the input device for that use.
- Voice recognition devices in the form of personal assistants, such as *Alexa* and *Siri*, are used in many homes. In a group of four, discuss how these devices are currently used in everyday life. One example would be to request music.
- Create a list of uses for voice recognition devices.

17

Other hardware used on the IoT

Learn

Devices	Key facts
Virtual reality devices	• Used to play games and give the gamer a more realistic experience. • Head-mounted devices and special gloves are used to send data to the game and receive feedback from it. The feedback comes in the form of vibration, sound or visual activity on the screen. • This helps the user become immersed in the game and improves their overall experience.
Digital cameras	• Produce digital images which can be stored, edited and analysed. • The quality of the camera will affect the quality of the images produced. • Digital cameras are used in security systems and weather stations in the IoT.
Webcams	• A digital camera connected to a computer or other device. It can send live pictures from its location using the internet. • The quality of images sent by the webcam is affected by the frame rate of the webcam. This is the number of pictures a webcam takes and transfers to the computer in a second. Typical frame rates are 30 frames per second (fps) although high end webcams can take as many as 60 fps. • The resolution of the camera is also important. Many webcams now have high-definition capabilities and can deliver high quality video images. • Webcams are used throughout the IoT to deliver live images of homes in security systems and for monitoring purposes.
3D Printers	• Provide physical outputs in **3D** format made from plastic or another material. • Used to make tools and equipment that have been designed on a computer. This type of equipment can be used to 'print' bones for replacement surgery.
Speakers	• Devices that connect to a computer and produce sound. • The sound generated comes from the computer's sound card. • Most smart phones have a built-in speaker. • Wireless speakers can be linked to the smart phone; this is common in many homes.

Unit 7.1 The Internet of Things: Merging the physical and digital world

DID YOU KNOW?

Smart phones have rear and front digital cameras. An important feature of the camera is the resolution, which is measured in pixels (or megapixels). The higher the resolution, the higher the number of megapixels, and the better quality the picture will be. A typical resolution is 40 MP. These cameras have many features. For example, they allow the user to zoom in on the subject, apply effects and use a flash. They also generate a lot of data about the photograph. A digital photo stores data about the location, date and time the photo was taken.

KEYWORDS

resolution: a measure of the quality of an image (or the amount of detail a camera can capture); relates to the number of **pixels** used to create an image – the greater the number of pixels, the better the quality of the image

pixel: short for picture element; refers to the individual dots used to make up an image or display on a computer screen

megapixel: one megapixel is one million pixels

Practice

> Copy and complete the following table for the devices named.

Device name	Photograph of device	Features	Uses	Advantages	Disadvantages
touch screen					
webcam					
3D printer					
SSD					

Find two versions of the same image using Google images. One version should have a higher resolution than the other. Open them, enlarge them. Do you see any differences in image quality?

> A local engineering business in MyBigCity needs to buy a 3D printer. You must research 3D printers online and recommend a printer to the company.

Your research should include reading reviews for the printer, considering the price of the printer and what it can do, and researching what engineering companies do.

o Ahmed works as a jeweller. He produces personalised 3D printed wedding rings. He uses 3D computer-aided design (CAD) software to create the unique designs before printing them onto wedding rings.

How could he make use of technologies such as touch screens and cloud storage to have a better service for customers?

Discuss your ideas with a partner – did you come up with the same or completely different ideas? How could your ideas make people's lives better and more enjoyable?

International Computing for Lower Secondary

Data storage

Learn

Many devices need to be able to store data. There are a number of different types of data storage. Each one has a different purpose.

Internal storage

When a device such as a computer is switched on, it needs to know what task to carry out to start the device. **Read only memory (ROM)** holds a set of instructions that will enable the device to start up. ROM cannot be modified as it is read only. ROM is **non-volatile**; this means that the data or instructions stored in ROM are not lost when the device is switched off. If the data in the ROM were to be lost when the device was switched off, then the device would never start up again.

When the device is being used it needs memory to hold the data and instructions that it is working on to carry out a range of tasks. **Random access memory (RAM)** holds this data and enables processing to take place. RAM is **volatile**; this means that the data or instructions stored in RAM are lost when the device is switched off.

hard disc drive

solid state drive

External storage

In order to store data permanently, devices have **hard disk drives (HDD)** and **solid state drives (SSD)**. **Universal serial bus (USB)** sticks and **flash memory cards** can also be used to store data when the device is switched off.

USB stick

flash memory card

Device name	Description	Capacity	Advantage	Disadvantage
Hard disk drive (HDD)	Magnetic storage device which stores a high volume of data on tracks. It rotates to allow data to be accessed on the disks. Read write heads are used to access the data.	Up to 10 terabytes	Much cheaper than the equivalent SSD.	Because of the continuous rotation to access data, the HDD can wear out more quickly than the SSD.
Solid state drive (SSD)	A storage device which has no moving parts. It uses semiconductors which store information by changing the electrical state of small capacitors. This is called flash memory.	Up to 4 terabytes	They are much faster than HDDs, and have a lower failure rate when reading data.	They are expensive and can increase the price of a device.

KEYWORDS

read only memory (ROM): a non-volatile storage medium; does not require a constant source of power to retain the information stored on it

non-volatile: data in memory is retained when the computer is switched off

random access memory (RAM): a volatile storage medium; loses any information it is holding when the power is turned off

volatile: data in memory is lost when the computer is switched off

hard disk drive (HDD): a form of external memory which permanently stores data

solid state drive (SSD): a form of permanent storage which has no moving parts and operates much faster than a traditional hard drive

universal serial bus (USB): a technology for connecting peripherals to a computer

flash memory cards: a storage device that uses non-volatile electronic memory to store data; cameras, for example, use these devices

terabytes: 1000 gigabytes

ROM: What is the ROM size of your home computer?

USB: What devices do you normally plug into the USB in your computer?

DID YOU KNOW?

Flash memory is used in SSDs, USB memory sticks, digital cameras and many more devices.

20

Unit 7.1 The Internet of Things: Merging the physical and digital world

Cloud storage is an important component used in the IoT.

The cloud has a huge number of computers connected to the internet. Data can be uploaded to the cloud and then it can be accessed from any location. Companies such as *Google* and *Microsoft* offer cloud storage accounts to users.

To use cloud storage you must set up an account and access it using a username and password. This helps keep the data safe.

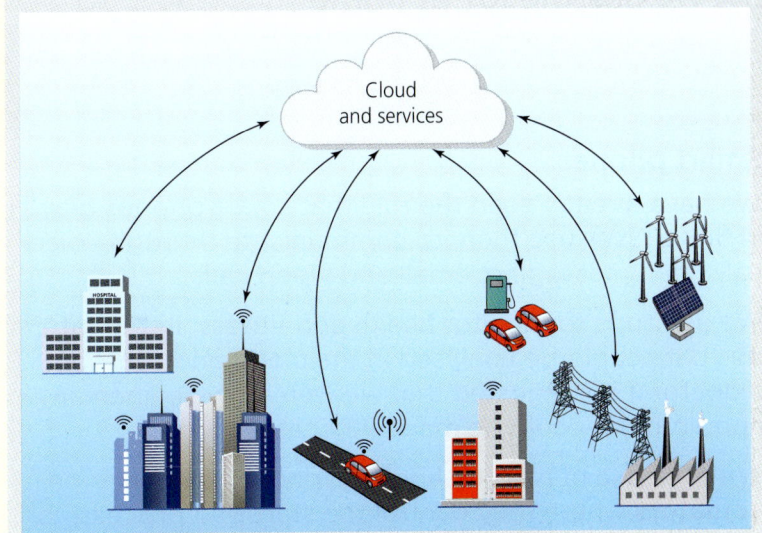

The advantage of cloud storage is that the data can be accessed anywhere on any device that can connect to the internet. Data is always there and can be recovered even if you have lost it from your device. Cloud storage is vital for the IoT as all of the data generated from the devices must be stored before it is analysed. The data can be accessed from anywhere allowing interconnection between devices.

Practice

- Primary storage (RAM and ROM) and secondary storage (hard drives, SD cards, USB flash drives, and so on) can be compared to your school locker (or bedroom at home) and your school bag.
  Your locker is like your secondary storage – you might store everything you may need for a school day, such as your textbooks for all subjects. Your school bag has all those things you need close by, such as your textbook for your current lesson, a pen and some paper.
  With a partner, note down all the things you keep in your school bag and what things for school you keep in your locker.

- Amy lives in MyBigCity. She is a wedding photographer. She takes photos using her phone or camera. As the images need to be detailed and high resolution, she needs lots of space to share the photos. From the following list, decide which input method, input device and storage device might be best for her to use and why.
  Touch screen/voice
  Webcam/camera
  Cloud storage or SSD

- Work with a partner to create a document which contains a list of uses, advantages and disadvantages for cloud storage. You should only prepare one document. You could share the document on a cloud sharing application or complete the document together on your school network.

International Computing for Lower Secondary

How we use the IoT at home

> **Learn**

Smart phones

We have already seen the role that smart phones play in the IoT. We use them to communicate through voice calls, text messaging, email and video calls.

We use apps to monitor health and fitness. In the future, this data could be analysed in the cloud and sent to a doctor if it suggested that we were unwell. Then an appointment could be made if necessary.

With the use of NFC technology, phones can become **actuators** where they control the start of a process; for example, when you use your phone to pay for items.

Central heating control systems

Many homes are equipped with a smart thermostat that is connected to the internet. The thermostat monitors a family's activities and learns about their habits and routines. It then automatically adjusts the temperature when people are at home or away, awake or asleep.

> Wouldn't it be great if this app could send a message to the maintenance company to tell them that there is a problem and schedule a home visit for the repair?

Overall this makes the heating more efficient and may save the family money on heating and air conditioning. The mobile app allows people to change switch-on times and temperatures remotely. It can also send a message to notify you if things have gone wrong with the heating system.

Care for the elderly

Safety

IoT devices can help keep elderly people independent in their communities. Simple devices such as a **motion sensor** can be installed so that an alert is sent to a carer if no movement has been detected for a long time. A smart watch has been designed which has a single button that can be pressed if a person has a fall. The message is received and processed by a company monitoring the device. The company will call a family member to let them know about the accident. Using these devices means that help will arrive quickly, potentially saving lives.

IoT devices can also track changes in air quality, temperature, **humidity**, or **carbon monoxide** levels, notifying the homeowner or care giver if levels fall below an acceptable level.

22

Unit 7.1 The Internet of Things: Merging the physical and digital world

Medication management

Smart pill boxes help make sure that elderly patients are taking their medication as prescribed. The pill box has sensors that can detect if a dose has been missed. The app will send an alert to the patient and the carer. Or a diabetic patient could use a smart watch to monitor their glucose levels and automatically log them online, no finger prick required. These devices may help seniors live with more independence and peace of mind.

Home security

Home security can be improved through the use of smart locks, cameras, and sensors. Alerts can be sent to homeowners when the doorbell rings. This means that they can see who is at the door even if they are not at home. They can also sense movement outside a property and send an alert if there is unusual activity near a property or if an alarm has been triggered. Homeowners using this technology can lock and open doors, see live video of the house or garden, and turn lights on or off from their smart phone.

DID YOU KNOW?

Wearable technologies are used across professional sports to track players' health and fitness. Players wear smart vests which can monitor many aspects of their training and match play statistics. Youth players can be monitored remotely to see if they are good enough to be signed to a major team.

KEYWORDS

actuator: a part of a system that is responsible for moving; for example, a robotic arm

motion sensor: a device that detects moving objects

humidity: the amount of water vapour present in air

carbon monoxide: a poisonous gas which is odourless and flammable

humidity: What is the humidity in your present location? Look on the Internet to find out.
carbon monoxide: Name something that emits carbon monoxide.

Practice

- Actuators are used in medical equipment, production machinery and in the transportation industry.
- Imagine how they could help in the working environment. With a partner, discuss the different ways in which a robotic arm could be used in a factory. You might consider:
  o how the arm can help speed up the process
  o how the arm can help to lift heavy objects
  o how many rest breaks the arm will need.

23

International Computing for Lower Secondary

- Create a list of advantages of using a robotic arm in the work place.
- Imagine a robotic arm that can set off the fire alarm if there is a fire in the chemistry laboratory (by breaking the glass in the fire alarm on the wall), and then operate a fire extinguisher to extinguish the fire. You have been asked to program the arm so that it will work.

    Describe the sensors that would be required to send information to the robotic arm. List, in logical steps, the different things that would occur when a fire is started. Think about the sensors used, what data is captured by the sensors, how the data is processed, the action taken by the arm, any outside communication that would be sent as a result of the fire.

- Coaches and managers at soccer and rugby matches make decisions based on player effort and performance. Players wear special devices that send information about their breathing, distance covered on the field and other performance data. The coaches analyse this data to decide whether or not to keep a player on the field.

    Research how wearable technology is used in rugby or soccer and make a list of six items of data that is collected about a player.

    You could use this website to help you:
    www.wearable-technologies.com

    As a manager of a sports team playing a game on the field, what data would you like to see collected about the player?

    Write a short report using a word processor showing how you would use data to make a decision about substituting a player.

    With a partner, discuss whether this is a fair way to make the decision. Then add the result of your discussion to the report.

Decomposition and algorithmic thinking

For this task you will need to think logically. What will need to happen first? What will happen as a result of something else happening? What might happen last?

An elderly patient who lives in MyBigCity has purchased a smart pill box. However, the pill box is not working as it should. If a dose of pills is missed, no alert is sent to the carer or the patient.

You must review the checklist of actions listed below. These will help you to find the source of the problem. Re-order the checklist, if necessary, and add any additional steps that you think are important. You might add steps to check the carer's technology as well. Remember that the IoT works with sensors, wireless networks, data analysis, smart devices and apps.

- Is the date and time on the box set correctly?
- Is the alarm on the box enabled or disabled?
- Is the pill box battery charged?
- Is the Wi-Fi in the patient's home turned on?
- Are there pills in the box?

Compare your checklist with another student. Do you have the same solutions? If not, what differences do you have and what were your reasons for your own design?

Unit 7.1 The Internet of Things: Merging the physical and digital world

Commercial uses of the IoT

> **Learn**
>
> Businesses use the IoT to try and achieve a competitive edge.
>
> It would be useful to receive a notification when things are wearing out or are not working properly. For example, instead of waiting until there is a leak in the kitchen, you could receive a notification that a pipe connector was deteriorating. Or, instead of your washing machine breaking down and leaving you with nothing to wash your clothes in, you could receive a notification that a part will need replacing after 10 more cycles.
>
> Or imagine you had one pen that was running out of ink – wouldn't it be good if there was a device that could let you know it was running out, so you could replace the ink or get a new pen?
>
> Well, in business it's just as important, as it makes customers happier and means they can be less wasteful and more environmentally friendly.
>
> This approach to keeping things working is called **predictive maintenance**. It aims to prevent the failure by monitoring data sent from the equipment regarding its performance. If the parts of the equipment are deteriorating, action can be taken to repair or replace these parts. So, the device won't fail and the equipment will keep running.
>
> Retail businesses across the world use IoT to improve customer satisfaction and store efficiency.
>
> ### Just walk out shopping
>
> Amazon has set up a number of shops without cashiers. In the shop, a system is set up to read tags on each item when a customer leaves the shop. The checkout system calculates the total amount spent on the items and automatically takes the payment from the customer via their mobile payment app.
>
>
>
> Creating an automated checkout system like this may reduce long queues and lead to greater customer satisfaction.

KEYWORD

predictive maintenance: continuously monitoring equipment to ensure that it is repaired before it breaks down

predictive maintenance: What type of equipment in your home or school would benefit from predictive maintenance?

International Computing for Lower Secondary

> **Smart shelves**
> All shops need to keep their shelves stocked with products for people to buy. Staff have to do this by looking at the shelves and replacing items. Smart shelves use RFID tags and readers to monitor products on display. They have weight sensors which send alerts when items are running low or have been placed on the wrong shelf. This saves money for the shop as checking stock and re-filling the shelves takes a lot of employee time.
>
> Some shops use robots to monitor the shelves and note if items are in the wrong place or running low in stock. This allows human workers to spend more time with customers.

Practice

Create a Venn diagram with three sections: A, B, and A and B (the overlap). In five minutes, list as many things as you can under each of the three sections.

- What are robots really good at, and why?
- What are humans really good at, and why?
- What are both robots *and* humans good at, and why?

A Venn diagram should look like this:

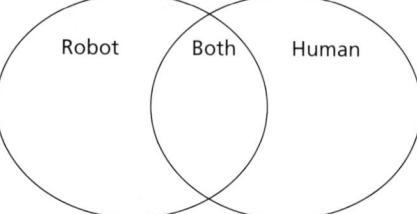

Decomposition

Decomposition means to break a problem down into smaller parts. Take one statement from what a robot is good at and one statement from what a human is good at, and break your statements down further into:

- what makes them good at that task?
- why would that (robot/human) task not be easy to do if you were a (human/robot)?

26

Unit 7.1 The Internet of Things: Merging the physical and digital world

Transport and the IoT

> **Learn**
>
> ### Driverless cars
>
> Driverless cars are vehicles which can drive themselves from one location to another without a driver.
>
> This complex technology is currently being developed. These cars have to make many quick decisions on the road. For example, the car needs to react if a pedestrian steps out onto the road, or work out how close to the pavement it should park.
>
> Therefore, driverless cars need many different types of sensor systems which monitor different aspects of the car's activity.
>
>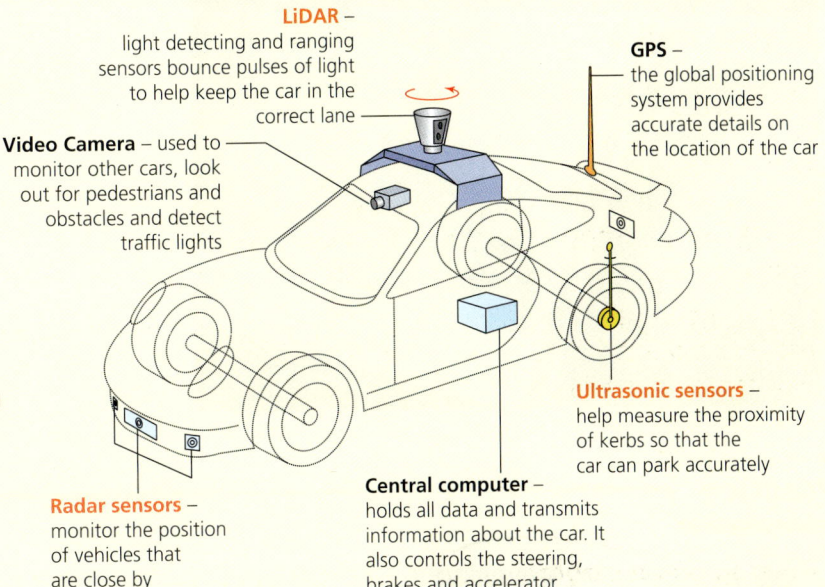
>
> **LiDAR** – light detecting and ranging sensors bounce pulses of light to help keep the car in the correct lane
>
> **Video Camera** – used to monitor other cars, look out for pedestrians and obstacles and detect traffic lights
>
> **GPS** – the global positioning system provides accurate details on the location of the car
>
> **Ultrasonic sensors** – help measure the proximity of kerbs so that the car can park accurately
>
> **Radar sensors** – monitor the position of vehicles that are close by
>
> **Central computer** – holds all data and transmits information about the car. It also controls the steering, brakes and accelerator
>
> Driverless cars could improve safety as they have a lower accident rate than human driven cars. Since they are connected to the internet they can select the shortest and best route for a journey. This could mean that there is less traffic congestion on major roads.
>
> ### Traffic control
>
> Traffic management is a major challenge for any big city because of the volume of traffic passing through and the traffic jams it causes.
>
>
>
> Smart cities use the IoT and data to control traffic flow around their roads. These cities are managing congestion by getting data from closed-circuit television (CCTV) cameras and sending data to traffic management centres. This allows the re-routing of traffic to settle the congestion. A well organised traffic system will allow more free-flowing traffic. There will also be less pollution, as pollution from cars is highest when cars are stopped but their engines are still running (at traffic lights, for example).
>
>
>
> Smart traffic lights use **real-time data** to distribute traffic load. Sensors mounted at key places in the city use IoT technology to gather data about congested areas. Analysis of this data will help generate different routes to avoid congestion. These alerts can be sent to travellers through the in-car communication system or to smart phones. The timing and sequence of traffic signals can be changed as a result of the data obtained. This will also help ease congestion.

27

International Computing for Lower Secondary

> **DID YOU KNOW?**
> In-car navigation was invented in 1909, when an engineer named J.W. Jones invented the Jones Live-Map in-car navigation system.

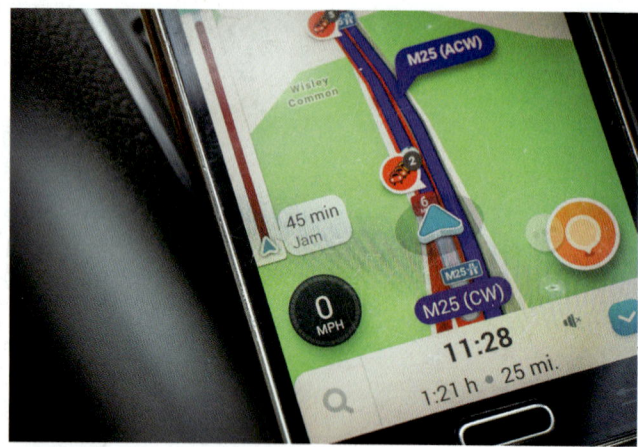

Practice

> Imagine you are travelling in a self-driving car. You have a cliff face that drops to the sea on your right and the mountains to your left. Another car comes around the bend in the opposite direction with failing brakes.
>
> How will your car react?
>
> It could turn inward and slam on the brakes to avoid a head-on collision, but this may cause the other car to go over the cliff. Or prepare for an impact which may keep both cars on the road but injure you and any passengers in your car.
>
> Humans act on instinct but, for a computer, a split second is enough time to make a logical decision. The outcome would be based on the way in which the car is programmed.
>
> In a group of four, discuss what the car should do. Copy and complete the table below.

	Answer	Reason
Should the car put its own passengers' safety first?		
What if the other vehicle is causing the crash?		
What if one car has more passengers than another?		
Should the driver be able to influence these decisions before getting into the car?		

KEYWORDS

radar sensor: a system which uses radio waves to determine range or distance

ultrasonic sensor: a device that can measure the distance to an object by using sound waves

LiDAR: works on the same principle as radar but uses lasers instead

real-time data: data which is processed immediately after collecting

video cameras: keep track of the vehicles and look out for pedestrians and obstacles on the road; they are also used to detect traffic lights

external aerials: receive information about the car's current location so that routes can be followed

video cameras: How could video cameras be useful at home or school?

DID YOU KNOW?
By 2040, 65 percent of the world's population will be living in cities. 1.3 million people move into cities every day. This is why governments are working on smart city initiatives.

Unit 7.1 The Internet of Things: Merging the physical and digital world

Go further

- Look at the infographic about a smart city. There are many different ways in which a city can be connected to the IoT to help its citizens. Research the term 'smart city' and write two sentences which explain what a smart city is.
- Create a presentation or movie which will promote Stockholm as a tourist destination because of its smart technology. You should use three headings; the first two have been started for you:
  1 Stockholm is an environmentally friendly city because …
  2 Stockholm is a safe city because …
  3 Stockholm …
- Answer the following questions:
  ❏ Why do we need smart cities? Justify your response.
  ❏ Are smart cities safe? What evidence have you found to suggest that they are?
- In groups of four, reflect on the question:
  In a smart city, does technology serve people or do people serve technology?

> Stockholm is one of the top smart cities in the world. Its citizens, businesses and services are connected through a complex network. Using the internet, read about how Stockholm has become one of the top smart cities in the world.

29

International Computing for Lower Secondary

- ◆ Use the graphic to focus your discussion.

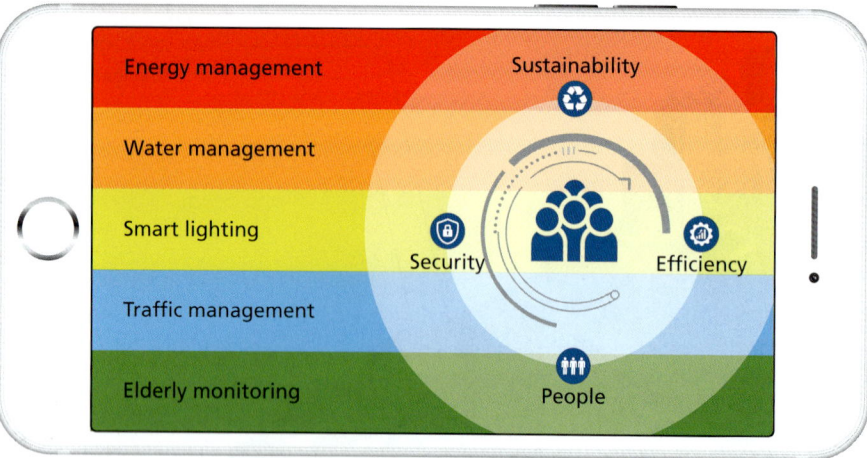

- ◆ Include the following in your discussion:
  - ❏ How can the environment be improved? (Think greenhouse gases, air quality, pollution.)
  - ❏ How can lives be saved? (Think medical care and crime prevention.)
  - ❏ How can commuters' experiences be improved? (Think timetables and smart trains.)
  - ❏ Do smart cities exclude people because they do not have the necessary technology? (Think about people who cannot afford devices to access all the data.)
  - ❏ Does the way smart cities collect data invade citizens' privacy?
- ◆ Decide whether your group wants MyBigCity to become a smart city or not.
- ◆ If you **agree** with making MyBigCity a smart city:
  - ❏ as a group, create a poster which will promote MyBigCity as a smart city; your poster should include the benefits to three of the following groups:
    - ◆ children
    - ◆ students
    - ◆ parents
    - ◆ local workers
    - ◆ commuters.
- ◆ If you **disagree** with making MyBigCity a smart city:
  - ❏ create a protest board to say why you are against MyBigCity becoming a smart city.

Unit 7.1 The Internet of Things: Merging the physical and digital world

Challenge yourself

Global positioning system (GPS) is a navigational system that relies on satellites to determine an object's location.

Devices that use GPS work by receiving signals from these special satellites that orbit the Earth. A minimum of 24 satellites are required for the system to function effectively but there are up to 30 satellites orbiting the Earth at any one time.

GPS continually emits signals that state the current time and where above the earth the satellite is positioned. This data is used in a complex calculation to provide the GPS coordinates of GPS receivers on Earth.

GPS receivers are embedded in most mobile phones and car satellite navigation systems. They can let you and others see where you are on the planet and can be used in route planning and location services like maps.

Scientists use GPS to gather data about earthquakes and businesses can use it to track delivery vehicles. Surveying and mapping was one of the first applications of GPS.

- Open *Google Maps* on your computer and find your location.
- Right click on the location and select 'What's Here?'. You can view your GPS coordinates.

GPS: Tell your partner about the last time you used a GPS to help you find your way or locate a place.

KEYWORDS

global positioning system (GPS): a radio satellite based navigation system that provides location details

GPS receivers: a device which works to locate four or more satellites and then uses a process called trilateration to calculate the distance to each; it uses this information to calculate its own location

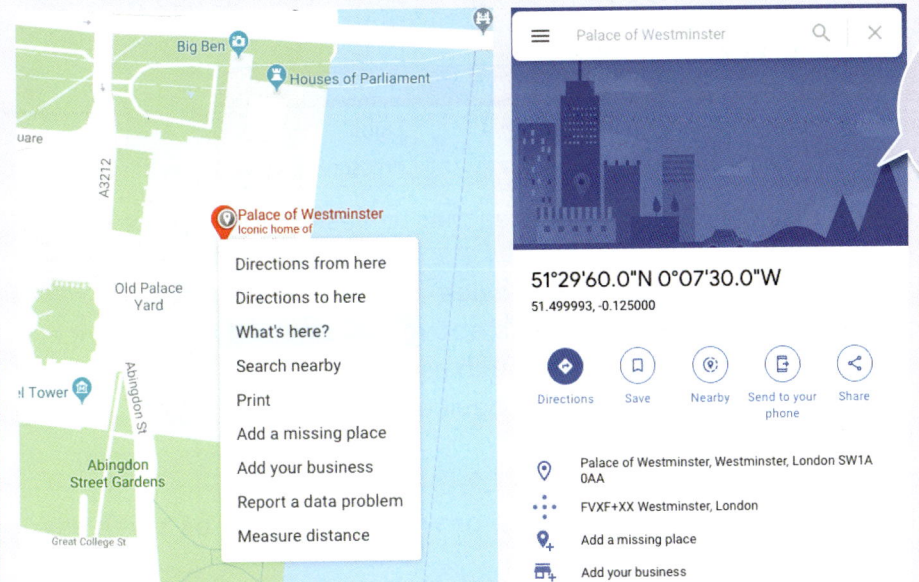

GPS co-ordinates give the latitude and longitude of your position on the planet.

- Research the meaning of the numbers that represent your GPS coordinates.
- List three other ways in which GPS could be used in MyBigCity to help businesses and citizens.

Think about using GPS receivers to track valuables, pets or even people.

31

International Computing for Lower Secondary

Final project

Winning the Smart City title for MyBigCity

The developers of MyBigCity want to enter the city into a competition and they need to provide the judges with examples of what could be done.

➤ Using the technologies listed in the table below, design a futuristic IoT device which will help the citizens of MyBigCity.

Input	Output	Storage	Connection	Sensor
Touch screen	3D Printer	Flash memory	5G	Light
Webcam	Speakers	Cloud storage	Wi-Fi	Pressure

➤ Use or adapt the **IotDesign.doc** provided by your teacher to design your device. Your design should:
  - give a brief explanation of the purpose of your device
  - explain how each of the technologies, in the table above, will be used in the device
  - provide details on how the device will function, such as
    - how the data will be captured using the input device
    - what data will be captured
    - how the data will be used and processed
    - what output will be produced from your device or what actions will be taken as a result of the data input
  - identify which group of citizens the device will help most and how it will help these citizens
  - explain what data will be collected using the device
  - include a draft outline drawing or picture of how the device might look.

➤ When you have finished your design, share it electronically on a cloud based facility such as *Google Drive*.

Unit 7.1 The Internet of Things: Merging the physical and digital world

Evaluation

- How well would your IoT device function in real life? Share your device idea with a friend. Ask them to comment on:
  o how easy or difficult the interface is to use
  o how easy it is to understand the software's basic functions
  o how the data collected could be used to improve peoples' lives
  o how the software caters for people with visual impairment; for example, people with colour blindness
  o how well the app reflects what happens in the real world.

- Use the feedback from your peers and your own thoughts to create a list of recommendations for improving your IoT device.

Definition check: Close your book and make a list of as many terms you have learned in this unit as you can. Compare them with your partner's list. Together try to define as many of them as you can. Check your definitions against the definitions given in the key word boxes.

Unit 7.2 Decomposing problems: Designing an app

About apps

The design and development of an **app** seems a difficult task. In fact, it could be described as a **complex problem**. A complex problem is one which is made up of many smaller problems.

Computational thinking is an approach to problem solving using logic and breaking down problems into more manageable tasks.

This approach can be used to design and create solutions for many different types of problems including designing apps, writing computer programs or for solving complex problems in everyday life.

You can refer to page 6 to review the principles of computational thinking.

KEYWORDS

app: short for application; referring to software applications often available on portable digital devices such as mobile phones

complex problem: a problem which is made up of many smaller problems

wireframes: a drawing or graphic which displays the design of a screen in an app or program

app: What is your favorite app? What can it do? Tell your partner about any good ideas you have for an app.

Learning Outcomes

In this unit you will learn to:
- use computational thinking skills to solve and review different types of problems
- understand thinking first and the importance of planning in problem solving
- create an accessible solution to a problem which considers the needs of all end users including those with impairment
- create structure charts to model processes using decomposition
- design a user interface using **wireframes**
- create simple algorithms and flowcharts to solve small problems
- use gestures and interactivity in an app.

34

Unit 7.2 Decomposing problems: Designing an app

SCENARIO

Sweet FeetZ Ltd is a small company which sells personalised socks. The company has two shops in the city. The socks have been selling well in the shops but people from further away have been telephoning to make orders. Completing telephone orders takes a long time and sometimes customers in the shops leave because the shop assistant is on the telephone with other customers. Yang, the owner, has tried using email to take orders but customers do not always provide the correct details and are not happy to send payment details in this way. On a few occasions, customers have not paid for goods and so Yang has lost money. Yang is now losing customers, so he has decided to approach an app development company in the city to help him.

As a member of the app development company you have been asked to design an app for Sweet FeetZ Ltd which allows the user to design, order and pay for personalised socks.

DID YOU KNOW?

In 2008, *Apple* opened its app store with only 500 apps. The *Google Play Store* was launched in October that year under the name *Android Market* and had only a handful of apps, including *Gmail*. There were 194 billion app downloads in 2018.

Do you remember?

Before starting this unit you should be able to:
- ✔ break larger problems into smaller problems which are easy to solve
- ✔ use a word processor
- ✔ make and edit a recording or video of yourself talking
- ✔ use the internet for research purposes.

How do I develop a mobile app?

Learn

Goal: Start by defining a clear goal for the app. Then work with a developer to create initial drawings or wireframes of what the app will look like. This is called a prototype.

Back-end: Now think about the back-end of the app. This is the part of the app which does the work but the user will not see it. It usually involves programming for things like the management of users and user accounts on the app. It will also involve the creation of the user experience for the app.

Data: During this process the developer will think about data management. How will the user's data be stored and used. For example, will it be shared with other websites or other businesses?

Front-end: The developer will create a user interface based on the designs you have agreed in the wireframes. This will be tested and evaluated to ensure that the app works as it is supposed to.

35

Computational thinking is applied at every stage of the design process. Think about Yang's problem and how computational thinking can be applied to help develop his app.

Decomposition will be used to look at the problem and break it down into smaller problems. For example, the app will have to provide a number of features for selling and also for customers to manage their accounts.

Generalisation is a way of solving problems based on what we have learned from solving previous problems. For example, Yang has already tried to solve the problem by allowing customers to email orders. This means he has a good understanding of how electronic ordering might flow, and he can use this to help the developer understand what is needed.

Abstraction allows us to remove detail that is not necessary for solving the problem. Yang will hold a lot of detail on his employees and their work schedule, but this information is not necessary to solve the current problem.

> **KEYWORD**
> **abstraction:** focusing on important details only and ignoring irrelevant detail which does not help produce a solution

Algorithms allow the developer to specify on a step-by-step basis how the problem will be solved. For example, in the case of customer management, each customer will have to register. The registration process may ask for details such as name, address and email address, and then the customer may be required to select a password. They will not be able to buy anything until this process is completed. Thinking about the step-by-step process and putting the steps into a logical sequence is algorithmic thinking.

Evaluation is an important part of the process. Each part of the app design can be evaluated before it is developed. The developer will:

- review the app design and ensure it is the most efficient way of getting the job done
- get feedback from Yang about the app design
- look at how the app may perform for different types of users and purposes; for example, customers and staff will use the app but they will have different needs
- make changes to the design based on all of the above.

Computational thinking is a problem solving skill or strategy that can be used to solve many complex problems.

Practice

- Apply algorithmic thinking to taking an order for socks on the telephone from a customer who wants to pay by credit card over the telephone. Write down the step-by-step process of how you would take the order, take the payment details and get the socks to the customer.

  You could start with:

  Ask for customer name
  Write customer name onto notepad
  Ask for customer address
  Write customer address onto notepad
  Ask customer what type of socks they want
  and so on ...

> You are using algorithmic thinking to break the process down. You are creating a step-by-step list of actions which will solve the problem of taking an order over the phone. This list is called an algorithm.

Unit 7.2 Decomposing problems: Designing an app

Socks for thought

➤ Aysha works for Yang at the shop. She needs to collect a delivery box of socks for Yang's shop.

She takes her dog, Jolly, and her cat, Anis, with her. Aysha collects the box and returns to her apartment block. She discovers that the main lift has broken. Aysha lives on floor thirty-five. The small service lift is working but there is only enough space for Aysha and either her cat, her dog, or the box.

If she leaves Jolly alone with Anis, the dog will bark and frighten the cat and the cat will be very upset. If she leaves Anis with the box, the cat will scratch it and tear the socks. If she leaves Jolly with the box, it will be safe, as he does not like to play with socks.

Aysha must work out a step-by-step series of actions for travelling up and down in the lift so that she can get herself, Jolly, Anis and the box safely up to her apartment. The service lift must be returned to the ground floor when she is finished.

Decomposition and algorithmic thinking

Challenge: Write the list of steps that Aysha must carry out to complete her task.

Swap your list with a friend and compare the number of steps required to complete the task.

Can you reduce the number of steps you need to complete the task? Think about which animals can travel together and always make sure that Aysha takes something with her in the lift. She should never travel alone in any direction.

target audience: Choose an app you are familiar with and try to determine its target audience. Are you a member of its target audience?

KEYWORD

target audience: the group of people at which the app or program is aimed

Target audience

Learn

When you decide to create a mobile app, there is a lot of work to do before you design it. An effective mobile app will enable users to carry out a specific set of related tasks. You need to consider the following questions.

➤ Who is the **target audience**?

The target audience is the group of users who you are targeting to use the app. They will have common characteristics.
- What sets your target audience apart from other potential users?
- What are their expectations and technical capabilities?
- What age are they likely to be?
- What will they need to use the app? For example, will they need a credit card?

➤ What tasks should the app perform?

These are the things that the user can do when making use of the app, such as signing up to the app or paying for purchases. It is important that you identify the tasks that the app can perform at the beginning. This

37

International Computing for Lower Secondary

means you can track the development process and you will know how you are progressing and when you are finished.

➤ What kind of similar apps are already out there?

You should investigate the competition. Look at apps that have been designed to do the same thing. Read reviews about similar apps to see what users think about them. This will help you with your own design.

Practice

➤ The *Amazon App* is used to sell products to customers from all over the world. Yang's app will be much simpler, but he still hopes it will reach countries all over the world. Review the *Amazon App* (or look at the *Amazon* website) and list the different features that it provides for a customer.

➤ Yang has decided to start small and only sell ski socks and sports socks online. These socks are the most popular. Create a list of characteristics about the target audience for the new Sweet FeetZ app.

➤ With a partner, review your lists of characteristics created above and create a single list on which you agree. Prepare this list for a presentation to Yang, the owner of Sweet FeetZ Ltd.

Creating user stories

Learn

A **user story** provides details about what the app will do from a user's point of view. There will be many different types of users for this app. For example, customers and staff.

KEYWORD

user stories: a description of what the app will do from the user's point of view

user stories: Write a user story for a simple app you use.

Consider two user stories for typical users of the app.

User Story 1 Details

Who – Job or Role: Customer (can be any type of user)

What – Goal : Purchase socks

Why – Reason: To keep warm in winter.

User Story 1 : As a customer I want to purchase socks to keep warm in winter.

User Story 2 Details

Who – Job or Role: Customer

What – Goal : Track my order

Why – Reason: So that I know when my socks will arrive.

User Story 2: As a customer I want to track my order so that I know when my socks will arrive.

38

Unit 7.2 Decomposing problems: Designing an app

- Create a useful and attractive **user interface** by drawing, on paper, what the design could look like. This drawing is called a wireframe of the app.
- Consider carefully what font, colour, style, buttons and icons you will use. This will ensure that users can easily find and understand the features. A cluttered screen with poor colour choice can be confusing to users.
- Get feedback on the design of your app and make improvements or changes to the design before going ahead.

Abstraction

Create a user story for a staff member who will use the app. Try to think about the kind of things that a staff member would have to do. What if prices changed?

Practice

- After looking at the *Amazon App* or website you should have some ideas about what customers might want to do on an app that sells products. For example, they may want to leave a review about a product, they may want to search for a product, or they may want to contact the company. Discuss with a friend the different ways in which a customer can use this type of app to help them shop.
- After your discussion, select two ways in which the customer can use the app (apart from purchase and deliveries) and create two more user stories for a customer user. Use the following layout:

> As well as customers, there are other types of users. The staff of Sweet FeetZ will have to manage the app.

Who (Job or Role): Customer

What (Goal) :

Why (Reason):

User story: As a customer I want to <INSERT Goal HERE> to <INSERT Reason HERE>.

International Computing for Lower Secondary

User interfaces and data collection

Learn

A well designed app will make good use of the whole screen. Consider the fact that many smart phone users use their thumb to navigate. You need to place important features within their reach.

▲ This app on the left has a lot of data on the screen and the functions of the different menu buttons are not clear. This app on the right is a lot simpler and makes use of subtle background colours. The screen is not too cluttered and the meaning of the icons is clear.

How will my app collect and use data?

Apps can track users and share their data. Data collected from apps can include information such as gender, age, location details and details of other apps contained on the device.

Mobile phones store sensitive information and if your phone is on this information is being broadcast all the time.

Most app users do not realise the extent to which their data is being collected and passed on to other countries.

An individual's privacy can be a matter for some concern. The GDPR is a European Union (EU) (and EEA) regulation. GDPR requires apps to:

➤ disclose their **privacy policies** to users
➤ acquire active **informed consent** before collecting or processing the data.

Gaining a user's consent, before collecting data, is very important.

GDPR: Briefly read a portion of GDPR. What does it say?

KEYWORDS

General Data Protection Regulation (GDPR): a law which protects the personal data and privacy of citizens

privacy policies: a legal document that explains how an organisation collects and uses an individual's data

informed consent: permission given when the individual knows exactly how the data will be used

privacy policies: When was the last time you consented to a privacy policy? Did you read the privacy policy?

40

Unit 7.2 Decomposing problems: Designing an app

KEYWORDS

profile: a collection of in-depth information collected about an individual online

ethically: acting in an honest and principled way

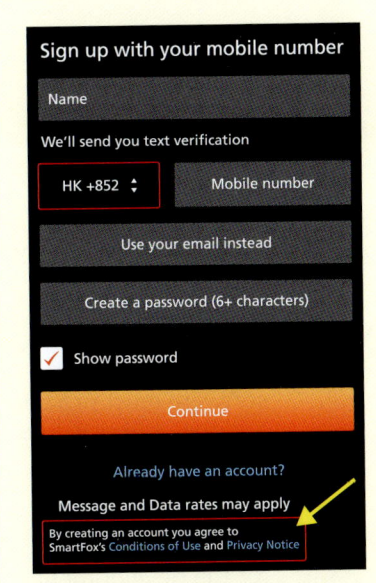

▲ An example of how a company could breach the GDPR law in the past.

▲ An example of a good privacy policy which acquires informed consent.

If an app collects enough data about an individual, that data could be used to build a **profile** of that person without the individual's knowledge or consent. The profile could be used to make decisions about that person without ever meeting them. Computer programs could make use of the profile when calculating insurance premiums or processing loan applications. GDPR does not allow children to be tracked in this way.

Data collection must be done **ethically** and without harming anyone. Data can only be shared if the individual has given consent.

Practice

- Make a list of the data that Yang's app might collect. Write down how Yang might use this data. A simple example might be to use the location data to find out where the people who are using the app live.
- Yang plans to start selling into the EU. He decides to analyse the data to see what the most popular socks are in different locations. He will then send advertisements to these people related to the socks they buy. With a friend, discuss whether or not it is legal in the EU. If it is not legal, what should he do to ensure he is following GDPR?
- Using the internet, research apps that allow customers to buy things. Most apps will:
  o allow customers to register or log in
  o record customers' payment details.
  Make a list of four other things that customers are able to do on these apps.
- What type of customer data is being recorded by the apps you have investigated? You can identify this by looking at the customer registration form. Most apps will collect location details and record preferences. For example, *Amazon* will keep a record of all the products viewed by the customer. *Amazon* may suggest similar products on the basis of what the customer has looked at.
- As a class, discuss how the companies could make use of the data collected.

41

Creating structure charts to model processes using decomposition

> **Learn**
>
> Sweet FeetZ wants to provide customers with an app which allows them to purchase custom made socks online and have them delivered. The problem needs to be broken down.
>
> App developers will meet with Yang, the **client**, and will interview him to try to understand what he wants the app to do. This is a part of the process which will help identify what tasks the app will perform.
>
> The list of tasks produced can be described as the **user requirements**.
>
> The user requirements can be used:
>
> ➤ at the end of the development process to determine whether or not the app does what is required
>
> ➤ as an agreement between the app developer and the client. If the app does not meet the user requirements, Yang may not pay the developers for the work they have done.
>
> Here is a list of the user requirements that Yang has agreed with the developers.
>
> The app must have the following features:
> - A sign up/register or login page
> - A feature for designing socks
> - A feature for previewing the socks that have been designed
> - A feature for paying for socks and recording delivery addresses
> - A feature for tracking deliveries
> - A feature for providing feedback about the app itself
> - The app must be easy to use

KEYWORDS

client: the person or organisation who requested the app and who will pay for it

user requirements: a list of tasks and features that the software must provide, and that a user would expect the software to do; it is created in agreement with the client who is paying for the development of the app

user requirements: Think of a simple app you frequently use. List a few of your user requirements for it.

Unit 7.2 Decomposing problems: Designing an app

Decomposition

The block diagram below shows how decomposition has been used to break the problem down into smaller problems. Each of these smaller problems must be solved so that the app will function correctly.

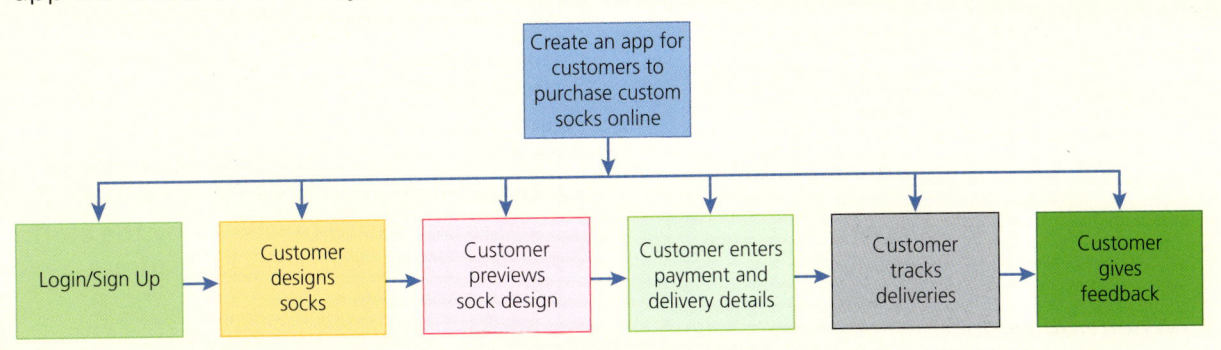

```
Create an app for customers to purchase custom socks online
    │
    ├─> Login/Sign Up
    ├─> Customer designs socks
    ├─> Customer previews sock design
    ├─> Customer enters payment and delivery details
    ├─> Customer tracks deliveries
    └─> Customer gives feedback
```

One large problem has been broken down into six smaller problems. Each of these smaller problems can be resolved individually.

It is common for clients to provide feedback on the design of the app. This helps to ensure it meets their requirements. Yang has reviewed the block diagram with the app developers. The developers have questions about how socks are designed. So, Yang has provided the following list of additional information.

- There are three sock sizes: small, medium and large.
- Children's socks are most popular at Christmas.
- The company frequently run out of plain black socks in size large.
- Some staff can be late for work so the shops may not open on time every day.
- Ski socks require customer to choose an image to be used as a pattern on the sock, and text to be written on the soles of the socks.
- Sports socks require customers to specify the colour of the heel, toe and stripe around the top of the sock. They also need text to be included on the soles of the socks.

Practice

- Look back at the list of additional information that Yang has provided. Remove the statements that will **not** help you to solve the problem; when you do this, you are using abstraction.
- For each statement that you have removed, write down a reason why this statement will not help to solve the problem.
- Compare your list with a partner and discuss why you have kept certain statements.
- Review the information about ski socks and sports socks in the list of additional information. Then, using the spaces provided, complete the list of actions that a customer must perform when completing the Customer Designs Socks section of the app.

International Computing for Lower Secondary

Select the sock size (small, medium or large)
Select the sock _____ (ski or sports)
If sock type is _____
Upload image
Upload _____
If sock type is sports:
1. Select heel colour
2. _____
3. _____
4. _____

▸ When you have completed the algorithm, check through it and see if there are any tasks that are repeated in more than one place. This is pattern recognition. This will help highlight shared tasks which only need to be completed or created once.

▸ In the future, Yang wants to include a staff section in the app. The staff should be able to log in to the app and change details about socks. They should also be able to change the prices, change the images of socks, add new socks, delete socks that are no longer in stock, and add details about special events or sales. Using decomposition, prepare a block diagram which will show the main problems to be solved by the staff section of the app. Use the diagram below to help you.

You should find one that is common to designing both types of socks.

Create staff section of the app

DID YOU KNOW?
The list of actions above is called an algorithm. It is a set of step-by-step instructions which represent a solution to the problem.

User interfaces and data collection

Learn

User interfaces
The user needs to be able to interact with a computer or smart device, for example, while using an app, browsing a website or using software on a computer. The user interface, sometimes called the UI, allows the user to interact with the device or software.

In the early days of computers there were **command line interfaces (CLIs)**. These provided basic screens with very little

KEYWORD

command line interface (CLI): a user interface which requires the user to enter commands at a prompt to operate it

44

Unit 7.2 Decomposing problems: Designing an app

text. The user had to know all of the commands in order to use the system. CLIs were used by computing experts; inexperienced users found it difficult to remember all of the commands to make the computer work effectively.

When **graphical user interfaces (GUIs)** were created, computer use became widespread. These interfaces made use of windows, icons, menus and pointers. They are much easier to use but use a lot more computer memory and processing power than the CLIs.

Look at the pictures below. Which interface would you prefer to use and why?

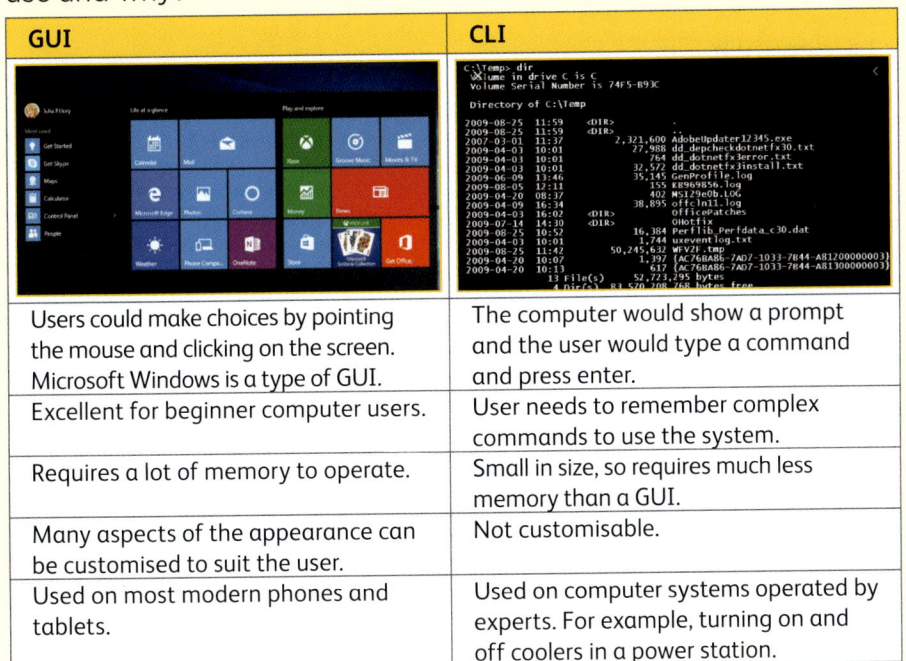

> **KEYWORD**
>
> **graphical user interface (GUI):** a user interface which makes use of windows, icons, menus and pointers on a screen; it is suitable for inexperienced users

GUI: Have you ever used a computer or website without a GUI. Tell your partner about your experience.

GUI	CLI
Users could make choices by pointing the mouse and clicking on the screen. Microsoft Windows is a type of GUI.	The computer would show a prompt and the user would type a command and press enter.
Excellent for beginner computer users.	User needs to remember complex commands to use the system.
Requires a lot of memory to operate.	Small in size, so requires much less memory than a GUI.
Many aspects of the appearance can be customised to suit the user.	Not customisable.
Used on most modern phones and tablets.	Used on computer systems operated by experts. For example, turning on and off coolers in a power station.

Practice

- Make a screen shot of your computer interface. Edit the screenshot and label all of the interactive features of the GUI. You should look for windows, icons, menus and a pointer.
- Using the structure diagram for the Customer section of the app on page 43, take one area and develop a GUI interface and a command line interface for it. Show how data would be collected.

  You can do this by using a word processor to create a wireframe of the screen. Use textboxes and shapes to show where and how the data would be entered, for example in a CLI it would be keyboard data entry.

  When you have designed the screen, fill the spaces for data collection on the wireframe with sample data.
- Consider the following situations and suggest which kind of interface would be most suitable:

  Turning coolers in a power station on and off.

  Video streaming service.

  Controlling central heating in a home.

International Computing for Lower Secondary

Using wireframes and getting feedback

Learn

When designing an app, you must consider the user interface carefully. Apps are operated using touch screen devices. Interface design must reflect the fact that users make selections using their fingers and thumbs.

Remember: Touch screen devices can be pressure sensitive or resistive.

Before an app is developed, designers create a detailed plan showing how each page or screen will look. These plans are called wireframes. Wireframes can be hand drawn or created using a word processor or special software.

Each wireframe should:
- have a title or number to identify it
- contain details about the
  - layout of buttons, icons and text on the screen
  - colour scheme and font to be used
  - graphics, videos and interactive elements to be used
  - layout of forms.

The wireframe below shows the Login/Registration/Home screen, which is the opening page of the App:

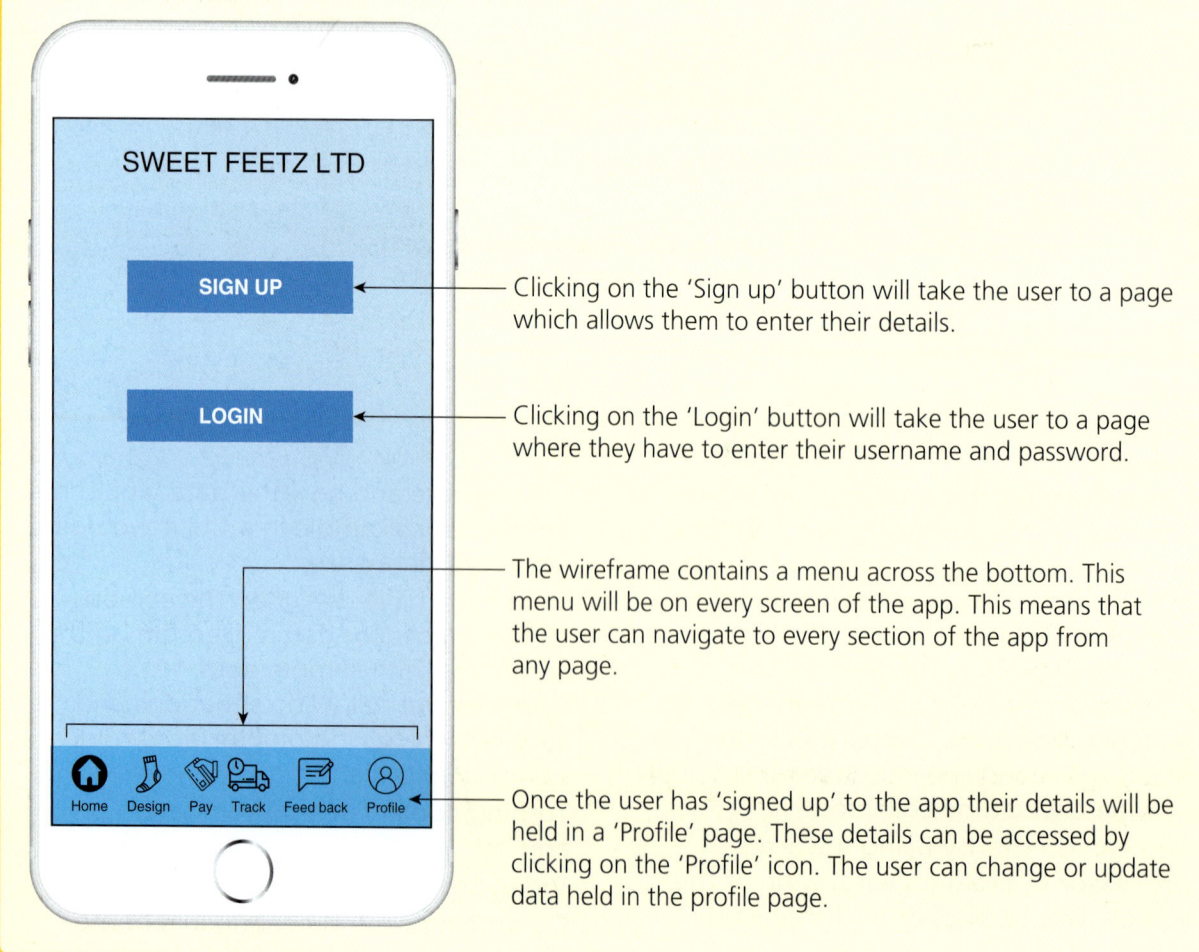

Clicking on the 'Sign up' button will take the user to a page which allows them to enter their details.

Clicking on the 'Login' button will take the user to a page where they have to enter their username and password.

The wireframe contains a menu across the bottom. This menu will be on every screen of the app. This means that the user can navigate to every section of the app from any page.

Once the user has 'signed up' to the app their details will be held in a 'Profile' page. These details can be accessed by clicking on the 'Profile' icon. The user can change or update data held in the profile page.

Unit 7.2 Decomposing problems: Designing an app

Practice

- Open the template **apptemplate.docx** provided by your teacher in *Microsoft Word*.
- Save the file as **SignUp.docx**.
- Using this file, create a wireframe for the Sign Up page.
  The Sign Up page should provide spaces for the user to enter their name, a username and a password. It needs a button to allow the user to submit their details. You can use textboxes, colour and graphics to show layout.
- Open the template **apptemplate.docx** again.
- Save the file as **Login.docx**.
- Using this file, create a wireframe for the Login page.
  The Login page should look similar to the Sign Up page but it should only ask for the username and password. You can use textboxes, colour and graphics to show layout.
- The first three wireframes (Home, Sign Up and Login) are now complete.
- There are different ways of collecting feedback from users; they could select a happy face or write a lengthy answer to a question. Look at the examples of feedback forms below:

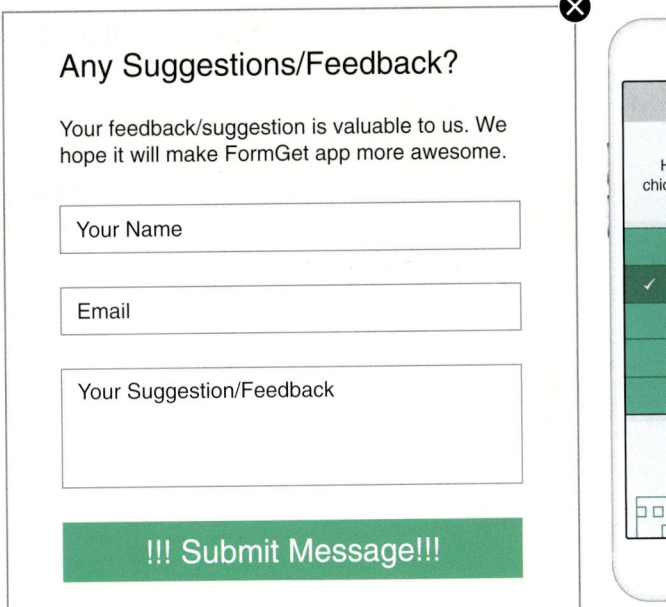

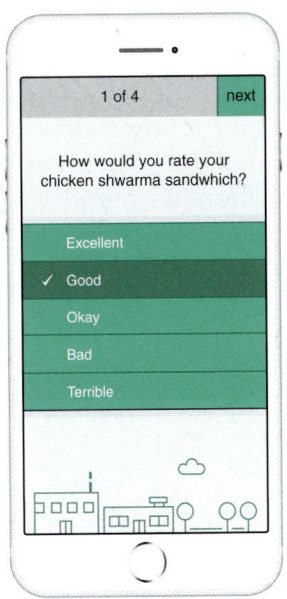

- Research how feedback pages on apps are arranged and how they allow users to provide feedback. Why do you think companies want feedback about their apps? Discuss with a partner how a company could use this feedback.
  o Open the template **apptemplate.docx** provided by your teacher in *Microsoft Word*.
  o Save the file as **Feedback.docx.**
  o Using this file, design a wireframe that will allow the app user to provide feedback about it.

47

International Computing for Lower Secondary

Designing socks and selecting options

Learn

A **selection** is used to make choices depending on the information provided by the user. In the case of the socks, the user must select either ski socks or sports socks. Different things will happen based on the choice of socks.

When you design solutions, you have to show how we deal with each of the choices the user can make. These choices usually take the form of questions, such as:

Do you want sports socks or ski socks?

The user's answer will determine which screen is shown: the sports sock screen or the ski sock screen. So, there are two pathways. Selection allows you to choose a pathway in the code.

When designing a solution, it is important that you can show all of the pathways in the solution.

Flowcharts

Flowcharts are methods of representing solutions to a problem.

A flow diagram (or flowchart) is a graphical or picture representation of the solution to a problem. Flowcharts use symbols to represent different operations, and flow lines to represent the flow of control or the pathways taken. Arrows on the flow lines represent the direction of flow, from top to bottom or left to right.

Some of the symbols used for flowcharts are shown below.

Can you remember what the user has to do if they choose sports socks? look at page 43 to remind yourself.

KEYWORDS

selection: a programming construct with more than one possible pathway; a condition is tested (using a question or criterion) before deciding which pathway to follow (which parts of the program or app will be executed next)

flowchart: a graphical representation of a solution to a problem which uses special symbols

flowchart: Draw a simple flowchart showing your decision making process in the morning from the time you wake up to the time you leave your home.

Graphic	Symbol	Purpose
→	Flow line	Indicates the flow of logic and connects the different symbols together.
(rounded rectangle)	Terminal (Stop/Start)	Represents the start and end of the flowchart.
(parallelogram)	Input/Output	Indicates input or output of data.
(rectangle)	Process	Indicates that an operation is to be done; there is usually text in the rectangle.
(diamond)	Decision	A decision box asks a question; there are two alternatives and a pathway is selected based on the response to the question.

Unit 7.2 Decomposing problems: Designing an app

Consider what happens when the user has to select a pair of socks.

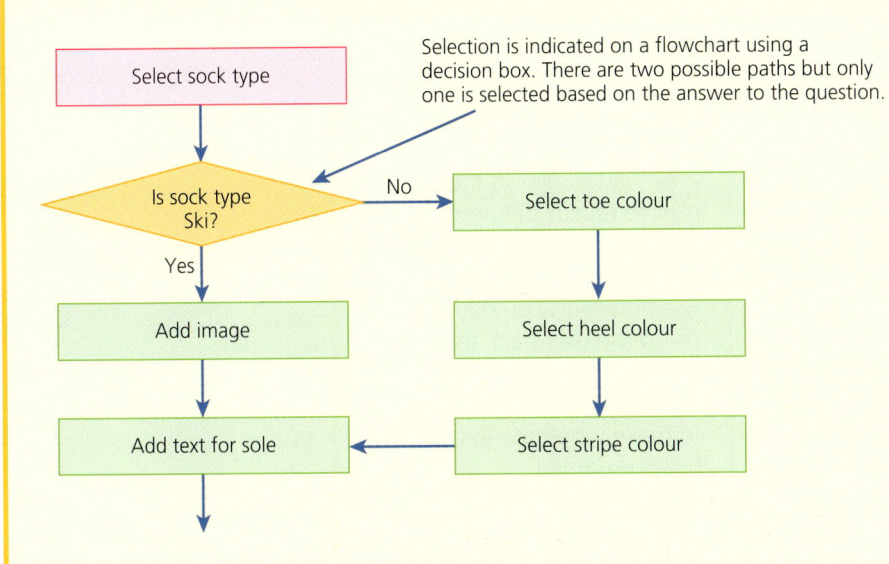

Selection is indicated on a flowchart using a decision box. There are two possible paths but only one is selected based on the answer to the question.

[Flowchart: Select sock type → Is sock type Ski? → Yes: Add image → Add text for sole. No: Select toe colour → Select heel colour → Select stripe colour → Add text for sole]

This is a section of the flowchart for sock selection. This part shows the decision box for the sock type and two pathways. Only one pathway is selected based on the user's response.

Selection is very important when designing solutions. It allows the designer to give the user choices to move through the app or program.

Another important feature of an algorithm is that it can allow a user to repeat a task or set of instructions. If a user wants to order more than one pair of socks, they will have to repeat the process. An algorithm must be able to show that parts of the program can be repeated if necessary.

Repetition is the process of repeating parts of the algorithm until a particular condition is met. Repetition allows the algorithm to **loop** around a set of tasks. This means that the designer only has to write the algorithm or code for the task once, and then it can be used over and over again.

The Sweet FeetZ app will allow users to preview their sock designs to ensure they are happy. If a user is not happy with the socks, they must repeat the process.

This section of the flowchart shows repetition. There is a loop in the flowchart. It allows the user to repeat the process by taking them back to the Select Sock Size process. The flowchart could have taken the user back to Select Sock Type instead. This is a choice for Yang to make when the app is being designed.

KEYWORDS

repetition: repeating a section of a program or app a number of times or until a particular criterion is met; it allows for looping in an app

loop: a feature of a programming language that allows for sections of code to be repeated

International Computing for Lower Secondary

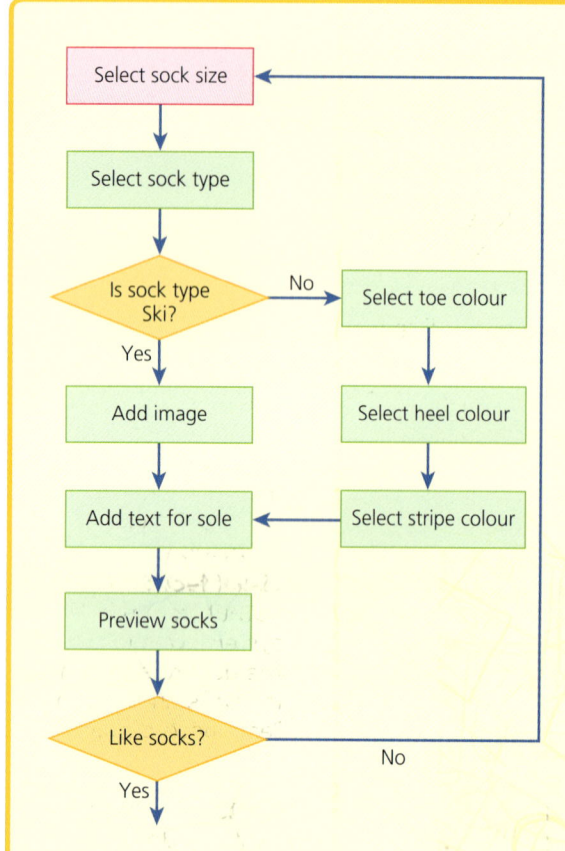

```
Select sock size → (loop target)
        ↓
Select sock type
        ↓
Is sock type Ski?
  Yes ↓                No → Select toe colour
  Add image                     ↓
        ↓               Select heel colour
  Add text for sole ← Select stripe colour
        ↓
  Preview socks
        ↓
  Like socks?
  Yes ↓   No → (back to Select sock size)
```

This section of the flow chart shows repetition. There is a loop in the flowchart. It allows the user to repeat the process by taking them back to the Select Sock Size process. The flowchart could have taken the user back to Select Sock Type instead. This is a choice for Yang to make when the app is being designed.

Practice

- Use a word processor to draw a flowchart that represents a solution to the login screen based on the following information:
    - When the app opens, it needs to check if the user is registered.
    - If the user is registered, they are taken to the login screen.
    - If the user is not registered, they are taken to the registration screen.
- You can use textboxes or shapes to create the flowchart symbols.
- Discuss your solution with a partner.
- Identify any selection or repetition which you have included in the solution.

Unit 7.2 Decomposing problems: Designing an app

Using interactivity and gestures to keep the customer happy

Learn

A successful app must be interesting and engaging. Here are some features that can be added to improve the user experience.

- Interactivity: The more **interactive** your app is, the more likely it is to grab the attention of potential customers.
- Gestures: **Gestures** can improve interactivity; for example, tap, touch, swipe, drag, double tap, pinch. These well-known gestures help users to interact with apps.

Guilt-free gluten-free penne pasta is sautéed in olive oil, tomatoes and basil. it's an easy and healthy dinner.

Calories 465g | Protein 27g | Fat 12g

Gluten-Free   Egg Free

Tomato Penne Pasta

▲ This picture invites the user to make a swipe down gesture to see the recipe for Tomato Penne Pasta.

- Animation: When paired with gestures, animation makes the user's brain think it is interacting with real objects.
  - Animation provides **visual feedback** to the user. If the app does not use animation, users may not have enough feedback to tell them that they have successfully completed a gesture or action.
  - A common gesture is pull-to-refresh. When paired with animation, the user feels that the list is being actively refreshed while they are watching. Most email apps use this gesture.

KEYWORDS

interactive: allowing two way flow of information between the device and the user; an application which accepts input from the user

gestures: actions on a touch screen which allow people to interact with smart phones; for example, swipe down

visual feedback: output from the system which allows the user to see what is happening and to react accordingly

Gestures: What gestures do you normally use on a tablet or on a computer when you don't use a mouse?

51

- ➤ Sound: Sound is used by humans to communicate and make sense of their world. It can provide feedback to an action or behaviour. Using sound provides a multi-sensory interaction for users.
- ➤ **Accessibility**: Approximately one in seven people worldwide have some sort of disability. Some of these people will use your app. As an app designer, you should think about the following.
  - **Content resizing**: Allow users to resize content. All users benefit from this, but it especially helps users with visual impairments.
  - Colours: Colours are a great way to get an important message across. However, if someone is colour blind, the choice of colour is especially important. Also, if the Sun is shining on a screen, some colours are difficult to see – especially for the visually impaired.
  - **Touch target size**: Users with limited mobility and vision impairments may find it difficult to touch small items, or touch targets, on the screen. The recommended minimum size for touch targets is 7–10 mm. Designers should also leave a space around these targets so that people do not press them by accident.

> **KEYWORDS**
>
> **accessibility:** providing features which will assist those who have impairments or disabilities
>
> **content resizing:** a feature which allows the user to select the size of the text or images on the screen
>
> **touch target size:** the size of the area on the screen which is set aside for tapping an item

Unit 7.2 Decomposing problems: Designing an app

Practice

This is the wireframe for the Select Sock Size process. The app designer has decided to include interactivity and gestures to assist the user on this screen of the app.

➤ As the app designer, you must provide a document containing information about the Select Sock Size wireframe.
  o Look at the wireframe above and discuss with a friend how the designer intends to make use of gestures and animation.
  o Using a word processor, create a report to describe how gestures and animation are going to be used in the app.
➤ Yang wants to ensure that the app is designed for everyone. He has asked you to review the Select Sock Size wireframe and comment on how this could be improved for people with visual impairment:
  o Open the document **SockSizeTemplate.docx** provided by your teacher in *Microsoft Word*.
  o Edit the wireframe and describe how you would use content resizing, colour, target touch sizing, and sound to help visually impaired people to use this page.
  o You can do this by adding textboxes and arrows containing ideas for improvement.

53

International Computing for Lower Secondary

Go further

- ◆ Look at this section of the flowchart for the app:
- ◆ Describe how selection and repetition have been used to help provide a solution for the app.
- ◆ Look at the Calculate Cost process. The cost is calculated by multiplying the number of pairs of socks by the cost of the socks. Both ski socks and sports socks cost the same. You can decide on the price of the socks. Use the **apptemplate.docx** document to design a screen, for the app, which will display the cost for the customer.
- ◆ After the cost is displayed, the customer will have to enter their delivery details and pay for the socks. Complete the flowchart so that the customer:
    - ❏ enters delivery address details
    - ❏ enters payment details
    - ❏ is asked if they want to go back to the start and design a different pair of socks. If they answer yes, the flowchart arrow should go to the top of the flowchart. If they answer no, the flowchart should stop.
- ◆ Swap your flowchart with another student and compare your designs. Discuss how well your flowchart represents the solution.
- ◆ In a group of four, identify the remaining screens which need to be designed. Each person in the group should create a wireframe for one screen not already designed. Before attempting to do this, the group should decide on the colour scheme and the interactivity elements to be used.

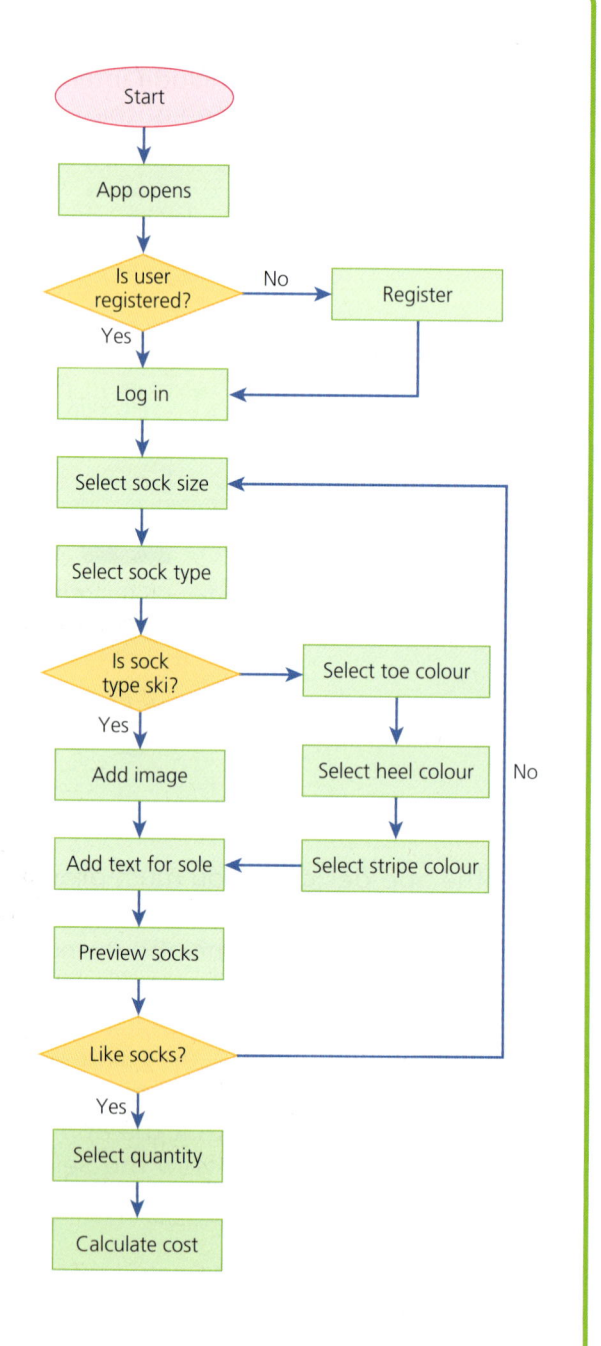

Flowchart:
Start → App opens → Is user registered? — No → Register; Yes → Log in → Select sock size → Select sock type → Is sock type ski? — Yes → Add image → Add text for sole → Preview socks → Like socks? — Yes → Select quantity → Calculate cost. If No to "Is sock type ski?": Select toe colour → Select heel colour → Select stripe colour → Add text for sole. If No to "Like socks?": back to Select sock size.

54

Unit 7.2 Decomposing problems: Designing an app

Challenge yourself

In order to ensure that the app is a success, it is necessary to evaluate it. Many mobile app users open an app once and never return. Nowadays, users expect a lot from an app. It should be easy to use, load fast and make good use of interactivity. In fact, the best apps need fewer clicks to complete a task.

Good apps …	What you should (or should not) do
… are easy to understand	Do not provide the users with information overload. Do not clutter the screen with too much information and buttons. Give each screen one function.
… have a good navigation system	Make sure your navigation system is clear and that users can move from one page to another easily. This is why you included a navigation menu at the bottom of each page of the Sweet FeetZ app.
… require few clicks to complete a task	If a task has a lot of screens or steps, then it should be divided up into two tasks. One example in your Sweet FeetZ app is the payment process which could be divided up into entering delivery details and checkout. The user should know where they are in the process. For example, step 1 of 5.
… use the information already collected	For example, if a user is logged in then their address or location may already be available. Some online taxi companies do not ask the customer about their location as the app will already provide this.
… make good use of interactivity	Make good use of interaction. Tap targets should be the right size and remember to design for thumb use.
… are accessible	The app should be designed for all people regardless of disability.
… meet the client's requirements	The app should meet the needs specified by the client.

- Create a podcast or movie in which you evaluate your app design under each heading. You should talk about each of the wireframes you have designed and say how they meet the criteria for a good app. You could use a sound recorder on a computer, or a phone or tablet to do this. Ask your teacher's permission before using a device in class.

- Swap your evaluation with another student and discuss how each of you have or have not designed a good app.

- Use the discussion to come up with two important improvements for your app.

Definition check: Close your book and make a list of as many terms you have learned in this unit as you can. Compare them with your partner's list. Together try to define as many of them as you can. Check your definitions against the definitions given in the key word boxes.

Unit 7.3 HTML: It's all news to me

About web news and HTML

We have access to news **apps** on mobile devices, dedicated news websites and social media applications to support the spread of news items.

Thanks to all of these, we have access to news articles about current events almost as soon as the event occurs and often as the event is happening.

reach: Find the reach of your favorite website.

Learning Outcomes

In this unit you will learn to:
- appreciate the **reach** of online articles and realise the implications of the immediacy of news presented online
- consider the impact of online news, how we access news online and be able to identify fake news
- understand how images are represented in binary form
- understand lossy and lossless compression approaches used to reduce file sizes
- understand the technical terminology relating to the internet, the intranet and the world wide web
- interpret and amend **website source code**
- break down a website address into its various components
- select appropriate digital image resources for inclusion in online applications and understand the importance of using folders to help organise **digital assets**
- create your own basic website using **HyperText Markup Language (HTML)** for a given audience
- understand how to apply **Cascading Style Sheets (CSS)** to improve the consistency of content in a web page.

KEYWORDS

reach: the number of people who visit a web page

website source code: the HTML code which is used to control the layout of any online web page

digital assets: any digital resources used to create an application; it is any text or multimedia files saved in binary format

HyperText Markup Language (HTML): the language used to create documents which can be published on the world wide web

Cascading Style Sheets (CSS): a language used to describe how the content of a HTML document will be presented

Unit 7.3 HTML: It's all news to me

SCENARIO

You are a new technology journalist with a newspaper called The Local Times. The editor of the newspaper is concerned about fake news and how it can impact on the stories other journalists are writing. He has asked you to help train other members of staff in recognising fake news stories, such as the ones shown below.

Coca-Cola is to launch three new flavours of its sugar-free Zero brand, claims the Sunday Mirror.

The avocado, sourdough and charcoal flavoured soft drinks have been conceived to appeal to the "brunch-loving, super food-snacking millennial", the newspaper says.

"Revolutionary" VAR headsets will be used by referees at the World Cup in Russia, claims a football "exclusive" in the Sun on Sunday. The $5000 gadgets will employ virtual reality to allow officials to see replays instantly on a 3D screen, speeding up decisions, we are told.

As a technology specialist, the editor also wants you to help develop a news website, and to help other journalists understand the importance of online news presentation and how people access news online. You will work through some exercises to help you identify fake news stories and learn about HTML. You will then create your own news website using HTML and digital assets you have found on the internet.

> **Do you remember?**
>
> Before starting this unit, you should be able to:
> - ✓ type web addresses into an internet **web browser** to locate a specific website
> - ✓ use an internet **search engine** and appropriate key words to locate information or resources on a specified topic
> - ✓ enter text correctly in volume.

DID YOU KNOW?

Newspapers and journalists must follow strict fact-checking guidelines before publishing news stories. But because it's possible for anyone to publish something online *without* fact-checking, there are many stories online which are untrue. They are fake news.

KEYWORDS

web browser: a software application which allows users to locate, access and display information on the world wide web; interprets HTML code and displays the web page content

search engine: a program which can be used to access information on the world wide web by taking key words entered by the user and searching for websites containing those key words

search engine: Which search engine do you use most often? Why do you use that search engine?

57

International Computing for Lower Secondary

Accessing news

Learn

More and more people access news articles online rather than waiting to catch up on the day's news on television.

People prefer to access news articles online for many reasons. Some of these include:

- immediacy – news is available as it happens and updates are available immediately
- interactivity – news articles often come with links to related content, so you can **surf** between related articles
- personalisation – personalised lists of news articles are selected and shown to you based on your previous viewing history and hobbies
- multimedia – articles often include **sound bites**, video clips, and **live streams** which help bring the news to life
- multiple sources – using the internet, you can search for alternative articles using key words to verify content and read different viewpoints

sound bites: Tell your partner about the last sound bite you listened to?

KEYWORDS

surf (the internet): the process of navigating through content on the world wide web by following **hyperlinks** on web pages

sound bites: short extracts from a longer piece of audio recording

live streams: using the internet to provide live video or audio from an event as it is happening

hyperlink: a word, phrase or image that once clicked on will take the user to another location, page, website, or open a document linked to the current file

Hyperlink: Find a hyperlink on your favorite website.

Practice

- Before you can understand how fake news is able to spread so quickly, you need to consider the various methods commonly used to access news articles. As a class, select a topic or famous individual. You will search the internet for news articles about the topic or individual.
  Examine at least three online news apps or web pages about the same news topic
  o Complete a table like the one shown on the next page; your teacher can give you a blank copy of the table.
  o Follow any hyperlinks on the web pages you find and complete the next row using that article.

Hyperlinks may appear as images or titles which can then be clicked on to take you to another part of the article or another web page.

58

Unit 7.3 HTML: It's all news to me

Article title	Website	Websites linked to	Reliability rating (scored 0–5)	Reliability rating explained
Alien Visitors	www.mynews.com	www.newnews.com www.oldnews.com www.dailynews.com		*Comment on the content provided* *Did the site include images or video to provide proof of the story* *Did the story seem biased in any way?* *Has the website been updated recently?* *Did all hyperlinks work?* *Did hyperlinks take you to relevant stories, advertisements?*

- With a partner discuss:
  o what reliability rating you gave each of the articles
  o why you gave that rating
  o which article you gave the highest reliability rating to and why you think this was the most reliable article you viewed.
- As a class, discuss the range of apps or websites (such as YouTube, Instagram, BBC News) that you and your family members use to access news. Which is the most popular?
- Discuss the following and, as a class, record your findings.
  o What websites or apps do older family members use to access the news?
  o How often do they check the news apps?
  o Why do they check the news app with this level of frequency?
  o Do they use **push notifications** to alert them to 'breaking news' stories? What impact does this have on them if they are doing another task?
- Much access to online news is **phone-led** as this is convenient; it allows users to access news at any time and in any location. Complete the table shown on the next page. Place the correct phrases in the appropriate column to illustrate the pros and cons of accessing news articles via mobile devices (add your own pros and cons to complete the table). Your teacher will give you a copy of this table to complete.

push notifications: Which push notifications do you use? Is it distracting?

KEYWORDS

push notifications: a message which appears on an app to let you know something new has occurred

phone-led: where access to something is led by your phone (or apps you access on your phone) rather than decisions you have made

59

Pros and Cons of accessing news articles online

- Able to scroll and swipe through content quickly
- Multimedia content illustrates news articles
- Tend to remain on same app, scrolling around between many linked articles
- Can be distracting; I don't always realise how long I have been online
- Articles are short
- All the articles I read online are accurate
- Data about the articles I read is being collected by other organisations
- Often too many articles are shown and you can be desensitised
- Fear Of Missing Out (FOMO) is one of the main reasons people access news online

Pros	Cons

Unit 7.3 HTML: It's all news to me

Navigating the news world

Learn

When you access news articles online you need to be sure you can successfully handle some of the cons associated with this type of news presentation. The diagram below identifies the technical terms for some of the main problems of online news articles.

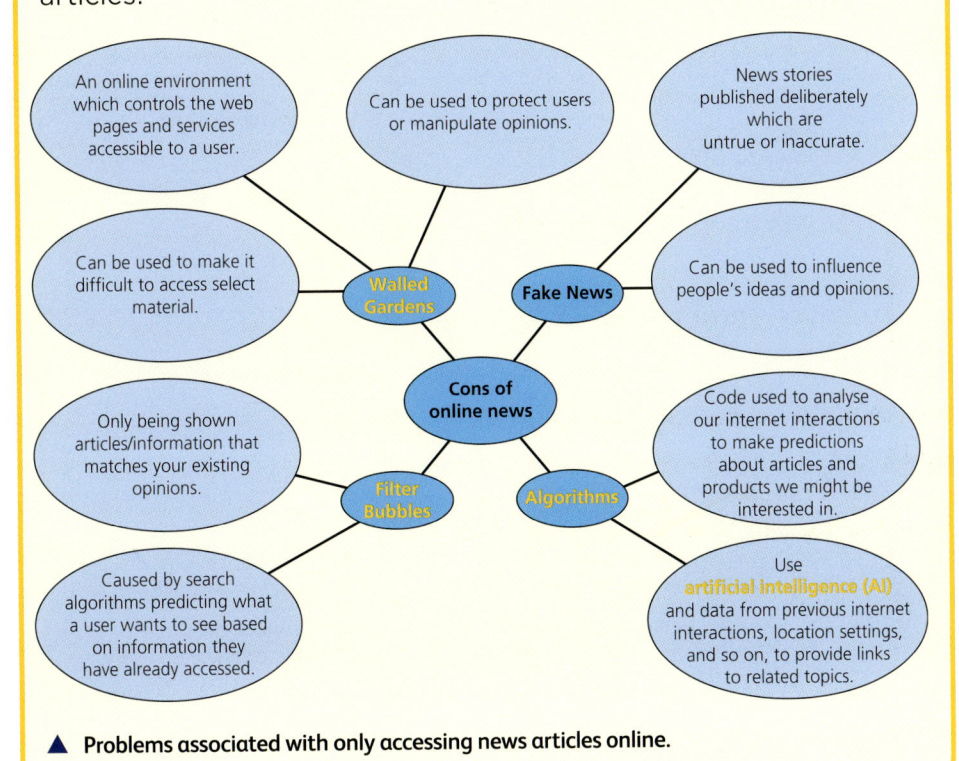

Cons of online news

- **Walled Gardens**
  - An online environment which controls the web pages and services accessible to a user.
  - Can be used to make it difficult to access select material.
- **Fake News**
  - Can be used to protect users or manipulate opinions.
  - News stories published deliberately which are untrue or inaccurate.
  - Can be used to influence people's ideas and opinions.
- **Filter Bubbles**
  - Only being shown articles/information that matches your existing opinions.
  - Caused by search algorithms predicting what a user wants to see based on information they have already accessed.
- **Algorithms**
  - Code used to analyse our internet interactions to make predictions about articles and products we might be interested in.
  - Use **artificial intelligence (AI)** and data from previous internet interactions, location settings, and so on, to provide links to related topics.

▲ Problems associated with only accessing news articles online.

ISP: What ISP do you use at home?

KEYWORDS

walled garden: virtual fence put in place, often by an **internet service provider (ISP)**, to make it difficult to access material which displays a certain opinion or set of facts

internet service provider (ISP): a company which provides services to support internet access, for example companies which provide broadband access, mobile phone and 4G or 5G services

filter bubble: often generated because of artificial intelligence (AI) algorithms which predict the sites/ articles a user would be interested in based on those previously accessed; can limit the formation of broad opinions and ideas

algorithm: a computer program used to find patterns in the data accessed by a user to make predictions about similar articles/ websites they might be interested in viewing; uses an element of **machine learning** and artificial intelligence

Practice

- In this task you will look more closely at the problems of online news sites and consider how, as users, we can avoid some of these downfalls. Carry out some research on the internet to find out how to avoid each of the problems shown in the diagram above.
  For example, use a search engine of your choice to enter in the key words 'Avoid Filter Bubbles'
- Your teacher will provide you with a file called **ConsOfOnlineNews**. Develop the diagram further by using the findings from your research to include details on how each of the problems identified in the diagram can be avoided.

International Computing for Lower Secondary

Abstraction and pattern recognition

Think like a news algorithm!

In the diagram below, analyse the articles accessed by a user on the left hand side of the screen. Predict which articles on the right hand side of the diagram you would recommend for them the next time they log on.

- Make use of pattern recognition to find multiple instances of the same word.
- Make use of abstraction to categorise similar words under a common word.
- Say why you would make these decisions.

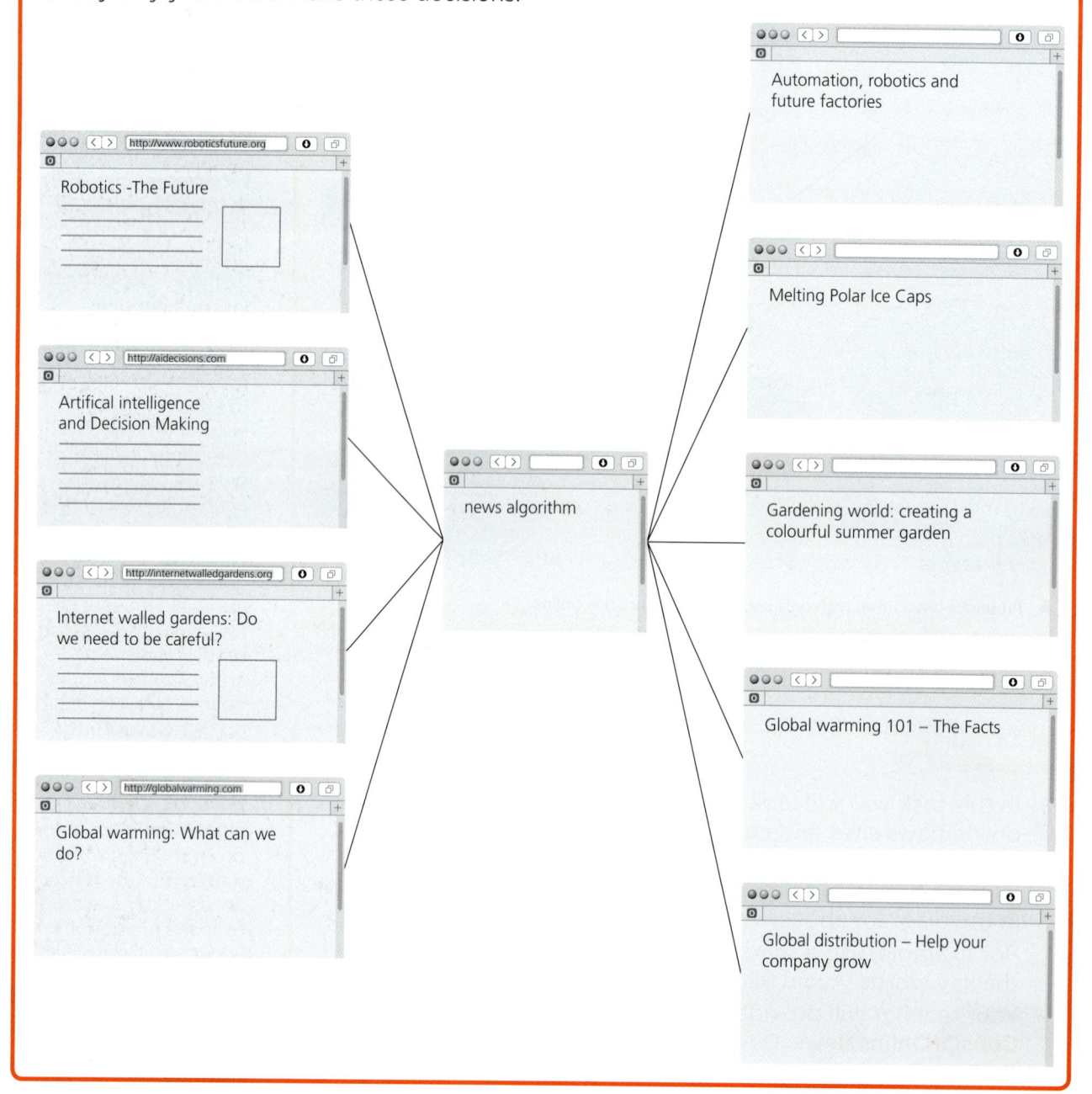

Left side (articles accessed):
- http://www.roboticsfuture.org — Robotics - The Future
- http://aidecisions.com — Artifical intelligence and Decision Making
- http://internetwalledgardens.org — Internet walled gardens: Do we need to be careful?
- http://globalwarming.com — Global warming: What can we do?

Centre: news algorithm

Right side (possible recommendations):
- Automation, robotics and future factories
- Melting Polar Ice Caps
- Gardening world: creating a colourful summer garden
- Global warming 101 – The Facts
- Global distribution – Help your company grow

62

Unit 7.3 HTML: It's all news to me

Social media and journalism

Learn

Internet news sites and social media presentation of news has changed not only the way we access the news but also the way journalists operate.

- Journalists can provide news stories to their audiences immediately – through online news websites and apps and social media news items can be shared millions of times within minutes of them being posted online.
- Journalists have the ability to live stream news via **social media** websites.
- **Social media influencers** can impact on **trending** stories.
- Audiences don't have to sit and wait for news to be sent to them in newspapers or read out on the evening news. Instead they can post news stories themselves on social media sites, or email news stories to journalists.
- Journalists often use **social media harvesting** to gather breaking news stories, which sometimes come from the audience.
- Journalists and audiences need to be more aware of fake news stories, **click bait** and other distracting online content as this can distract from the real news stories.

KEYWORDS

social media: websites and apps where users can create and share their own multimedia content

social media influencer: an individual with a large following on social media whose online posts can influence opinions or decisions

trending: a topic which is currently popular online

social media harvesting: collecting data from social media sites to help identify trends in news stories, often done using algorithms

click bait: a headline that may not be entirely true or truly reflect the contents of the article it leads to, but which is designed to encourage a reader to access that link

social media: Compare the social media you use with those that your partner uses.
social media influencer: Choose someone you follow on social media and find out how much of a following he/she has.
trending: What topics are you aware of that are currently trending?
click bait: Have you recently clicked on something to find it was just click bait? Tell your partner about your experience.

Practice

- The diagram on the next page represents all of the new stories which have appeared on a journalist's social media feed overnight. Each number in the news feed represents an occurrence of story. Some stories are trending.
- With a friend, analyse the journalist's news feed. Help them identify any news items that are trending so they can write a follow-up story.

63

International Computing for Lower Secondary

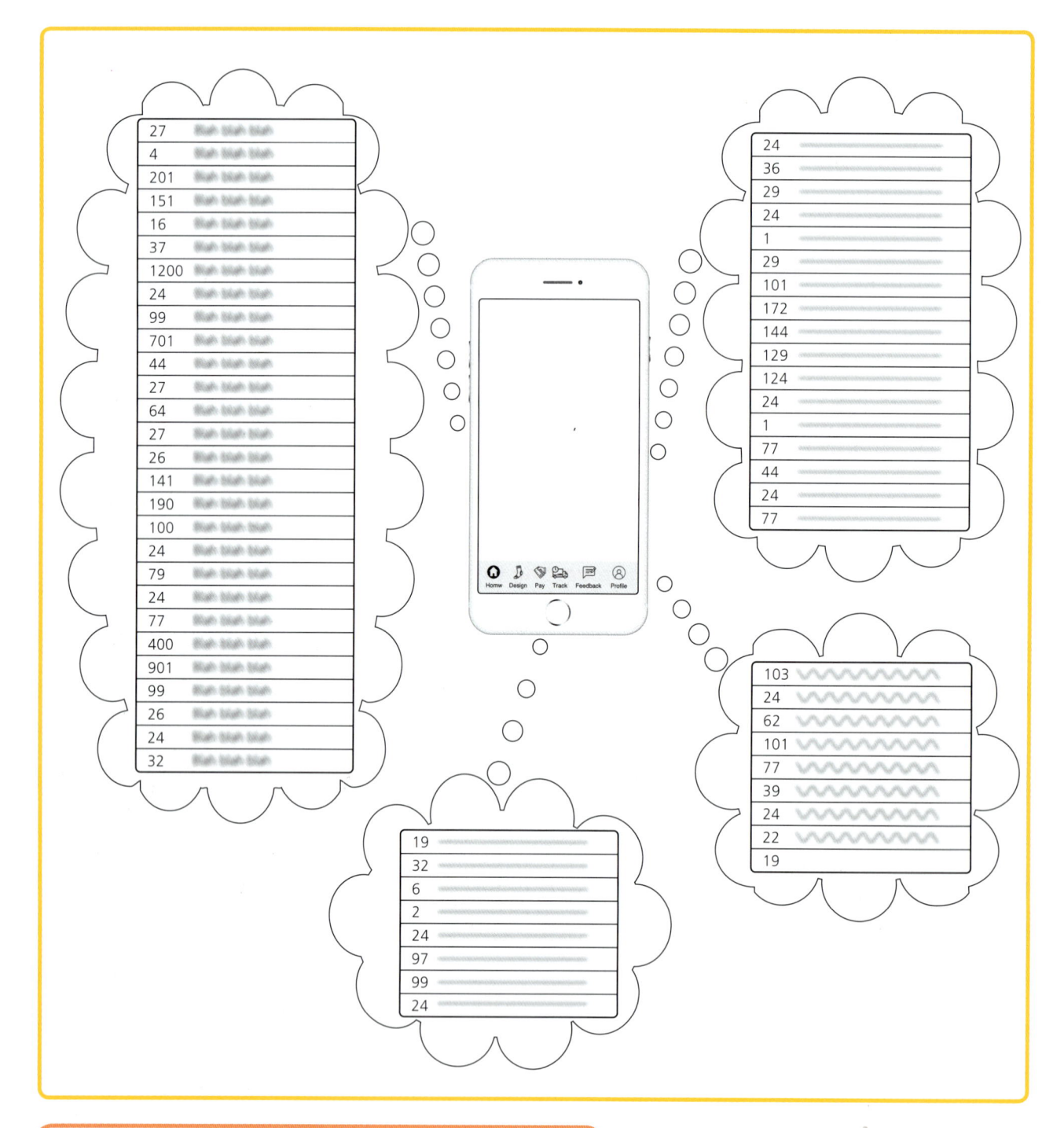

Thought bubble 1 (left):
27	Blah blah blah
4	Blah blah blah
201	Blah blah blah
151	Blah blah blah
16	Blah blah blah
37	Blah blah blah
1200	Blah blah blah
24	Blah blah blah
99	Blah blah blah
701	Blah blah blah
44	Blah blah blah
27	Blah blah blah
64	Blah blah blah
27	Blah blah blah
26	Blah blah blah
141	Blah blah blah
190	Blah blah blah
100	Blah blah blah
24	Blah blah blah
79	Blah blah blah
24	Blah blah blah
77	Blah blah blah
400	Blah blah blah
901	Blah blah blah
99	Blah blah blah
26	Blah blah blah
24	Blah blah blah
32	Blah blah blah

Thought bubble 2 (top right):
24, 36, 29, 24, 1, 29, 101, 172, 144, 129, 124, 24, 1, 77, 44, 24, 77

Thought bubble 3 (bottom right):
103, 24, 62, 101, 77, 39, 24, 22, 19

Thought bubble 4 (bottom centre):
19, 32, 6, 2, 24, 97, 99, 24

Phone icons: Home, Design, Pay, Track, Feedback, Profile

Pattern recognition and decomposition

Write down an algorithm on how the journalist will make sense of their news feed (for example, using tallies). As part of your algorithm, think about:

- pattern recognition; identifying repeating entries or grouping similar entries (abstraction)
- decomposition; how you and your friend are going to divide up the tasks for analysis.

64

Unit 7.3 HTML: It's all news to me

The fake news phenomenon

Learn

Fake news stories are stories which are untrue.

Sometimes, parts of a fake news story can be true but the rest may be inaccurate as the person writing the story has not fully checked the facts. Other fake news stories are completely inaccurate and are only written to increase the number of people visiting a website; in other words, they can be used as click bait.

The problem with fake news is:

- it can be difficult to tell which stories are true and which are fake; this can be confusing and damaging, especially for young viewers
- it can be harmful to the subject's reputation
- if journalists cannot identify fake news stories, they may unknowingly write articles based on untrue facts; this can lead to websites not being trusted when they post real news stories.

How can we as internet users spot fake news?

- Always confirm the story using another reliable source, such as a reputable website or the television or radio news
- Do you think the story sounds realistic or believable?
- Use the website address to check the reliability of the source; for example:
  - is it a well-known domain name?
  - is the domain name correctly spelt?
  - is the top-level domain well recognised; for example, .orgcom instead of .com or .org?
  - do any images or videos used to illustrate the story look fake or edited?

Practice

Produce a poster or infographic to help students in your school identify fake news stories.

Your poster should:

- grab the attention of the audience quickly, perhaps with a clever or sensational title
- include a small number of copyright-free images
- make use of clear and easy-to-read fonts
- contain a small number of points which are easy for a younger audience to understand.

> When using a search engine such as *Google* to select images, you should ensure the images can be used without breaking copyright laws. To do this, go to the home page and select images. Enter in your key words for your search, click on 'Any licence' on the right hand side and choose 'Free to share and use'.

65

International Computing for Lower Secondary

Getting to know your URLs

Learn

In this section you will be introduced to the various parts which make up a **uniform resource locator (URL)** and gain an understanding of what makes a good URL.

All websites have a URL. This is the technical term for a reference to a web resource.

To access a website, you enter the website's URL into the address bar of a web browser.

Part 1 protocol: a set of rules used to support the transfer of data across the internet.

Part 3 sub domain: this tells the user what page of the website they are visiting. In this case we are accessing the KS3 (Key stage 3) page of the Hodder website. Not all web pages will include a sub domain.

Part 5 top-level domain: this tells users what type of organisation owns the site and what country their server is located in; for example, this is a company with a server based in the UK.

address bar

`https://www.keystage3.hoddereducation.co.uk/thisbook/unit3.html`

Part 2 web server or **web reference:** this identifies the type of computer storing the document; in this case a www server

Part 4 domain name: this tells visitors to the web address who owns the site, in this case Hodder Education.

Part 6 folders/pathway: the folder on the server which is storing the resource we are accessing; for example, in this case, the page we are accessing is in a folder called 'this book' and the page we are accessing is 'unit3'

Part 7 file extension: this tells the browser what type of file it is displaying, in this case a HTML page

---

DID YOU KNOW?
URLs were defined in 1994 by Tim Berners-Lee. He invented the world wide web.

KEYWORDS

uniform resource locator (URL): an address which tells browsers where to locate individual resources on the world wide web

web server: a computer which manages resources on a network and acts as a central storage place for resources on a network

66

Unit 7.3 HTML: It's all news to me

Pattern recognition and abstraction

A URL is a layer of abstraction. It hides the web server or hosted location's IP address.

This layer of abstraction helps us, because website addresses are easier to remember than IP addresses in the form of numbers.

Practice

- Users don't always know the exact URL of the website or web page they are trying to access, so they will attempt to access the website using a search engine.

  Organisations using the internet want to increase the amount of **website traffic** to their websites. They try to do this by making their website more 'visible' to search engine users; this is called **search engine optimisation (SEO)**.

  To help with this, organisations should follow the hints below.

website traffic: How much website traffic does one of the sites you use get?

KEYWORDS

website traffic: the number of web users who visit a site

search engine optimisation (SEO): steps taken by organisations to help increase the number of visitors to their website

1. Search engines will look for key words in your domain name, then your sub domain before any other part of your web page. So include your key words in the domain or sub domain!
2. Do not include spaces in your web address. If you want to separate keywords, use hyphens (-) or underscores (_).
3. Keep the URL short and simple.
4. Keep page URL's relevant to the content.
5. Remove 'stop words' such as *and*, *or*, *the*, *but*, and so on.

- With a friend, discuss the made-up URLs listed below. State whether each is search engine optimised and user friendly.
- What can be done to improve each web address?
- Produce an alternative web address which is both user friendly and search engine optimised.

A web address for a new online shop selling sportswear for teenagers. The shop is called Teen Sports Wear:
http://www.youwear.com/ksjdfsuek/sdfss.html

A URL which links to a new music streaming website called music4you. This URL links to a web page with links to songs by a new artist called 'Music Master':
http://www.four_____you.edu/Song list.com

A URL for a school blog which Stage 7 students in your class need to complete as part of a homework on website design:
http://www.blogsite.com/HYUJGDL/HOMEWORK/YEAR9BLOG.jpg

67

International Computing for Lower Secondary

> ▸ The editor has asked you to identify a URL for The Local Times news website. Label each of the parts of the newspaper's new URL to show you have included a:
> - protocol
> - domain name
> - web server reference
> - top level domain.
>
> ▸ Go to http://whois.domaintools.com/ and type in your proposed URL to see if it is already being used by another organisation.

Wi-Fi: What Wi-Fi network do you use at home?

Internet, intranet or world wide web?

Learn

We often use the terms internet and world wide web (www) to mean the same thing. They are, in fact, very different.

The **internet** is a global network of networks all interconnected using connections such as **satellites**, **fibre optic cable** and **Wi-Fi** connections. Anyone with the correct technology and communication links can access the internet.

Electronic devices connected to larger networks can gain access to an **internet router** using a Wi-Fi connection or, if there are a lot of users, they may be connected via a **switch**. A switch is a device that can take many signals from lots of devices and organise them so they can travel down one single communication line. Devices can be connected to a switch using an **ethernet cable**.

The www is made up from all of the multimedia applications which run on the internet. Pages from www applications are created using HTML code and can be viewed using web browsers. Once a user has accessed a www resource they can use hypertext links to navigate from one resource to another. The http protocol is most often used to transfer content across the internet.

An **intranet** is a private network used within an organisation. An intranet makes use of internet technologies but is said to have a **closed user group**. In other words, users need authorisation in order to gain access to the content on the intranet site. Users of an organisation's intranet can log on to the intranet from inside the organisation but they can also log on remotely using internet communication technologies, as shown in the diagram on the next page. Many organisations use intranets to share information with employees, to support communication and file sharing among colleagues.

KEYWORDS

satellites: an object which orbits the Earth which can transmit communication signals across the globe

fibre optic cable: cable which consists of one or more strands of glass used to transmit data using pulses of light along long distances

Wi-Fi: a wireless networking technology which transmits data using radio signals

internet router: a hardware device that can connect a local network to the internet

switch: a device that can take many signals from lots of devices and organise them so they can travel down one single communication line

ethernet cable: high speed cable used to connect devices on a network over short distances

intranet: a private network used mainly by the members of an organisation

closed user group: a method of restricting access to a network or communication group by providing only those authorised with a username and password

Unit 7.3 HTML: It's all news to me

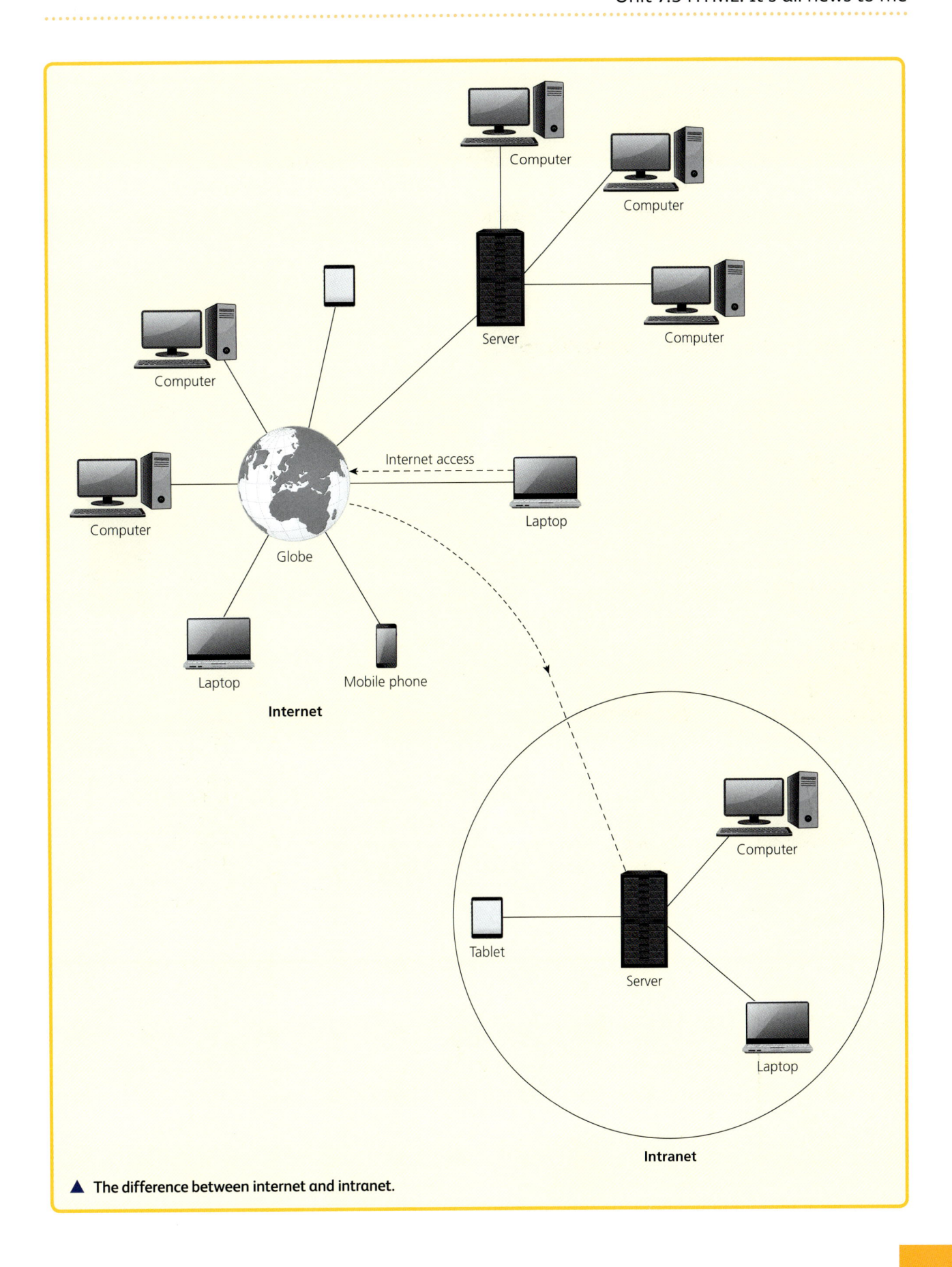

▲ The difference between internet and intranet.

International Computing for Lower Secondary

Practice

The editor of The Local Times has asked you to produce a graphic. It should show the technology needed to allow readers to access the news pages from digital devices, once the web pages are published.

➤ Use what you have learned about the technology needed to allow users to connect to the newspaper website. Do this by labelling the communication media used at each point in the diagram below (labelled 1–5). Some terms may be used more than once.

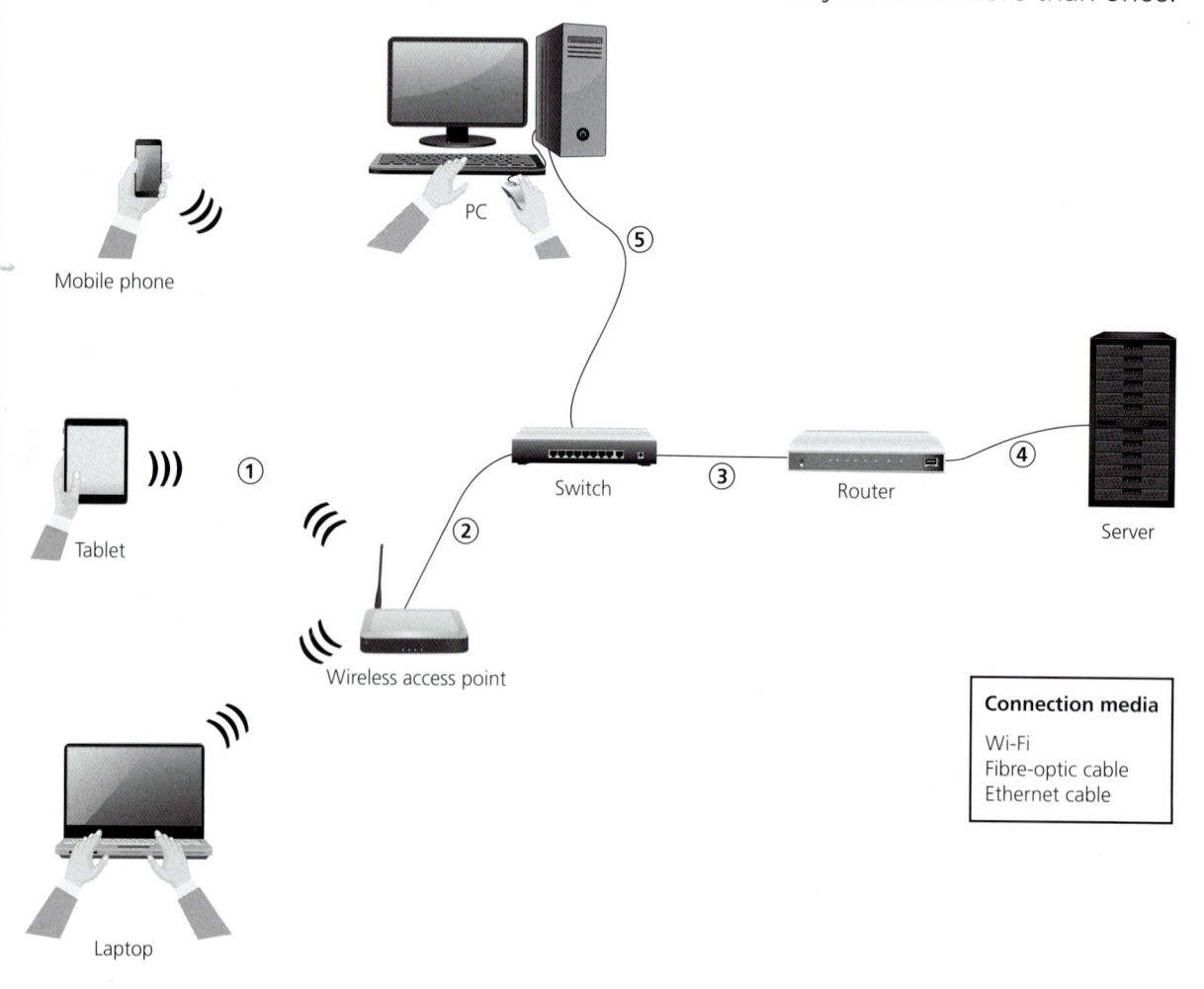

Connection media

Wi-Fi
Fibre-optic cable
Ethernet cable

Unit 7.3 HTML: It's all news to me

Multimedia file types for web pages

Learn

Multimedia files are often large. So, when adding multimedia content to web pages, it is important to consider the file types used to store and, therefore, transmit the content.

Images are displayed on screens using one of two alternative approaches: bitmap graphics or vector graphics.

Bitmap graphics

Bitmap graphics (or raster images) are stored as tiny dots called **pixels** (short for picture element). The pixels are organised on a grid on screen. Each pixel has its own colour value.

KEYWORDS

bitmap graphics: graphics produced using a rectangular grid of pixels

bit: the smallest amount of data a computer can store, represented as either 0 or 1

colour depth: a measure of the number of bits used to represent colour in individual pixels in an image

▲ Individual pixels can be viewed when you zoom in on bitmap images.

The number of pixels making up an image is measured in pixels per inch (ppi). This value is the image's resolution. The higher the resolution, the better the quality of the image.

In the example below, each pixel is represented by only one **bit**, 0 or 1. Thus each pixel can only be either black or white. So, the image below needs 100 bits to store it. This image is said to have a **colour depth** of 1, as a single bit is used to represent each pixel.

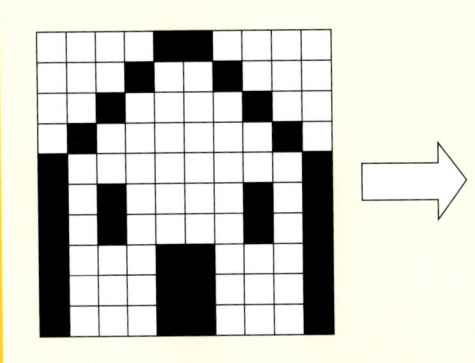

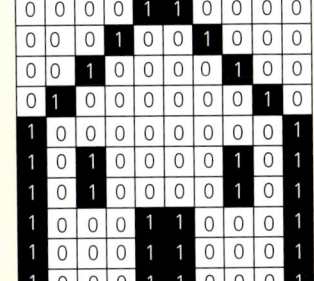

71

International Computing for Lower Secondary

The bitmap grid showing the house image contains 10*10 pixels, each pixel has a colour depth of 1 so this image needs 100 bits to store it:

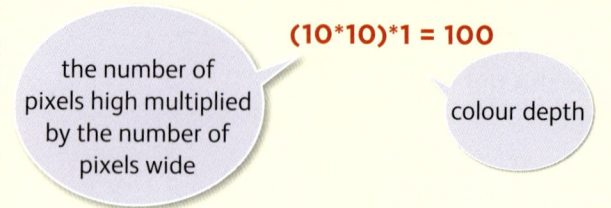

(10*10)*1 = 100

- the number of pixels high multiplied by the number of pixels wide
- colour depth

If we want the image to be represented in colour, we need to use more bits for each pixel to allow us to represent more colours. Bitmap image files can get very large!

If we want to store an image with more than two colours, we would need to include additional bits. For example, if we had a colour depth of two we could represent four colours:

- 00 = white
- 01 = black
- 10 = green
- 11 = red

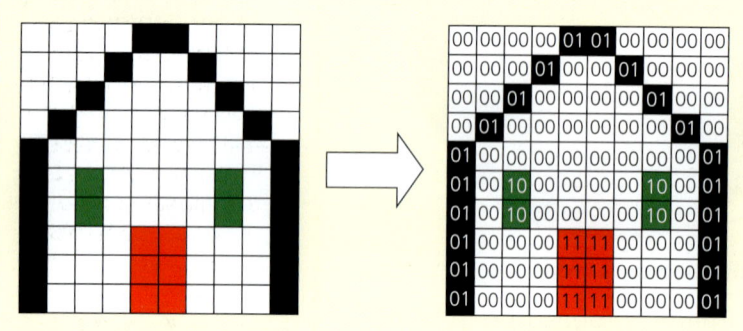

Complete the calculation to show how many bits you would need to store the same image with a colour depth of two.

(_____ * _____) * _____ = _____

Vector graphics

Vector graphics are made up from objects placed on the screen using commands which contain details about the location of the object on screen, colour information and details relating to line length, and so on. They do not hold information regarding every pixel on the screen display, so are smaller in file size.

The above image could be replicated in vector format using commands such as:

- from the bottom left of the screen, draw a straight line six-tenths of the length of the screen
- draw a diagonal line at 45° up to the top middle of the screen
- ... and so on.

KEYWORD

vector graphics: graphics made up from a series of objects placed on a computer screen

Unit 7.3 HTML: It's all news to me

Can you complete the description of this image with commands like these? Notice how, in this case, we can ignore all of the pixels which are shaded white.

The table below shows some of the main differences between bitmap and vector graphics.

Bit map	Vector
Larger file size as information stored about every pixel.	Smaller file size as details stored about objects and location.
Can be edited at pixel level.	Individual objects making up the image can be edited by for example moving, resizing or recolouring.
High quality colour representation.	Limited colour representation.
When bitmaps are stretched the pixels are stretched distorting the quality.	When vectors are stretched, we just change the line length, for example, and it is redrawn without distortion.

Web designers may use both vector and bitmap images on a web page. Where **web space** is limited, however, they may try to avoid bitmap images if possible. Web developers will sometimes use compressed file formats to help keep page **load times** short.

File **compression** can sometimes lead to a reduction in the quality of the image – this is called **lossy compression**. If no loss in quality occurs when an image is compressed, this is called **lossless compression**.

Some compressed image file formats include:

File type	Compression type	Support animation	File size	When to use
JPEG (Joint Photographic Experts Group)	Lossy	No	Very small	When graphic has a high number of colours or contains photographs; supported by most browsers.
PNG (Portable Networks Graphics)	Lossless	Yes	Small	Storing graphics for web images.
GIF (Graphics Interchange Format)	Lossless	Yes	Small	When the graphic has a small number of colours.
TIFF (Tagged Image File)	Lossless	No	Large	Good quality images often used in printed resources.

Many web pages include video and audio files which can also take up a lot of web space.

Web users enjoy viewing high resolution videos but if you have limited web space or are not using optimised video files this can slow down your load times. Including too many non-optimised sound file types can have the same impact.

load times: Use Google to search a topic and determine the load time that Google used to find the results for that search.

KEYWORDS

web space: the amount of space on a computer's hard disk used to store your web pages and multimedia content which makes up your web space

load times: a measure of the time taken to download and display the entire contents of a web page

compression: the removal of some unnecessary data to help reduce the amount of storage taken up by a file

lossy compression: a method of reducing file size of a graphic which results in some loss of image quality

lossless compression: a method of reducing file size of a graphic which does not result in loss of image quality

image optimisation: reducing file size without losing image quality

International Computing for Lower Secondary

When including video content on your web page, choose video file types which are compressed but which are also compatible with the most recent version of HTML (currently HTML5).

Commonly used optimised video and audio file types supported by HTML5 include:

Video file types	Audio File types
MP4 (Moving Picture Experts Group)	MP3 (Moving Picture Experts Group), which is a compressed file type
	WAV (Waveform Audio File Format)

Practice

- Consider what you have learned about image file types and uses. Recommend a suitable file type for the six images shown here.

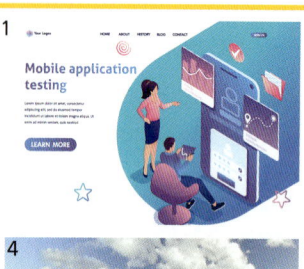

Pattern recognition and abstraction

When completing a task such as this (where images are being constructed using smaller parts or bits), we start to identify patterns in the image we are creating. Our mind starts to complete the image for us which makes the task easier to complete.

We use abstraction when representing images in bitmap format as the image is not a true representation of the scene we are showing on screen. In doing this, we use codes to represent colours and pixels to create an abstract representation of the image.

Key:
00 = blue
01 = red
10 = yellow
11 = green

Unit 7.3 HTML: It's all news to me

Your teacher will give you a copy of the document called **CreateYourOwnBitMap**.

Use the key provided in the document to help you complete the bitmap image represented. The image has a colour depth of two.

A copy of the bit pattern for the image is shown on the previous page.

You will also be provided with your own bit map grid and a space to create your own key for an image with a colour depth of 2.

In the blank grid at the bottom of the page, create your own image and key and ask your partner to colour your image for you.

Getting to grips with HTML

Learn

Web pages are text based files which are used to describe the content of a web page and how it should be displayed in a web browser. Web pages are described using HTML. HTML uses special **tags** which tell the browser how to display web page content in a browser window. HTML tags can be used to create **internal hyperlinks** and **external hyperlinks**, add images and **embed** video or sound to a web page. They can also be used to change the appearance of text on a web page; for example, they can change text size, colour, font and style.

We can also add CSS to HTML tags to add colour to page backgrounds and text.

There are many ways of referencing colours when writing HTML. At this stage, we will use colour names.

NAVY	BLUE	AQUA	TEAL	OLIVE	GREEN	LIME	YELLOW
ORANGE	RED	MAROON	FUCHSIA	PURPLE	BLACK	GRAY	SILVER

WHITE

KEYWORDS

tags: hidden key words in a web page which tell the browser how to display the content on the page

internal hyperlinks: hyperlinks which when clicked on take the user to a resource on the same website

external hyperlinks: hyperlinks which when clicked on take the user to a resource on another website

embed: the process of inserting a file created with one application into a file created by another application

Internal hyperlinks and external hyperlinks: Go onto a website and find an internal and external hyperlink.

75

Practice

- The editor of The Local News has asked you to create a two page website to explain some of the issues associated with fake news. In addition to guidance on identifying fake news, the web page should include video and sound files and a range of hyperlinks.
- HTML is a text based language, so we can use a text editor to enter the HTML code. In this example you will use the application Notepad++.
- Create a folder to store your website and its content; give this folder a sensible name, such as 'FakeNewsWeb'.
- Open Notepad++.
- Select the language you wish to use which, in this case, is HTML.

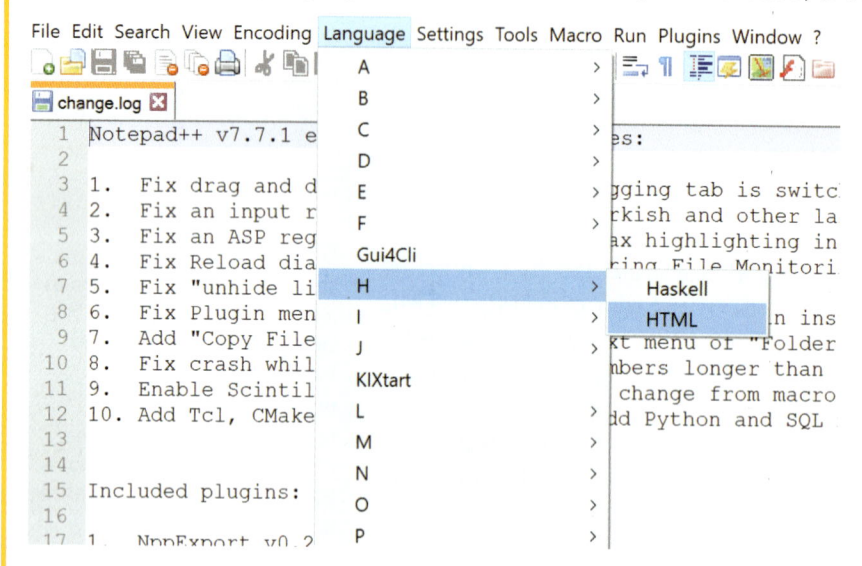

> **KEYWORD**
> **metadata:** data about data

- Enter the following HTML code into the Notepad++ window:

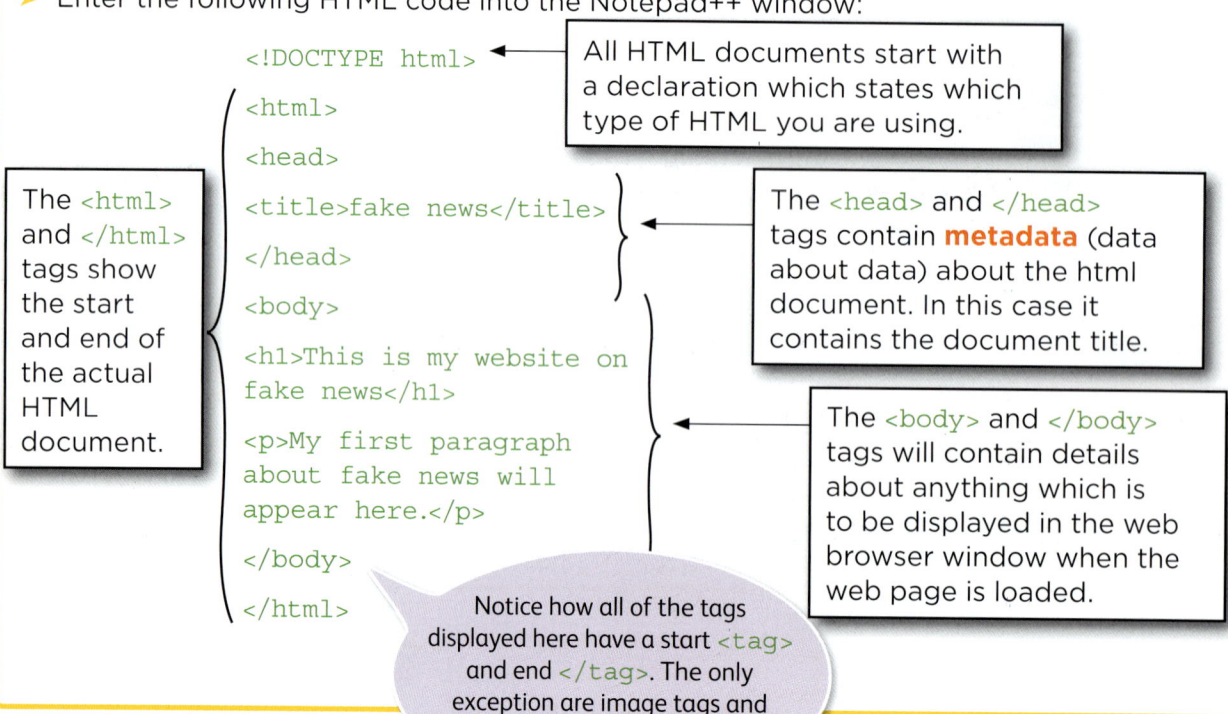

```
<!DOCTYPE html>
<html>
<head>
<title>fake news</title>
</head>
<body>
<h1>This is my website on fake news</h1>
<p>My first paragraph about fake news will appear here.</p>
</body>
</html>
```

All HTML documents start with a declaration which states which type of HTML you are using.

The `<html>` and `</html>` tags show the start and end of the actual HTML document.

The `<head>` and `</head>` tags contain **metadata** (data about data) about the html document. In this case it contains the document title.

The `<body>` and `</body>` tags will contain details about anything which is to be displayed in the web browser window when the web page is loaded.

Notice how all of the tags displayed here have a start `<tag>` and end `</tag>`. The only exception are image tags and `<br/>`; we will see how they are used later in this unit.

Unit 7.3 HTML: It's all news to me

- Click on 'File' and 'Save As' to save this page as '**index.html**'.
- Browse to your 'FakeNewsWeb' Folder and select 'Hyper Text Markup Language file' from the 'Save as type' drop down list, as shown below.

> It is good practice to store the home page of a website as **index.html** as this is the page all browsers will look for first when a website is being loaded.

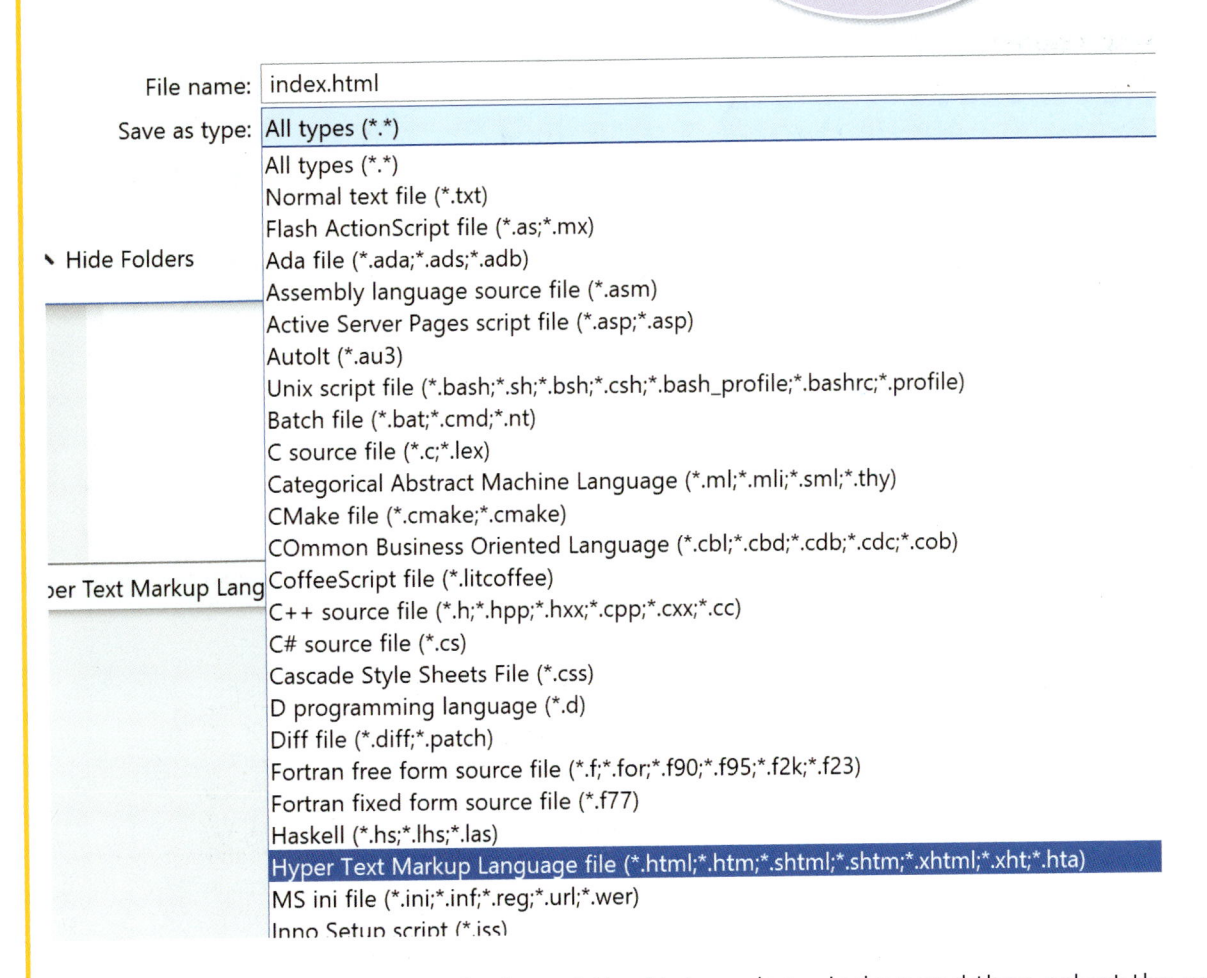

File name:	index.html
Save as type:	All types (*.*)

All types (*.*)
Normal text file (*.txt)
Flash ActionScript file (*.as;*.mx)
Ada file (*.ada;*.ads;*.adb)
Assembly language source file (*.asm)
Active Server Pages script file (*.asp;*.asp)
AutoIt (*.au3)
Unix script file (*.bash;*.sh;*.bsh;*.csh;*.bash_profile;*.bashrc;*.profile)
Batch file (*.bat;*.cmd;*.nt)
C source file (*.c;*.lex)
Categorical Abstract Machine Language (*.ml;*.mli;*.sml;*.thy)
CMake file (*.cmake;*.cmake)
COmmon Business Oriented Language (*.cbl;*.cbd;*.cdb;*.cdc;*.cob)
CoffeeScript file (*.litcoffee)
C++ source file (*.h;*.hpp;*.hxx;*.cpp;*.cxx;*.cc)
C# source file (*.cs)
Cascade Style Sheets File (*.css)
D programming language (*.d)
Diff file (*.diff;*.patch)
Fortran free form source file (*.f;*.for;*.f90;*.f95;*.f2k;*.f23)
Fortran fixed form source file (*.f77)
Haskell (*.hs;*.lhs;*.las)
Hyper Text Markup Language file (*.html;*.htm;*.shtml;*.shtm;*.xhtml;*.xht;*.hta)
MS ini file (*.ini;*.inf;*.reg;*.url;*.wer)
Inno Setup script (*.iss)

- Click on the 'Run' menu at the top of the Notepad++ window and then select the web browser you wish to use to display your web page, such as 'Launch in IE'.

File Edit Search View Encoding Language Settings Tools Macro **Run** Plugins Window ?

Run...	F5
Launch in Firefox	Ctrl+Alt+Shift+X
Launch in IE	Ctrl+Alt+Shift+I
Launch in Chrome	Ctrl+Alt+Shift+R
Launch in Safari	Ctrl+Alt+Shift+A

International Computing for Lower Secondary

- This will open a browser window and display your web page.
- Display your Notepad++ window and your browser window side by side on your desktop so you can see both at the same time.

> Do this by resizing both windows so they each cover half the width of the desktop, and then place them side by side.

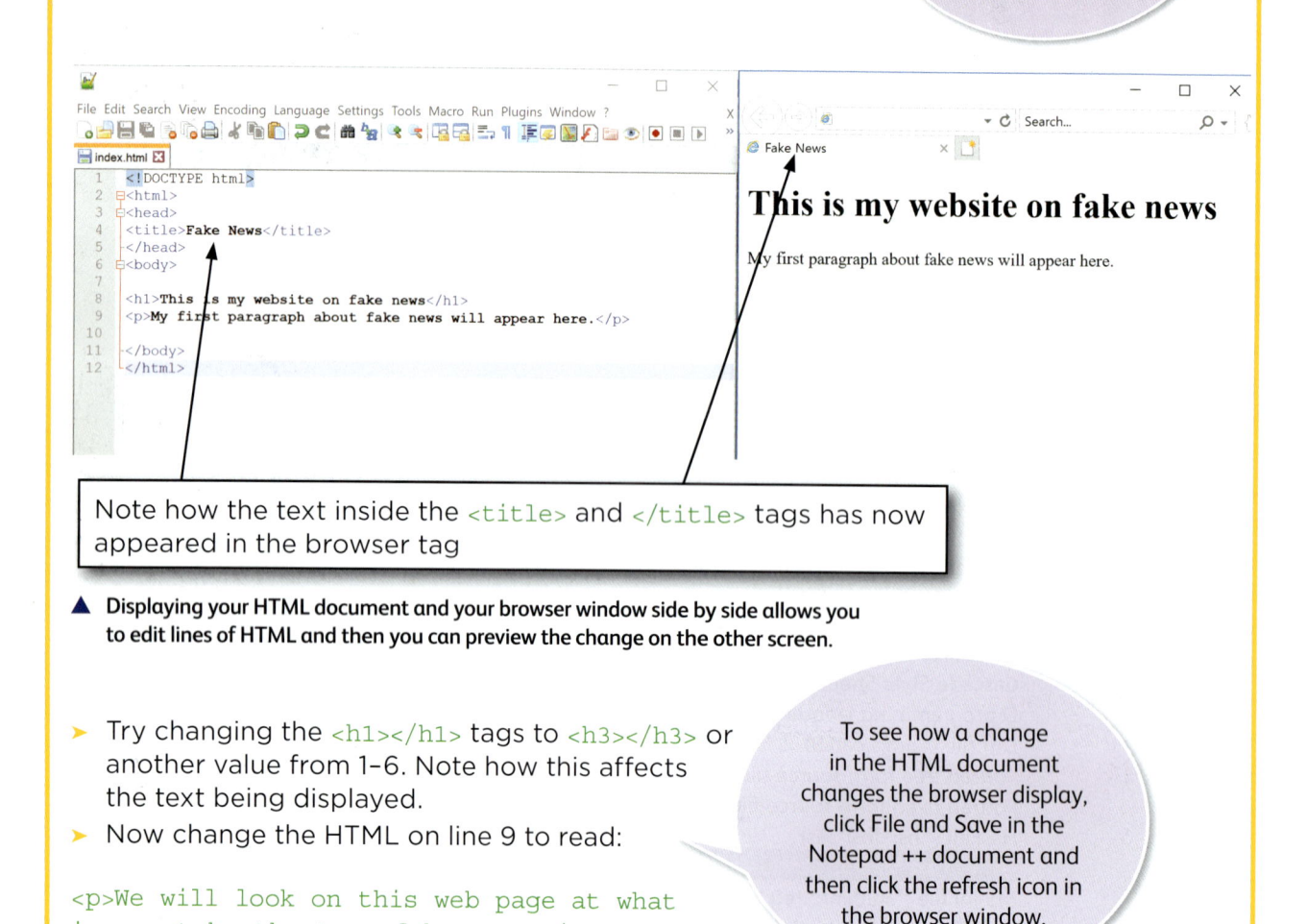

Note how the text inside the `<title>` and `</title>` tags has now appeared in the browser tag

▲ Displaying your HTML document and your browser window side by side allows you to edit lines of HTML and then you can preview the change on the other screen.

- Try changing the `<h1></h1>` tags to `<h3></h3>` or another value from 1–6. Note how this affects the text being displayed.
- Now change the HTML on line 9 to read:

```
<p>We will look on this web page at what is meant by the term fake news.</p><p>We will look also at some of the problems caused by fake news and how we can identify fake news.</p>
```

> To see how a change in the HTML document changes the browser display, click File and Save in the Notepad ++ document and then click the refresh icon in the browser window.

- Note: Do not make a new line or press the enter key.
- Save your **index.html** document. You can do this by going to 'File' and then 'Save'.

Unit 7.3 HTML: It's all news to me

- Click the refresh icon in your browser window.
- Your page display should be similar to the one below.

This is my website on fake news

We will look on this web page at what is meant by the term fake news.

We will look also at some of the problems caused by fake news and how we can identify fake news.

> What has happened to the text were the `</p>` and `<p>` tags were inserted? `<p></p>` creates a paragraph of text; all of the text between this opening and closing tag set will be part of a paragraph of text separated from other text using a blank line.

- Now change the HTML on line 9 to read:

```
<p>We will look on this web page at what is meant by the term fake news.</p><p>We will look also at some of the problems caused by fake news <br/>and how we can identify fake news.</p>
```

> The use of the `<br/>` tag has forced all of the writing after it onto a new line, even though it is in the same paragraph.

- Save your HTML file again and hit the refresh icon in the browser window.
- Notice how your display has changed again.
- We can use HTML tags to add emphasis to text; for example:
  o the tag set `<b></b>` displays words in bold
  o the tag set `<u></u>` displays text with an underline
  o the tag set `<i></i>` displays text in italics.
- Change line 9 to read:

```
<p>On this web page, we will look at what is meant by the term <u>fake news.</u>.</p><p>We will also look at some of the <b><i>problems caused by fake news</b></i><br/>and how we can identify fake news.</p>
```

> Some of the words are now emphasised: fake news, and problems caused by fake news.

DID YOU KNOW?

All tags (apart from `<br/>`, which indicates take a new line) must have a start and end tag.

KEYWORD

home page: the first page to be launched when a website is loaded by a web browser

79

Adding style to HTML pages

Learn

So far we have looked at how we can combine HTML tags to improve how we display text in a HTML document.

In the example below, the HTML document now includes the `<b></b>`, `<i></i>` and `<u></u>` tags.

```
<body>
<h1>This is my website on fake news</h1>
<p>On this web page, we will look at what is meant by the term <u>fake news.</u>.</p><p>We will also look at some of the <b><i>problems caused by fake news</b></i><br/>and how we can identify fake news.</p>
</body>
```

Practice

- Open NotePad++
- Open your file called index.html
- Edit your `<body tag>` so that it reads as shown below.

```
<html>
<head>
<title>Fake News</title>
<style>
body { color: white;
background-color: black;
}
</style>
</head>
<body>
<h1>This is my website on fake news</h1>
<p>On this web page, we will look at what is meant by the term <u>fake news.</u>.</p><p>We will also look at some of the <b><i>problems caused by fake news</b></i><br/>and how we can identify fake news.</p>
</body>
</html>
```

> Note the spelling of 'color'. HTML uses American standard spelling for words such as 'color' and 'center'.

- You have added the tag set `<style></style>` inside the tag set `<head></head>`. You can use this to define the colour of the body of the HTML document and the text as shown.

Unit 7.3 HTML: It's all news to me

> # This is my website on fake news
>
> On this web page, we will look at what is meant by the term <u>fake news.</u>
>
> We will also look at some of the *problems caused by fake news* and how we can identify fake news.

▶ Use what you have learned about fake news on page 65 to add an additional text to your HTML page which describes fake news and some of the problems it causes. Use at least two of the following HTML tags in your paragraph `<b></b>`, `<i></i>`, `<p></p>`, `<u></u>`

> When adding a style definition to a HTML tag in the head section of a file we use { } to group the style definitions together. In this example, you have applied two styles to the body of this HTML document: one to change the colour of the text, and one to change the colour of the background.

Go further

Web pages are multimedia documents which can include images, sound and video. Your teacher will give you copies of three files called **FakeNewsImage.jpg**, **FakeNews.mp4**, and **sound_bite.mp3**, to include in your web page.

> Using folders to store the digital assets will make them easy to locate later.

◆ Inside your folder called 'FakeNewsWeb' create another folder called 'Assets'. Copy the image, video and sound file into the Assets folder.

◆ Add the following HTML to your document at a location where you would like the image called FakeNewsImage to appear on your web page

```
<img src = "Assets/FakeNewsImage.jpg" alt="identifying fake news">
```

- Image tag does not need a closing tag `</>` the way other tags do.
- Tells the browser where to locate the file called **FakeNewsImage.jpg** which will be displayed on your web page.
- Displays the text 'identifying fake news' when the user places their mouse over the image on screen. This is useful if the image fails to load or is slow to load.

◆ Save **index.html** and refresh your browser display to view the image. It is quite large!

> Always include the full location of the folder your image is stored in. For example, in this case you are telling the browser in this line of HTML to go to the Assets folder to locate the image called FakeNewsImage.jpg.

International Computing for Lower Secondary

- Make the following changes to the `<img src>` tag previously entered. This time add additional information to the img tag by specifying the height and width of the image in pixels when it is displayed on screen.

  `<img src = "assets/FakeNewsImage.jpg" alt="identifying fake news" style="width: 500px; height: 600px;">`

- Search the internet for an additional image to help illustrate your fake news **index.html** page. Insert this image into your **index.html** page and add appropriate 'alt' text to describe the image.

  > Remember what you learned in pages 73–74 and be sure to select an appropriate file type.

- The `<audio></audio>` tag can be used to embed sound files in a HTML document. Add the following HTML tags to **index.html**.

```
41
42   <img src = "assets/FakeNewsImage.jpg" alt="identifying fake news" style="width: 500px; height: 600px;">
43   <p> </p>
44   <audio controls>
45       <source src = "assets/sound_bite.mp3" type=audio/mpeg>
46   </audio>
47
```

- The `<video></video>` tag works in the same way as the `<audio></audio>` tag. Add the following HTML tags to '**index.html**' to play the mp4 video called **FakeNews.mp4**:

  `<video width = "200" height = "200" controls>`
  `<source src = "assets/FakeNews.mp4" type = "video/mp4">`
  `</video>`

  > Adding the `<p></p>` tag places a blank line between the image and the sound bite. `<audio controls></audio>` inserts the mp3 file with user controls so the user can choose whether or not to play the sound file.

- Save your **index.html** file and refresh your browser window to ensure everything displays correctly.

Unit 7.3 HTML: It's all news to me

Challenge yourself

The editor of The Local Times has asked you to work as part of a team to create a new website providing information on fake news. The editor has asked you to decide on the content of each web page. The web pages should be linked together to create a website that includes hyperlinks to external websites which relate to fake news in some way. Work with a partner or in a small group to complete this task.

Decomposition

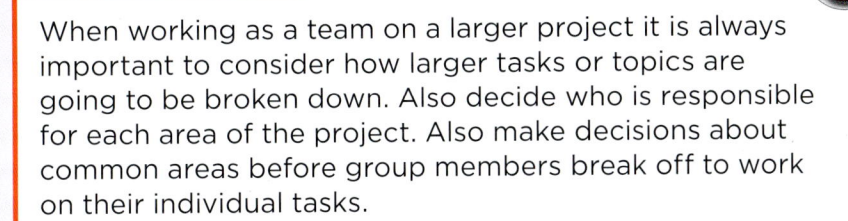

When working as a team on a larger project it is always important to consider how larger tasks or topics are going to be broken down. Also decide who is responsible for each area of the project. Also make decisions about common areas before group members break off to work on their individual tasks.

KEYWORD

navigation links: hyperlinks which allow users to move from one web page to another

As a group …

- examine the topics studied in this unit and select one topic to help you plan your web page content
- create a folder called 'GroupProject' which will be used to store your group's completed website
- decide on a consistent style for your web pages and discuss why this is so important and how you will achieve this.

Now, individually …

- create a folder for the web page you are responsible for developing. Use this folder to save your web page and any images, videos or sounds you wish to include in your web page (your website should include at least two of these)

Remember: one student must be responsible for creating the page called **index.html**. As a group decide on the content of the pages to be completed by other members of your team.

For example, what CSS styles will you use? How will you use bold, italic and underline tags? What colour will your page background be?

Make sure you are using compressed file types such as jpg, mp3 or mp4.

83

International Computing for Lower Secondary

- search the internet for suitable images, sounds, videos you wish to use and save them into your folder
- create an additional web page for your site. In Notepad++, click 'File' and 'New', give the web page an appropriate name, and save it into the folder containing your image, sound and/or video files
- add content to your web page relating to your chosen topic
- when your web page is complete, copy your entire folder into the 'GroupProject' folder; you are now ready to add **navigation links**.

Each group member is responsible for creating a link between their page and the index page.

- Under the title tag, at the top of **index.html**, use the following HTML tag to create a link to the second page of the website:

```
<a href="page2.html">Click Here to go to Page 2</a>
```

Edit here to show the name of your web page (include the folder if necessary). Remember your web page is saved inside a folder. Include the full location much like you did on page 82 when you were adding image and sound files.

Edit here to contain the title of your web page or the text which will appear on the web page for the user to click on to access your web page.

- Create a similar hyperlink between the page you created back to the page called **index.html**.
- The example below shows you can use `<a></a>` to link to external websites:

```
<a href= 'https://www.myfakenewswebsite.com>Click here to view my fake news website</a>
```

- This line of HTML displays the text 'Click here to view my fake news website' in the browser window. The text is displayed as a hyperlink so that, when the user clicks on it, they will be taken to a web page called www.fakenewswebsite.com
- Add a similar hyperlink to your web page (underneath your last paragraph of text). Your hyperlink should take the user to a web page containing facts about fake news.

> Go to page 76 to remind yourself how to create and save a new web page.

> Remember to embed at least two of the following into your web page: image, video or a sound file.

> The `<a></a>` tag is used to create a hyperlink to another HTML resource. The href attribute is used to tell the browser where to find the resource it is supposed to be displaying.

> This web address does not exist; but try using this tag to add a link to your web page to a fake news story you have found online.

Unit 7.3 HTML: It's all news to me

Final project

The editor of The Local Times was so impressed by your training that he has asked you to create a news story which will be published on the newspaper's website. The article can be a real news story or a fake news story. You can use it to test other people's ability to recognise a fake news story.

Your website should:
- be a single web page created using HTML
- make appropriate use of heading tags, text layout tags and style tags and descriptors covered in this unit of work
- include appropriate images in an optimised format to help illustrate your story (these can be downloaded from the internet)
- include a video and sound file in an optimised format (the video clip and sound file should be no more than 10 seconds long). Use the internet to locate suitable video or sound files for this part of the task.
- include a hyperlink to a website containing a similar story to yours to help convince readers your story is true
- include suggestions for search engine optimised URLs for your website

> Remember file optimisation on pages 73. Ensure the video files and sound files are in mp4 and mp3 format.

> Page 84 will tell you how to create a hyperlink to an external website.

> Remember search engine optimised URLS on page 67

85

Evaluation

- Ask a friend to evaluate your website and make comments on:
  - the suitability of the graphics, audio and video assets you have included
  - whether the navigation is easy to follow
  - load times
  - use of colour (background and text), font used, and so on
  - whether they think the news story is fake or real, and why.
- Make a list of any changes you made to your website based on the comments you received.
- If possible, publish your web page to your school website or a class electronic notice board for others outside your class to see.
- You have also now experienced developing web pages as an individual and as part of a group. Write a short commentary on the following:
  - What were the pros and cons of working as a group when developing a web page?
  - As a group, how did you ensure all of your web pages looked the same?
  - Which approach would you prefer and why?
  - How would you change your approach to a group project in the future?

Definition check: Close your book and make a list of as many terms you have learned in this unit as you can. Compare them with your partner's list. Together try to define as many of them as you can. Check your definitions against the definitions given in the key word boxes.

Unit 7.4

Block it out: Creating a game

About Scratch

Scratch is a visual programming language. It allows you to program your own animations, games and other **digital solutions** using blocks of code instead of typing lines of code.

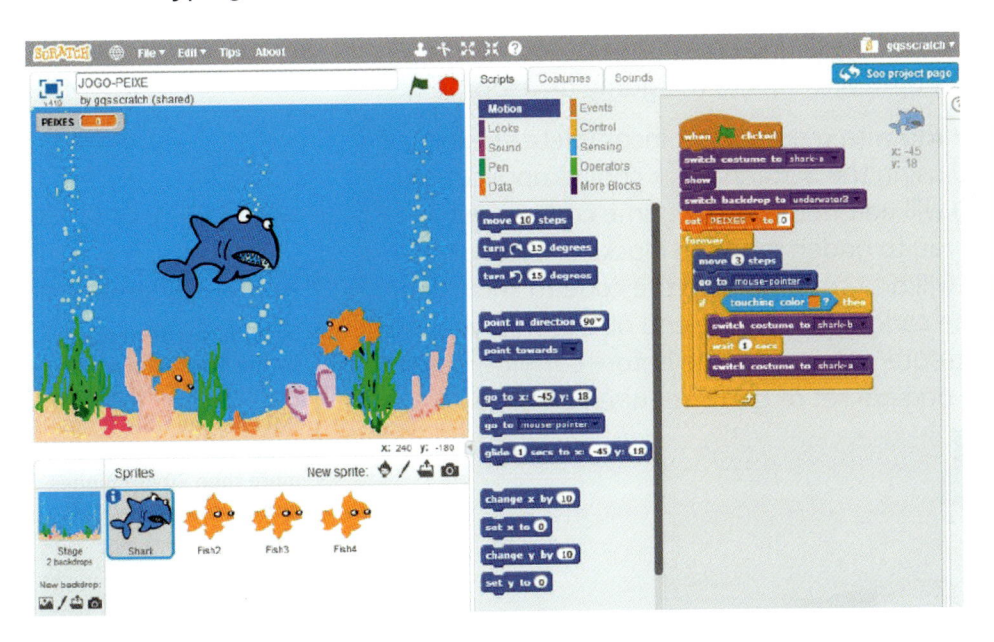

Learning Outcomes

In this unit you will learn to:
- consider user requirements when producing an **application**
- create code in Scratch which
  - manages **user interactions** and feedback in a computer game (for example, scores and sound **feedback**)
  - allows scrolling backgrounds
  - invites **input** from a user to control an element of the game
  - uses **procedures** to create reusable code
  - uses lists to handle information
- **debug** code using Scratch
- add comments to coded solutions to help others understand the code
- test an application during the development process
- evaluate an application by considering the original user requirements.

KEYWORDS

digital solution: a digital artefact made from instructions for a computer to solve a problem

application: a computer program designed for an end user; for example, child, teenager, adult

user interactions: describes how a user can provide instructions to a program and receive information from a program

feedback: a message or information about an action or event; for example, increased score in a game

input: data which is entered into a computer using a device such a keyboard, mouse, touch screen, joystick

procedure: a set of coded instructions used to tell a computer how to carry out a process; sometimes called function or sub program

debug: the process of identifying and removing errors from a computer program

Feedback: Find an example of feedback given to you from an Internet-based game you play.

International Computing for Lower Secondary

SCENARIO

You are a new employee in a game development company. You have joined a team of programmers who are part way through developing a computer game. The game is a single player **pick up game** designed to help improve hand-eye co-ordination and reaction times in 7–10 year olds. The team are working to a very tight deadline; they need to complete the game as quickly as possible.

Your challenge is to examine the existing code, understand what it does, correct any errors, and then complete the game development.

Your teacher will provide you with a number of incomplete versions of a Skate-IT game created using the Scratch block coding application. Throughout this unit you will edit and test the game code as you develop it. This will help you to understand the blocks of code used to create the game. You will add comments to the code to show your understanding of how the code works. At the end of the unit, you will have an opportunity to create your own game before carrying out an evaluation based on the original set of game requirements.

> **KEYWORD**
>
> **pick up game:** a game which requires the user to navigate around a screen and collect objects in order to score points

> **pick up game:** Name a pick up game you play.

> **DID YOU KNOW?**
>
> Scratch was developed by the Massachusetts Institute of Technology (MIT) in the USA; it has been translated into more than 70 languages and is used worldwide.

Do you remember?

Before starting this unit, you should be able to:
- ✓ decompose problems (break larger problems into smaller, more manageable chunks)
- ✓ identify patterns in solutions to problems
- ✓ create **algorithms** to show the steps involved in solving problems
- ✓ evaluate solutions to problems
- ✓ carry out the following in Scratch:
  - Open an existing Scratch project.
  - Create simple code in Scratch to support animation and some user interaction.
  - Be able to view existing code attached to **sprites** in a Scratch program.
  - Edit sprites and backgrounds.
  - Upload your own sprites and backgrounds.

> **KEYWORDS**
>
> **algorithm:** step-by-step instructions, which when followed will solve a problem
>
> **sprite:** an image in a Scratch project that can be changed or moved (such as a skateboard image)

Unit 7.4 Block it out: Creating a game

User requirements and target audiences

Learn

Before you develop an application, you need to think about who the target audience is, and what the target audience want the application to do (the user requirements).

> **Skate-IT: game description**
>
> The game should have a scrolling, animated background designed to look like a pathway on a skate park. Skaters need to avoid randomly-appearing, moving footballs coming from outside the play park.
>
> The skater must be an animated sprite that can move up, down, left and right on the screen. Skaters should avoid touching track borders at the top and bottom of the screen; they will automatically be sent back to the middle of the screen if they do.
>
> To help keep the skaters hydrated, glasses of water will appear at random times on the screen.
>
> Skaters gain five points for every glass of water they collect.
>
> Skaters lose five points if they collide with a football. The football speed increases each time a football touches another object on the screen.
>
> The object of the game is to score as many points as possible.
>
> Game players can decide how long they wish to play the game for; the game will automatically stop once that time is reached and the score will be displayed on screen.
>
> Only users whose names are on an authorised list of players will be allowed to play the game. Anyone else who tries to play the game will be told they are unable to play.

Practice

Before you can start working on the game development, you need a clear idea of the user requirements. With a friend, read through the detailed game description above and complete the list of user requirements started below.

The user requirements state that the skate park game must:

- only allow users to play the game if their name appears on a list provided by the developer
- provide a message to tell users they are unable to play the game if their name is not on the list
- allow the user to decide how long they want to play the game for.

International Computing for Lower Secondary

Animation with loops and sequencing

Learn

Objects that move around in a game are called sprites. You will now look at how to animate a sprite in a Scratch project.

Animations are created by presenting slightly different versions of the same graphic one after another in sequence and in quick succession.

The skater sprite (character) in the Skate-IT game is called animatedskater. This sprite has been created using two versions of the same character, each with a different version of the same costume. One is shown straight after the other in quick succession, just like frames in an animation.

Different versions of the same costume.

You can make a sprite appear to move by swapping between these two costumes quickly using code to form a **script** for the sprite shown on screen.

Lines of computer code are often carried out one after another. This is known as **sequencing**. There may be times when you want lines of code to be repeated. To do this you can use a coding structure called a loop (called **iteration** by programmers). In the example below, a **forever block** is used to make the animation continue throughout the entire game (creating a forever loop) until the user exits the game. The previous programmer was trying to use iteration to help animate the animated skater in the game.

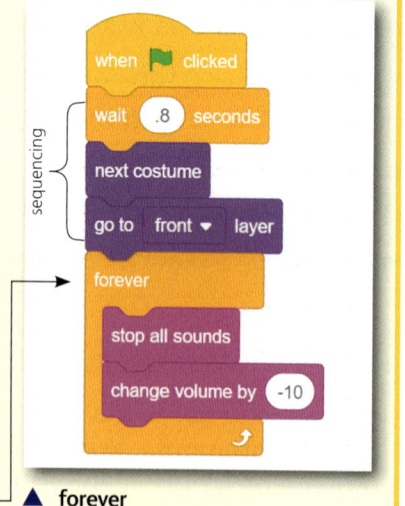

▲ forever

A `forever` block allows you to create a loop; any tasks you want the program to repeat until the end of the game are placed inside the `forever` block. You can do this by clicking on the code block and dragging it to the correct place inside the forever loop.

KEYWORDS

script: lines of code which determine how objects, such as sprites, move and interact with each other on screen

sequencing: lines of code often carried out one after another

iteration: a code construct that repeats code many times in a loop

forever block: an indefinite loop where tasks repeat until the end of the game

Unit 7.4 Block it out: Creating a game

Practice

- Look at the code in the Learn box again. The blocks of code are in the wrong order and some of the blocks are not needed.
  o Discuss with a friend what you think each block of code shown is designed to do.
  o Which two blocks of code do you think will not be needed to animate the skater character?
  o Which block will make sure the skater can always be viewed on the screen?
  o Predict what the code might do incorrectly.

  > Look back to page 89 for a reminder of how the animated skater should appear on screen. Which blocks have nothing to do with appearance?

- Open the file **skaterstart.sb3**, provided by your teacher. Press the green flag to run the code to test the animatedskater sprite.
  o Were your predictions about how the code would run correct? If not, discuss with a friend where you think you went wrong.

One of the most important jobs for a programmer is debugging a computer program. This is to make sure it works correctly. When debugging a computer program, the programmer must predict how they expect the code to operate before they run the code. If the code does not perform the way they expect, then they must make changes. Then they run the code again.

> This file contains two sprites: the animated skater and a sprite called Test. Ignore the Test sprite for now. We will look at the test sprite at a later stage.

- You will now debug the code to ensure the animatedskater sprite appears on screen correctly throughout the game.
  o Click on the animatedskater sprite and go to the code window for this sprite.
  o Remove the blocks of code which do not help animate the skater.
  o Reorder the remaining blocks to animate the skater.
    - The Test sprite is included to help you test that the animated skater appears at the front of the stage at all times. Move the Test sprite so that it is covering the animatedskater sprite and run your code. Run and stop your code a number of times to see what happens to the animated skater on screen. Try placing the `go to front layer` code block inside the `foreverloop` block to ensure the animatedskater sprite remains in front of any other objects on screen.
    - Place the `wait` block and the `next costume` block inside the `foreverloop` block. Does it matter, in this example, what order they appear inside the loop?

  > To remove a block of code: click on the code block, drag it off the coding area and onto the blocks panel of your screen. It should now disappear from your coding area.

91

International Computing for Lower Secondary

- o Change the value in the `wait` block to see how that impacts the animation.
- o Run the animation to test your code. When you are happy with how your sprite appears, delete the Test sprite (it is not part of the final game).
- o Save your Scratch project with an appropriate name.

> Set the value to a number which makes the animation obvious but not too fast!

Computer programs are not always started and finished by the same team. So, it is important to add comments when coding; these help different coding teams understand what the code is meant to do, especially when debugging. Comments help describe the code, but they are not executed as part of the program.

▶ Add a comment to each block of code to explain what it does: right click on the block and select 'Add Comment'.

▶ Edit the colour of the T-shirt on the skater in one costume.
- o Click on the animatedskater sprite in the sprite window.
- o Click on the Costumes tab; you will see the sprite has two costumes.
- o Use the paint tools to edit the T-shirt colours on one or both of the costumes.
- o How does this change the animation?

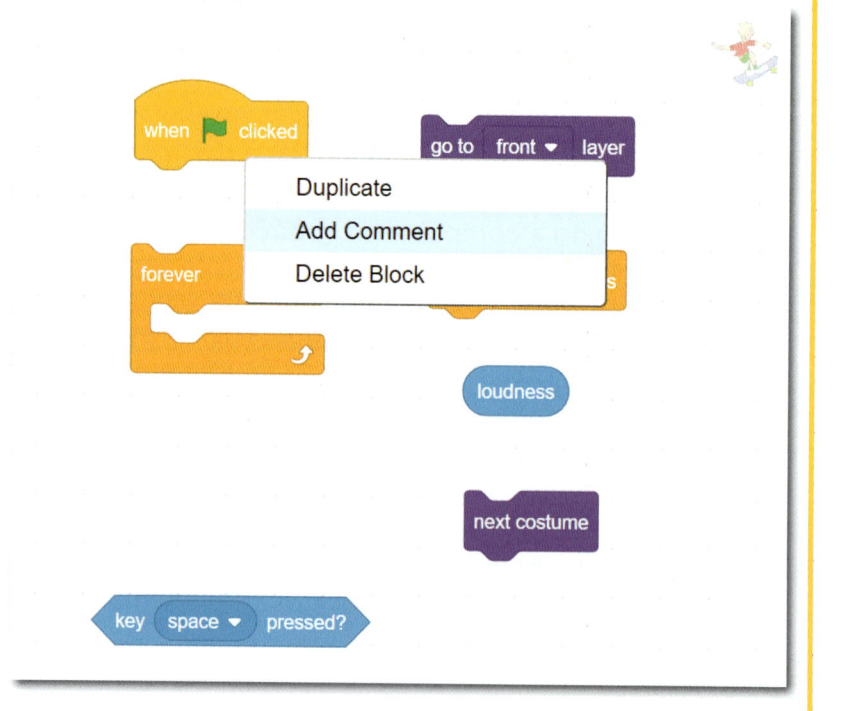

Abstraction

Sometimes, it helps to focus on fewer details to achieve the same desired effect. This process is called abstraction. For example, you have chosen two costumes to show two different directions that the sprite can travel in. You could, of course, have many more costumes – such as costumes showing the skateboard at different angles, or costumes showing the skater's feet up or feet down, and so on.

With a friend, discuss how you could make other changes to make the sprites look different, and to make the sprite appear more realistic.

Unit 7.4 Block it out: Creating a game

Making decisions and managing movement

> **DID YOU KNOW?**
> The screen used to create your game is called a stage. The stage is divided up into pixels. You can then use (x, y) co-ordinates to pinpoint locations on a Scratch stage. A Scratch stage is 480 pixels wide and 360 pixels high. The centre of the screen has the co-ordinates (0,0). You can instruct a sprite to move to a particular set of co-ordinates, or to move by a particular number of pixels by changing the x or y co-ordinates.

KEYWORD

stage: area on a Scratch project where the game is created and displayed

Learn

The person playing the game must instruct the computer to move the sprite. For example, the player can use the keyboard to give the computer instructions about the direction, distance, or location that they want the sprite to move to.

`go to x: -191 y: 10`

You can move sprites around the stage using a number of different code blocks. As shown below, a sprite starting at location (0,0) can be moved to another location using the `go to` block.

New location on stage X:–191, Y:10 After the go to block has been carried out

Starting point X:0, Y:0

(X:–240, Y:0), (X:0, Y:0), (X:240, Y:0), (X:0, Y:180), (X:0, Y:–180)

Scratch programmers use a code block called `go to x: ___ y: ___` if they wish to move sprites to a certain location on the stage.

You don't always know where the sprite will be when the gamer makes a decision to move it. If this is the case, you can use the `change y` or `change x` blocks instead, as shown in the example shown on the next page.

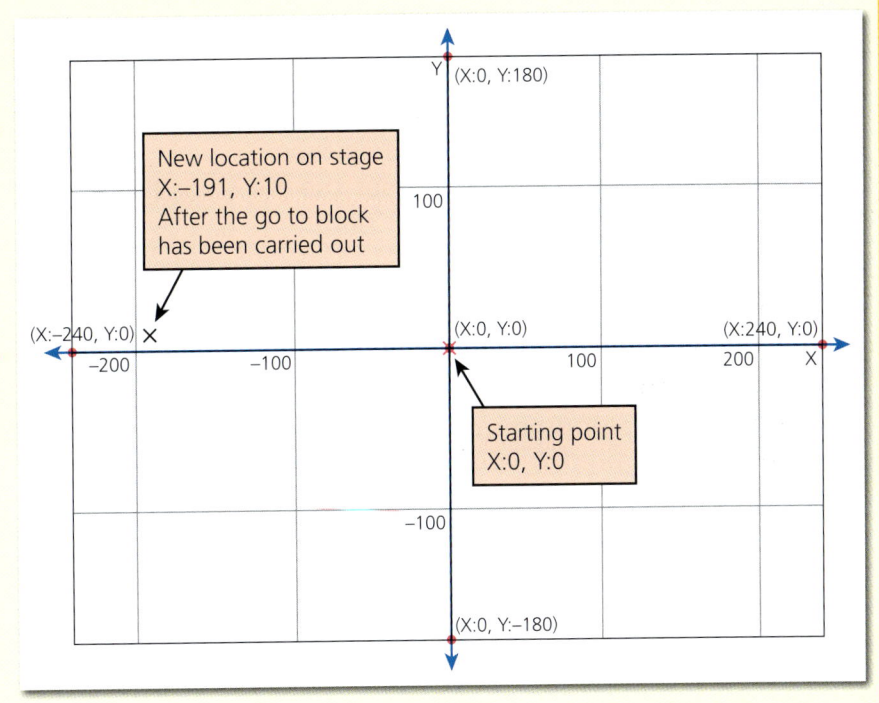

In the code shown on the next page we are using an `if` statement to test a condition; has the up arrow been pressed?

There are two possible answers to this question; yes or no. Depending on the answer, the program can do one of two things:
- Change the y: co-ordinates by five.
- Do not change the y co-ordinates.

93

International Computing for Lower Secondary

*If statements are an example of **selection** in coding*

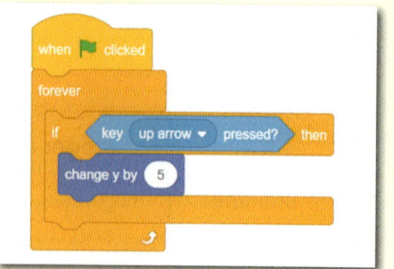

- This example uses the change by block.
- Add these code blocks to your animatedskater sprite. Save your program and test your code by clicking on the Green Flag and then pressing the Y key on your keyboard.
- Now change the value to −5 and run the code again to see what happens when you press the up arrow.

Programmers sometimes use diagrams called flowcharts to help them design code. Flowcharts use symbols to show the steps of a program; two of these symbols are shown here.

You can create a simple flowchart to show the condition being tested in a selection statement. The flowchart will help you decide what to do if the game player presses the up arrow key in your game.

Remember to change your 'change y by' value back to 5 before you move on to the next task. Otherwise your animatedskater sprite will move in the wrong direction

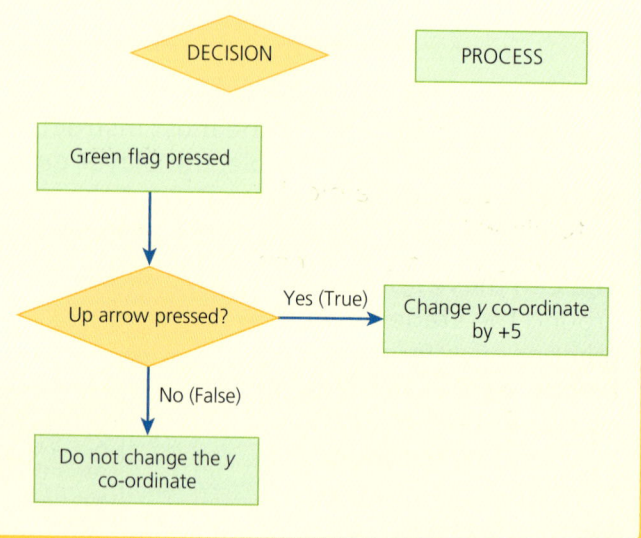

DECISION   PROCESS

Green flag pressed

Up arrow pressed? — Yes (True) → Change *y* co-ordinate by +5

No (False) ↓

Do not change the *y* co-ordinate

Algorithmic thinking

When designing algorithms programmers sometimes plan the code in their head and predict what they think the code will do when it is run. We can also use flowcharts as a way of designing code in a diagrammatic way.

Before producing the code for the up arrow key, a programmer might produce a flowchart design like the one shown below:

After the condition is tested and a decision is made about which pathway to take, this code block continues to test for the up arrow being pressed until the program is no longer running

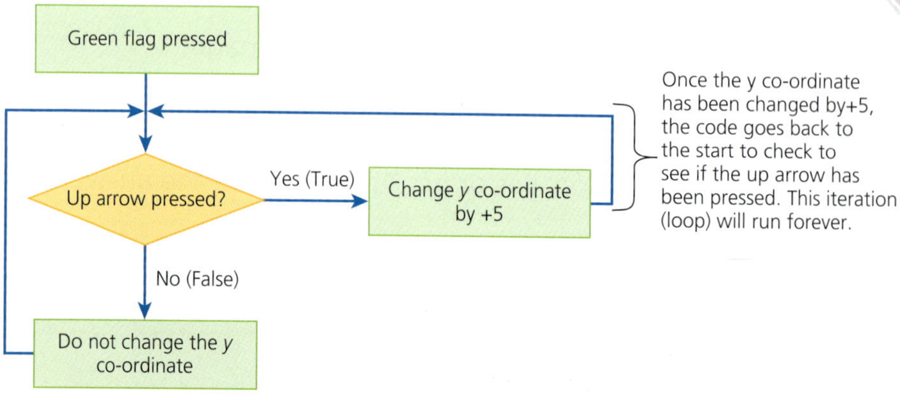

Green flag pressed

Up arrow pressed? — Yes (True) → Change *y* co-ordinate by +5

No (False) ↓

Do not change the *y* co-ordinate

Once the y co-ordinate has been changed by +5, the code goes back to the start to check to see if the up arrow has been pressed. This iteration (loop) will run forever.

Unit 7.4 Block it out: Creating a game

Practice

You now need to make sure the person playing the game can move the skater around the screen. There are two ways of controlling movement in the skate-IT game.

1. Moving the skater up and down the screen, using the `if` and `change y by` code blocks.
2. Scrolling the background image to make it look as though the skater is moving across the screen. You will do this using the `forever` and the `go to` code blocks.

Open the copy of **skatermove.sb3**, provided by your teacher.

▶ Press the green arrow to play the game.
▶ Press the up arrow and then press the down arrow on your keyboard. Check to see how the skater moves on screen. What is wrong with the way the skater moves when your press the up arrow and then the down arrow?
▶ Look at the code blocks used for animated skater, shown below. Edit the code blocks to allow the sprite to move correctly up and down the screen.
▶ Add code blocks that allow the sprite to move forwards and backwards on the screen.

> You can do this by adding **if** statements for forward and back (use the left arrow and right arrow keys to help with this).

▶ Test your code by:
  ○ pressing the up, down, left and right arrow keys to make sure the sprite moves in the correct direction
  ○ pressing other keys on the keyboard to make sure the sprite does not move.

`If-then` blocks allow you to ask questions to decide if lines of code need to be executed or not. Here, you are asking the program to keep checking if the user is pressing the up arrow or the down arrow. If they are, they need to change the y co-ordinates of the skater by the value given in the `change by` block.

The value used to move the skater if the user presses the down arrow key is incorrect. How can you make him move down the screen?

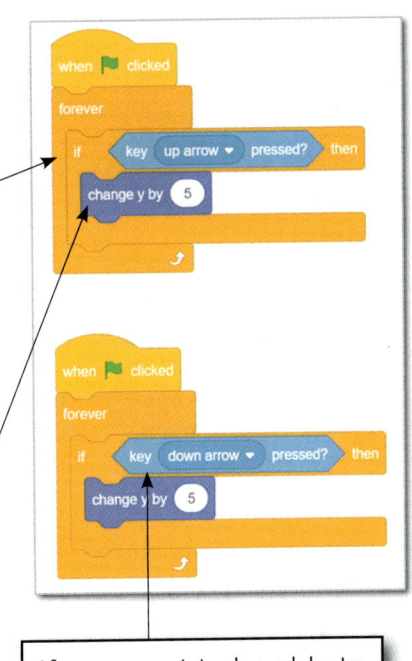

If you want to be able to move across the screen you will need to add extra `key press` blocks.

International Computing for Lower Secondary

Pattern recognition

- ✪ Look for a pattern in the code used to help make the skater move up and down on the screen.
    - ○ Look at how the `forever` block is used and how many times the `when clicked` block is used.
    - ○ What can you do to combine this into one `forever` block of code?
    - ○ Edit your code so you have one forever loop with four if statements inside it.

> Look for the similarities in the code. Add the if statement for key down into the same `forever` block as the key up if statement. Do the same for the if statements for forward and back.

- ✪ Click the green arrow again, but this time focus on the scrolling background. You will notice two purple circles appearing repeatedly on the screen.
    - ○ Edit the sprites called background1 and background2 to remove the purple circles. Replace these with lots of smaller dots to represent small stones on the ground.
    - ○ Press the green flag to check you are happy with how the scrolling background looks on screen.
- ✪ Look at the code for sprites called background1 and background2. The first `script` block for background1 is hiding the original sprite and then making a clone of the original sprite after five seconds.

The second block of code for background1 displays the clone at *x,y* location 480,0. This is where it is on the screen.

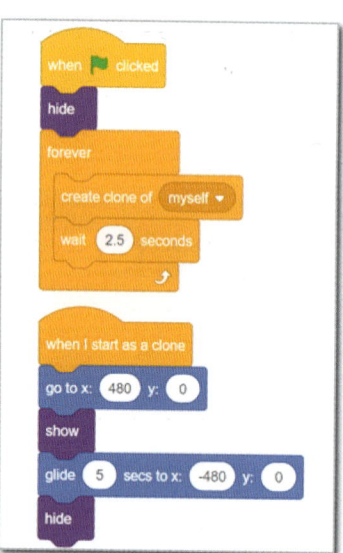

> If both clones are made after five seconds, one will appear above the other.

▲ background1 (left) and background2 (right)

- ○ What do you think the `glide` block does?
- ✪ Compare the `wait` block used in background1 and background2. Think about why the time in the `glide` block for background2 is 2.5.
    - ○ Try changing the wait values and the glide values in each block of code for each background.
    - ○ Press the green flag to see how this changes how the background is displayed.
- ✪ When you are happy with the skater's movement, and the appearance of the scrolling background save your game with an appropriate name.

Unit 7.4 Block it out: Creating a game

Avoidance tactics

Learn

Decisions about running lines of code are made by asking questions using **conditional statements**. The decision is based on testing a **condition**. If the condition is true, the lines of code within the `if` statement will be carried out. If the condition is false, the lines of code within the `if` statement will not be carried out.

For example, look at this conditional statement in a block of code:

> if key up arrow pressed?

The program carries out the following test when the up arrow key is pressed by the user:

> IF up arrow pressed = TRUE

The conditional statement is asking a question where the outcome can only be TRUE or FALSE. A conditional statement like this is called a **Boolean expression**.

Boolean expressions make use of Boolean operators (symbols) such as those shown in the table below. You will already know some of these.

Expression	Boolean operators
Equal to	=
Greater than	>
Less than	<
Greater than or equal to	>=
Less than or equal to	<=
Not equal to	<>
And	AND
Or	OR
Not	NOT

State whether each of the following statements are TRUE or FALSE

1. 6 > 8
2. 5 <> 6
3. 6 = 6

It is also possible to ask a program to assess more than one conditional statement using the following Boolean expressions.

➤ Using AND as part of a Boolean expression will only output TRUE if both parts of the condition are TRUE.

➤ Using OR will lead to a result of TRUE if either of the conditions are TRUE.

➤ NOT is carrying out a test on a condition to see if it is FALSE.

KEYWORDS

condition: a statement which evaluates to true or false; for example, x<10 is an example of a condition; if x is equal to 11, the condition will evaluate to false

conditional statements: used to make decisions about running lines of code; the decision is based upon testing a condition. If the condition is true the lines of code within the 'if statement' will be carried out. But if the condition is false the lines of code are not carried out

Boolean expression: a statement or expression which, when tested, produces a result of only either TRUE or FALSE

International Computing for Lower Secondary

Say whether the outcome of each of the following statements would be TRUE or FALSE for a statement with two conditions x, y.

1. x = TRUE AND y = FALSE
2. x = TRUE OR y = TRUE
3. x = NOT TRUE

More complex statements can be used to help decide if or what sections of code are to be carried out. For example, if you want the skater to move back to the start position if he touches either of the purple blocks, you could use the following **compound conditional** statement:

> Combined using a Boolean operator 'OR' to combine the conditions

If touching border1 OR border2 then

- condition 1 = touching border1
- condition 2 = touching border2

Complex conditional statements like this allow you to check if two or more conditions are met before another block of code is **executed**.

KEYWORDS

compound conditional: the use of **logical operators** to combine conditions before deciding if a block of code needs to be executed

executed: when code is translated to be run by the computer's processor

logical operator: words such as AND and OR which are used to combine two or more conditions

DID YOU KNOW?

Statements where the answer can only be TRUE or FALSE are called Boolean expressions. They are named after an English mathematician called George Boole (1815–1864).

Practice

- Open your skater game file – you should now have a sprite that can move up, down, forward and back, and a scrolling background on the stage. Play the game again. Look at what happens when the skater moves too far up or down the screen.
- With a friend, discuss the extra code blocks shown on the next page.
- How can you add these code blocks to the animatedskater script to stop the skater disappearing off the top and bottom of the screen?

   Tip: You need to develop your program to check if animatedskater is touching either border1 or border2. If either condition is shown to be TRUE, the sprite will be returned to the centre of the stage. Use following example example to help you:

> Create two rectangles called border1 and border2 for the top and bottom of the screen. What do you want the skater's *x, y* co-ordinates to be if he collides with those sprites?

98

Unit 7.4 Block it out: Creating a game

```
IF touching border1 = TRUE OR touching border2 = TRUE THEN
    set x to 0
    set y to 0
END IF
```

Use OR to combine the touching border1, touching border2 conditions. OR will produce a Yes or True answer if either condition is True.

Use the OR statement to combine two conditions. Use the If statement to test this combined conditional.

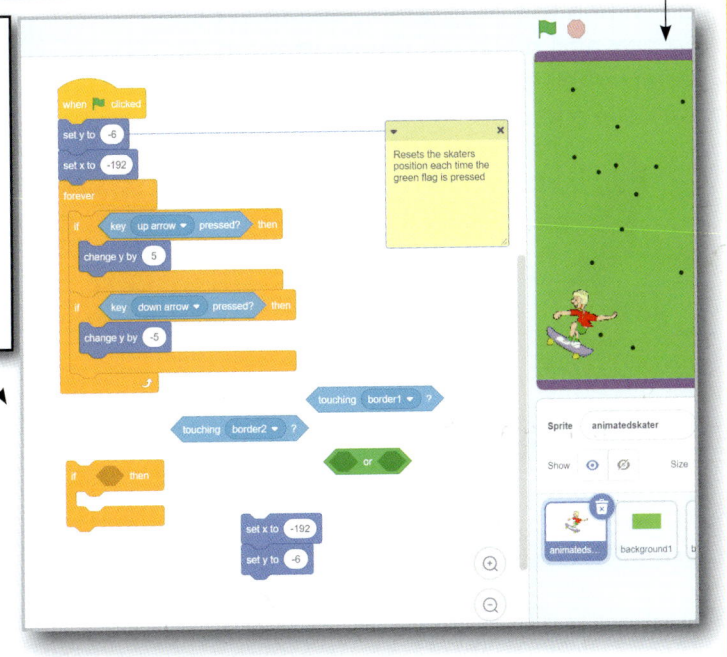

- ➤ Add additional borders to stop the skater moving off the left and right hand side of the screen.
  - o Create two additional borders called border3 and border4 for the left and right hand side of the screen.
  - o Add if statements to the animatedskater sprite which will return him to a new position on the screen if he collides with either of the new borders.

Algorithmic thinking

As well as flowcharts, we can use pseudocode to design code. Pseudocode contains details of the instructions to be carried out by a program. It shows the order in which they are to be carried out. It is not a programming language, but may contain some programming terms to help programmers understand the structure of a program.

International Computing for Lower Secondary

A variable amount

Learn

When creating programs, you often need to store **data items** so they can be used later in the program. When you want to store and use data values in this way, you create **variables**. When you create a variable, you need to give it a name. In programming this is called **variable declaration**. This name is used to identify a location in memory where the data item is stored, much like a box with a piece of paper inside. When the program needs to access that data item, it opens the box and reads what is written on the piece of paper. This paper, when put in the box, is known as **assignment** – giving the variable a value.

Variables can be used to store many different types of data, from text to numbers. They are called variables because, once they are set up, the program can use the stored values as part of the program and change the values while the program is running. Using the box and piece of paper analogy, it is like someone erasing the value written on the piece of paper, writing a new value on it, and putting the paper back into the box.

KEYWORDS

data item: information processed or stored by a computer

variable: a stored value which can change during the execution of a program

variable declaration: the process of creating a variable by giving it a name and in some programming languages a data type

assignment: the process of assigning a data value to a variable name

It is a good idea to give the variable a sensible name so you can remember what it is being used to store.

Practice

➤ In these next tasks you will:
  o add a new sprite called bouncingball
  o animate the new bouncingball sprite by causing it to move across the screen
  o create a variable called Ball Speed
  o use the Ball Speed variable to create code to change the speed of the ball when it interacts with another sprite on the stage.

Create a more interesting sprite if you have time. Perhaps your skater is trying to avoid animated frisbees or animals which randomly run across his path.

Unit 7.4 Block it out: Creating a game

Decomposition

The previous design team started to create the program to allow the ball to move. They selected most of the code blocks needed but did not manage to combine them to create the final code. Your manager thinks one code block is still missing.

Use what you have learned about Scratch so far to help figure out which additional code block you need.

Combine the code blocks on the next page so that, when the green arrow is clicked, the ball will go to its start position, point in a random direction and then repeatedly move in that direction testing for an edge to bounce off.

Decomposition

The following pseudocode will also help you complete the practice task. Break down the design provided by thinking about which code blocks would represent each line of the pseudocode shown.

```
when green flag = clicked
go to x: y: start position
point in random direction
hide variable ball speed
set ball speed to 1
repeat FOREVER
    move ball speed z steps
    IF touching edge
        point in random direction
        IF ball speed <5
            set ball speed to ball speed + 0.5
            end IF
    end IF
end repeat FOREVER
```

Remove this line if you wish to display the ball speed during the game.

Programmers sometimes put one IF statement inside another to test more than one condition. This is called a nested IF statement.

- Test your game by playing it once you have updated the ball script.

International Computing for Lower Secondary

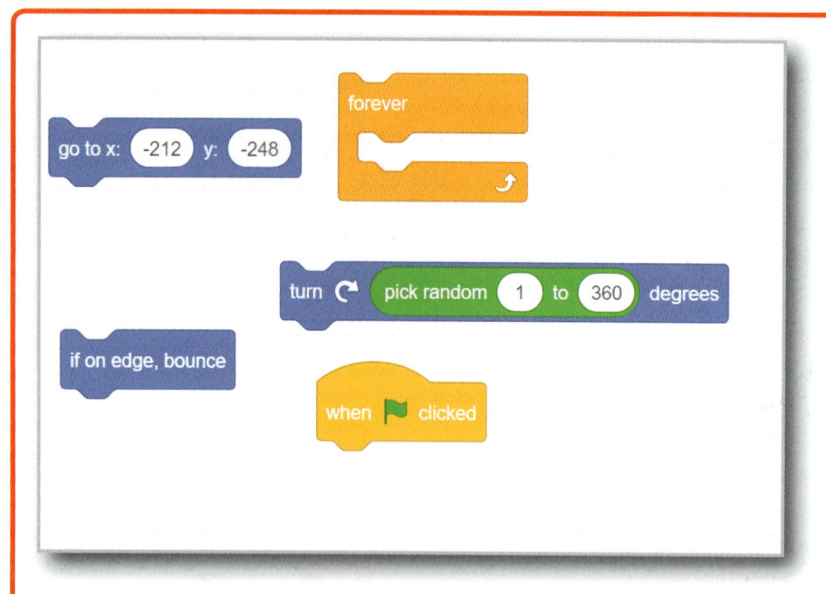

[Scratch blocks shown: go to x: -212 y: -248; forever; turn ↻ pick random 1 to 360 degrees; if on edge, bounce; when ⚑ clicked]

- ✸ Try changing the *x* and *y* values in the `go to` block and run it again to see how that changes how the code operates.
- ✸ Do the same with the values in the `pick random` block and the `move` block.
- ✸ What do you notice about the movement of the ball when you have played it a few times with the same values in each code block?
- ✸ Make the game more difficult by increasing the ball speed each time it bounces off another object on the screen.
    o You will need to add a variable to the game first; you can do this by clicking on the orange Variables group and select `Make a Variable`. Call this variable Ball Speed.

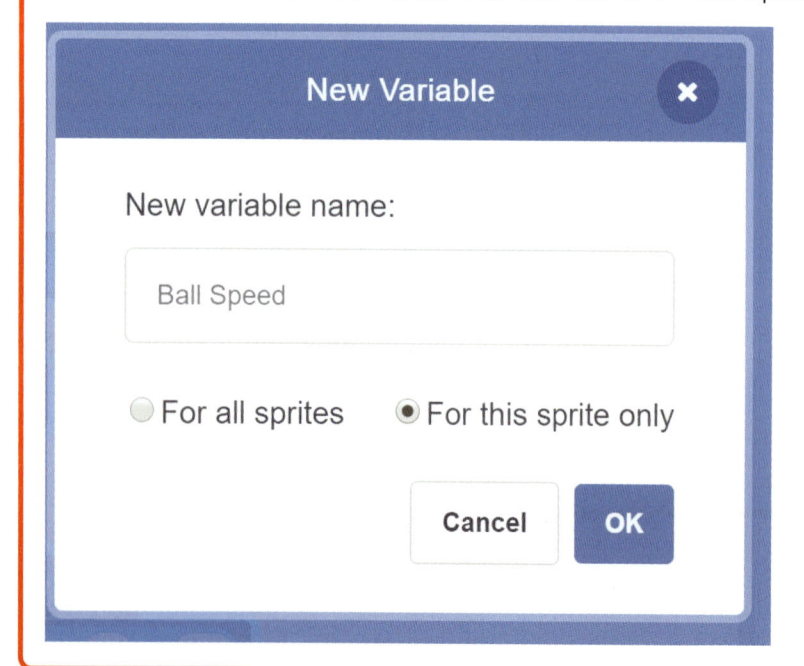

> Where else could you use the **pick random** block to change the start position of the ball every time the game restarted?

> Click on the white areas of the code blocks to change the values to, for example, a speed or direction of your choice. Test the game until you are happy with the way the ball moves and bounces.

New Variable

New variable name:

[Ball Speed]

○ For all sprites   ● For this sprite only

[Cancel]   [OK]

102

Unit 7.4 Block it out: Creating a game

Practice

- Create a new sprite called bouncingball. Draw a red circle to represent the ball (or use an existing ball in the sprite dictionary – click on the magnifying class to search the sprite dictionary). Create a new sprite by clicking on the Paint tool in the sprite panel. This will be used as a moving obstacle for your skater.
- Click on your bouncingball sprite and use the Code tab to add the appropriate code blocks into the script window for the sprite.
- Use the flowchart below to help you reorganise the code blocks to increase the ball speed when it bounces off the edge of the screen.

Paint tool

DID YOU KNOW?
Program designers use flowchart symbols to design blocks of code before they try to implement them.

Flowchart 1

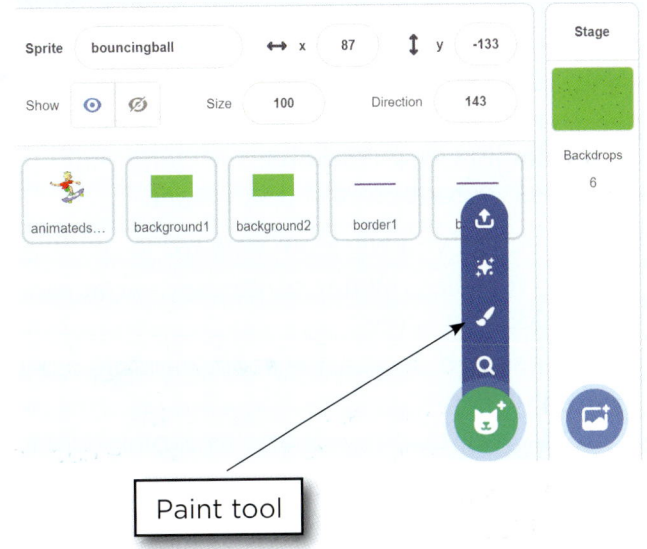

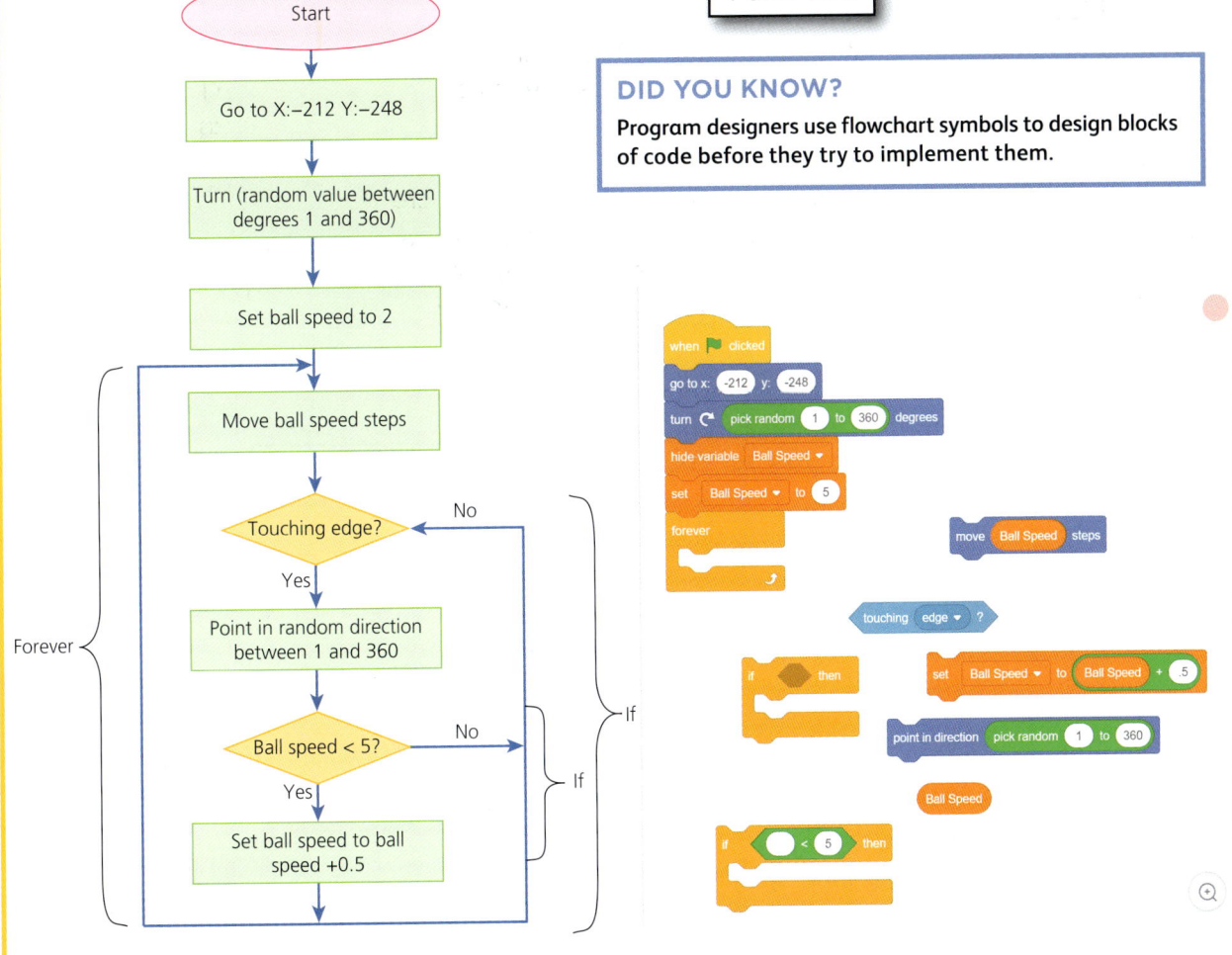

Start
↓
Go to X:−212 Y:−248
↓
Turn (random value between degrees 1 and 360)
↓
Set ball speed to 2
↓
Move ball speed steps ←──────┐
↓   │
Touching edge? ──No──→─────────┤
↓ Yes   │
Point in random direction   │
between 1 and 360   │
↓   │
Ball speed < 5? ──No──→────────┤
↓ Yes   │
Set ball speed to ball   │
speed +0.5 ────────────────────┘

Forever

103

International Computing for Lower Secondary

Keeping score

Learn

All good games need a competitive element. In this game, the skateboarder needs to move around the screen and collect glasses of water to help him stay hydrated. He gets five points for every glass he collects. But, each time he hits a ball, he loses five points. Glasses of water will randomly appear on the stage. To gain points, the skateboarder sprite must touch one of the glasses of water before it disappears.

In this section you will learn how to:

- make the Glass Water sprites appear at random times and locations on screen
- increase and decrease a score variable using on screen collision events
- create your own flowcharts to explain what a block of code is doing.

Practice

- Add a new sprite to your game. You can use the Glass Water sprite from the Scratch library, or you can create your own. You can do this by clicking on the magnifying glass in the Sprite panel.
- Add the code shown to your Glass Water sprite.
- Produce a flowchart to illustrate how the block of code operates. Use the example flowchart on page 103 to help you. Your flowchart should only include the following symbols.

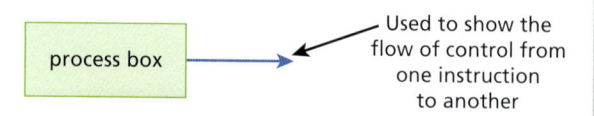

process box — Used to show the flow of control from one instruction to another

- You have learnt how to amend existing code and reorder code blocks to solve a range of problems. You will now learn how to use your new coding skills to create your own code block to add a scoring system for the game.

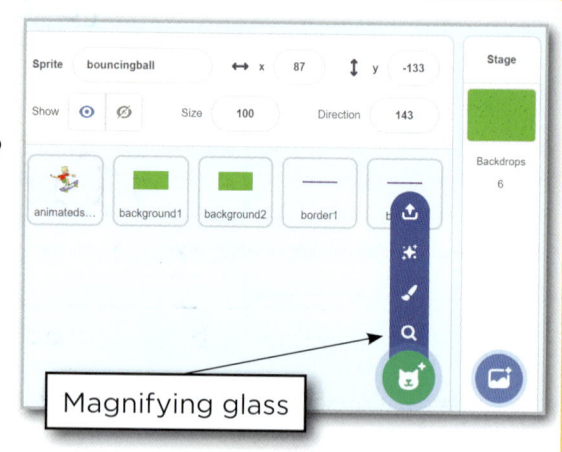

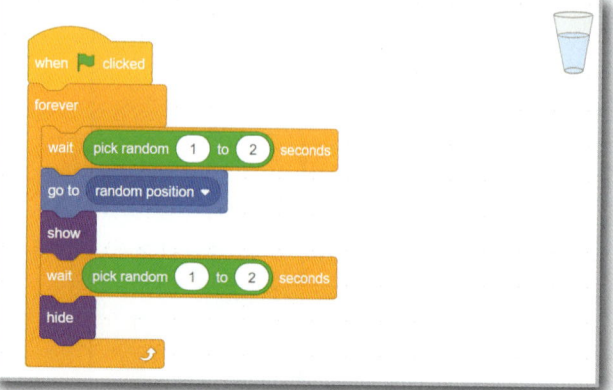

Unit 7.4 Block it out: Creating a game

- Click on your Glass Water sprite.
- Drag a new `when green flag clicked` block to your code window for the Glass Water sprite.
- Create a new variable called Score.
- Go to the `Variables` code blocks and click on the `set _ _ to _ _` code block.

Remember creating variables on pages 100–103?

- Drag the `set _ _ to _ _` block to the script window for the Glass Water sprite and place it under the when green flag clicked code block.
- Amend the values in `set _ _ to _ _` so that it sets the score variable to 0 when the green flag is clicked.
- Combine and edit the following code blocks to complete this task before adding them to your code for the Glass Water sprite.

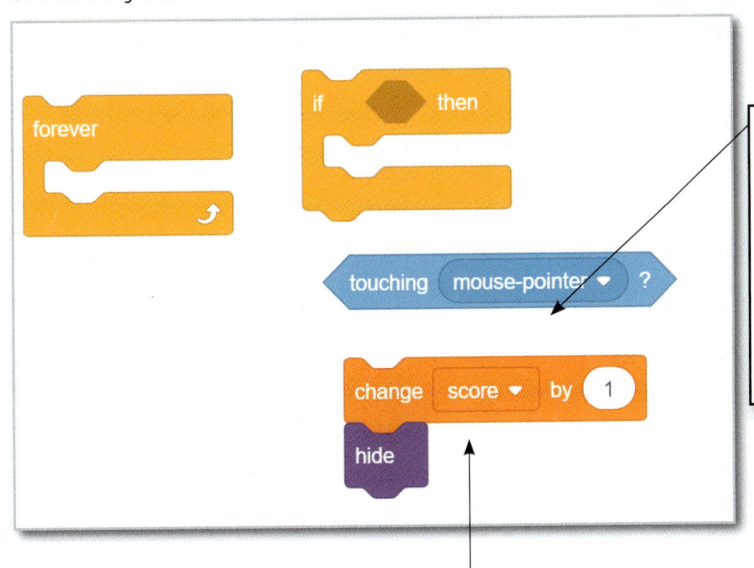

Create an `If` statement that tests to see if the Glass Water sprite is touching the animatedskater sprite (not the mouse-pointer).

If the condition is true, set the score variable to score +5.

Put the code inside a forever loop.

- Think about how you can make sure this happens for the duration of the game.

▶ Edit the existing code on the bouncingball sprite so that the value of the score is reduced by five if the animatedskater sprite collides with the bouncingball sprite.

Edit the code you have created for the Glass Water sprite to help you with this.

▶ Think carefully here about how you would use additional show and hide blocks to ensure the ball does not disappear off the screen permanently.

105

International Computing for Lower Secondary

Collecting user input for variables

Learn

Until now, you are the only person that has created and used the variables in your game.

User input is a very important part of a computer program. In computer games, for example, the user can provide instructions to the game using an input device, such as a keyboard. Input can then be used to control elements of the game. You have seen this already with keyboard instructions controlling elements of your game. User input can also be used to provide text or numeric (numbers) which can be used to control the game.

User input can then be processed by the computer program and **output** is produced and displayed for the user. Output is made available to the user in many forms using devices such as screens, speakers, printers, and so on.

In the following tasks you will add code to your game which will allow the user to control how long the game is to be played for.

Scratch uses the `ask...` and `wait` code block to collect data from the user. The example below shows the use of a variable called name being used to collect information from the user before the same information is output by the sprite.

KEYWORD

output: data which is produced by a computer program and made available to the user via a device such as a screen, speaker, printer, and so on

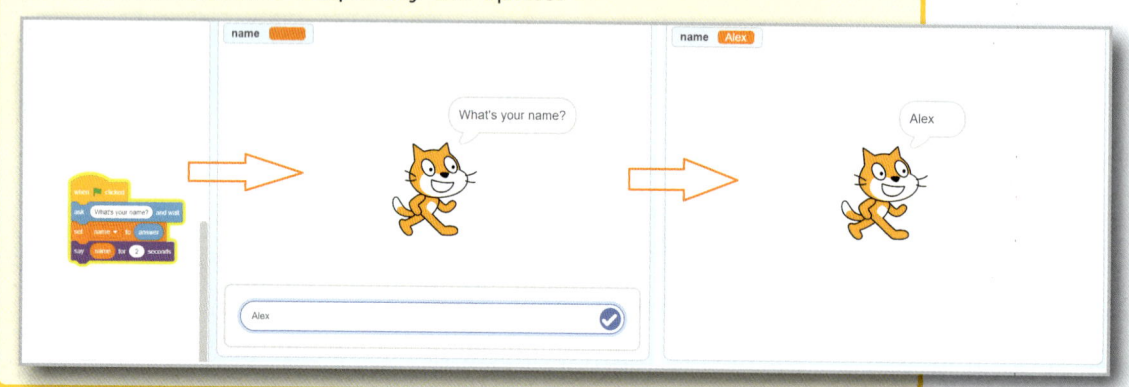

Abstraction

This diagram shows the input, process and output elements of this game. The process part of the program has underlying code. We might abstract that code as demonstrated here so that we can focus on the input and output and the experience of the teenager playing the game.

Input (for example, using keyboard) → Process → Output (for example, onscreen display)

Unit 7.4 Block it out: Creating a game

Practice

> Look back at pages 100–103 for help creating variables.

- Create your own short program to collect information from the user.
  - Create a new Scratch file by clicking on 'File' and then 'New'.
  - Create a new variable called name.
  - New Scratch projects always start with the Cat sprite, called sprite1. You can use this.
  - Add a `when green flag clicked` block to the code panel for the sprite.
  - Use the `ask… and wait` block to ask any question; in this case: 'What is your name?' The `ask… and wait` block temporarily stores the most recent text input with the `ask… and wait` block.
  - Use the `set` block from the variable code group to set the contents of the name variable to equal the answer given by the user. Look at the example code to help you with this (you can find the `answer` block in the sensing code group).
  - Use the `say` block, from the Looks group of code blocks to make the sprite repeat the word input by the user. You can set time to as long as you wish.

- Use the `ask… and wait` block to ask the user to input how long they want to play the game for. Look at the three examples of script below. Decide which one will correctly complete the three tasks listed here, and then add this code to your game.

- Use what you have learned in this practice panel to help you edit your own animatedskater game now so that it can
  - Collect information from the user about the length of time they wish to play for.
  - Store the value entered by the user in a variable called duration.
  - Use that value to count down to zero before telling the user the game is over and ending all scripts.

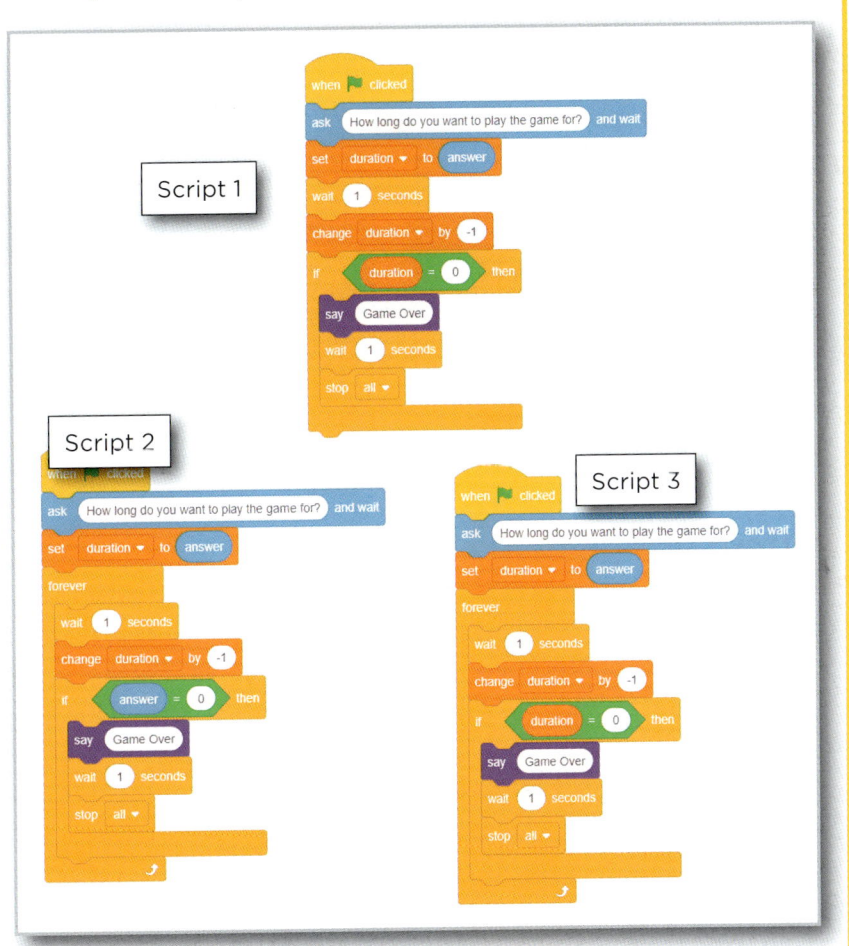

International Computing for Lower Secondary

Making my blocks

Learn

Solving problems is much easier if you take larger problems and break them down into smaller, easy-to-understand parts.

When you added controls for movement to your animatedskater sprite, you first thought about how you wanted the sprite to move around the screen. You then added blocks of code using `if` statements and conditions which repeatedly checked for input from any of the arrow keys used to control the skater.

Look at this code again with a friend.

Do you notice any patterns appearing in your code?

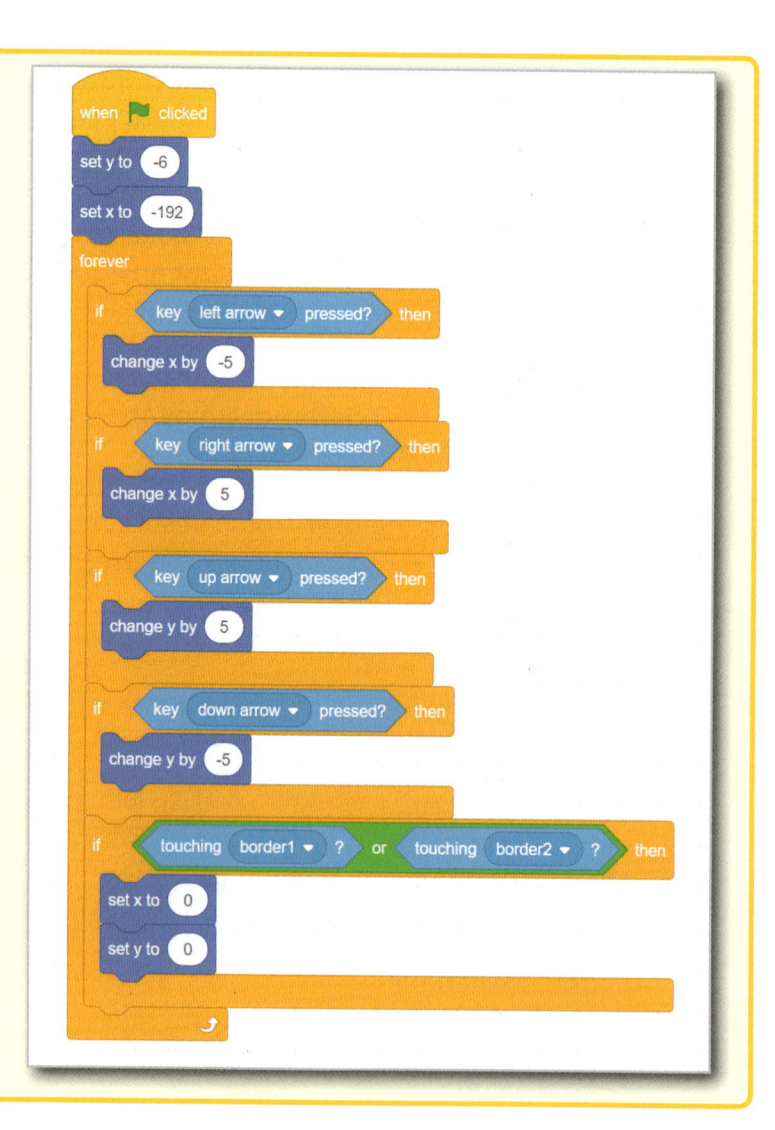

Pattern recognition

The code for each of these tasks is very similar and is being repeated over and over again. This makes the code very long and difficult to read.

You can make this code much more readable and efficient by using **procedures**.

Before writing a procedure you need to consider what name you will give to the procedure and what useful data needs to be passed into and/or out of the procedure (**parameters**).

Look carefully at the code for moving up, down, left and right.

KEYWORD

parameter: a special kind of variable used to pass data between procedures

108

Unit 7.4 Block it out: Creating a game

Practice

- You are going to write a procedure to allow you to handle movement of the animatedskater sprite. You will use it to replace some of the long lines of code in the `skater` code blocks.
  - Click on the animatedskater sprite.
  - Now click on the 'Code' tab.
  - Click on 'My Blocks' and select 'Make a Block'.
  - Name the block 'Move Skater'.
  - Click 'OK'. This creates a new block called `Move Skater` in the My Blocks panel and creates a new block definition in the code window for the animatedskater sprite.

  - Copy the `If up arrow pressed` statement block from the main body of the script for animated skater and add it to your new define up block.
  - Do the same for the `If down arrow pressed`, `If right arrow pressed` and `If left arrow pressed` statement blocks.
  - Now drag the `Move Skater` block from the My Blocks panel and drop it inside the forever loop which contained the original four if statements.
- Your code block for the animatedskater sprite should now have changed from the original code structure on the left to the new updated version with procedures on the right.

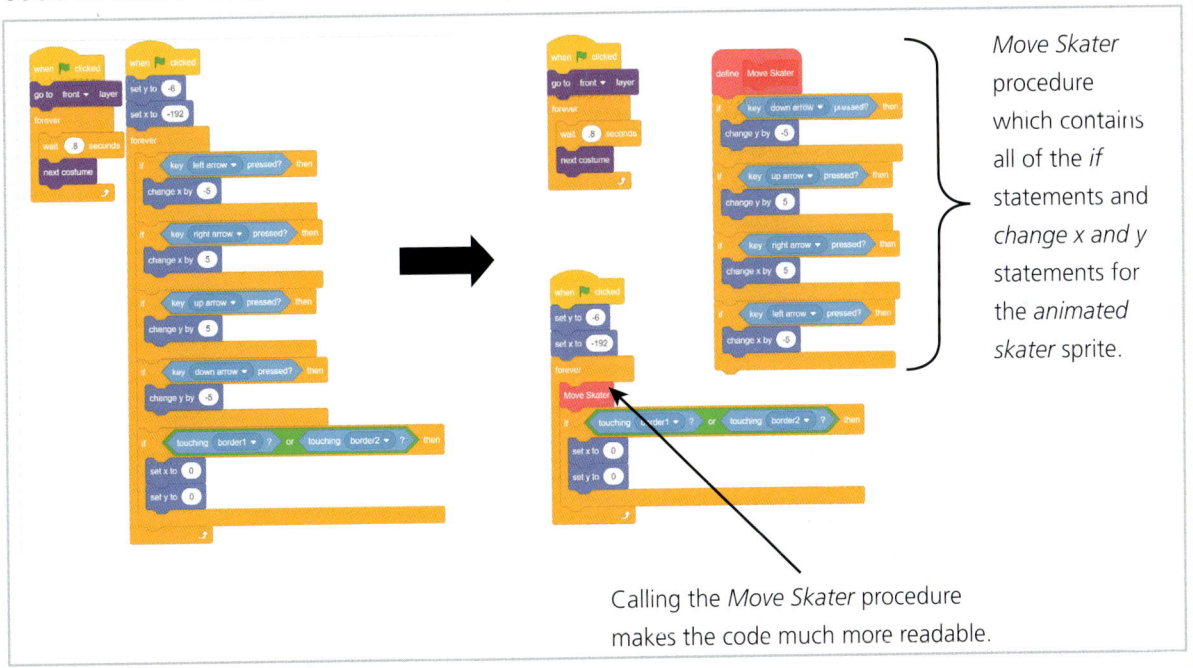

Move Skater procedure which contains all of the if statements and change x and y statements for the animated skater sprite.

Calling the *Move Skater* procedure makes the code much more readable.

109

International Computing for Lower Secondary

Go further

- Try increasing the difficulty level of the game even further by adding an additional obstacle or multiple animatedball sprites. Think carefully about the start location of the additional obstacle.

- To make the game more complex:
  - right click on the Glass Water sprite and select 'duplicate' so you now have more than one glass of water appearing for the skater to collect
  - edit the code associated with the duplicate to ensure it does not appear at the same time as the original
  - use the `change size` block in the looks panel (tip: you could change the size of the ball by a random amount each time it collides with another object).

> Consider using different wait times for the appearance of additional Glass Water sprites.

> The `hide` and `wait` blocks can help you with this problem.

- With a friend, plan a solution in a flowchart to show how you would edit the score code to take into consideration additional sprites. Use the flowchart example on page 103 to help you.
  - Remember to include a `when green flag clicked` block.
  - You will also need a `set score to 0` block immediately after.
  - You will need a loop. Inside your loop you should include `if` statement blocks to show how the code will be amended for each sprite.
  - Once you have planned your solution, implement your code.
  - Examine your game with a friend. Look carefully at how the score keeps increasing or decreasing for as long as the animatedskater sprite and the Game or bouncingball sprites are touching.

Unit 7.4 Block it out: Creating a game

Challenge yourself

KEYWORD

list: a data structure that allows us to store more than one variable; sometimes called an **array**

The game company has asked you to make some additions to the game. They would like the game to include a list of authorised users (people allowed to play the game). Anyone not on the list will receive a message saying, 'Sorry, you are not on our list of players! You cannot play this game!'

Scratch has a useful tool to store information one after another, called a **list**. Lists are referred to as **arrays** in some programming languages.

> Just like a shopping list, all of the items you need from the store are on a page, with each item on a new line.

Lists in Scratch are used to store a group of variables. They can contain any number of variables and can be used to store data made up from text or numbers or both. Variables stored inside a list can then be used by other parts of the program.

We are going to create a list of authorised gamers for the skater game. Users will only be able to play the game if their name appears on the list.

- Click on the Variables panel on the Scratch interface.
- Create a new variable called name.
- Click on the Variables panel on the Scratch interface. This time click on 'Make a List'.
- Call your new list gamer list. This will appear on the main Scratch stage.
- Use the + button to add a number of names to your list.
- Edit this script to include an `ask` block which will collect the game player's name at the start of the game. Place this after the `when clicked` block at the start of the code, as shown below.

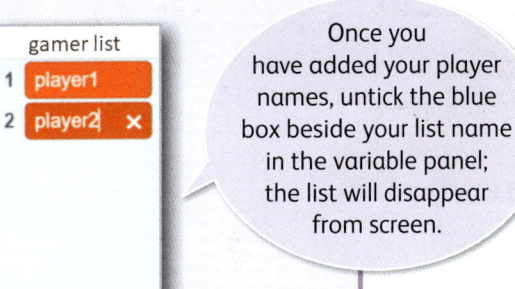

> Once you have added your player names, untick the blue box beside your list name in the variable panel; the list will disappear from screen.

> Return to the script you created on page 107 where the user could enter in how long they wanted to play for

111

- Under the `ask` block use the `set` block as shown below to assign the answer given by the user to the variable name.
- Now use the pseudocode shown below to help you complete the missing part of this code.

```
If gamer list contains answer
      Say 'Hello!
Are you ready to play today?'
ElseSay 'Sorry you are not on our list of players!
You cannot play this game!'
      Wait 1 second
      Stop all code
```

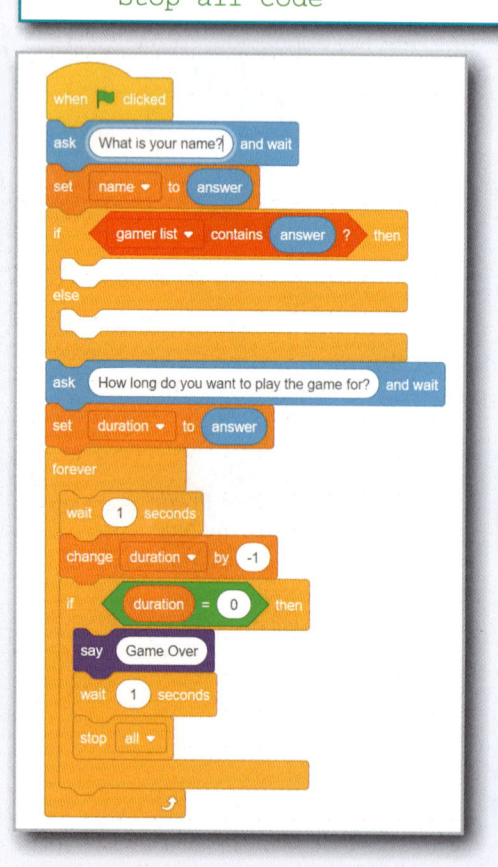

> **DID YOU KNOW?**
> Some programming languages have data structures called arrays. Arrays usually only allow for the storage of one data type. Lists can hold data of any type, such as a mix of text and numbers.

- Test the game by running the code and entering a name which:
  o **is** included on the list, to make sure the correct message is displayed
  o **is not** included on the list, to make sure the correct message is displayed.

Unit 7.4 Block it out: Creating a game

Final project

The gaming company have now asked you to create another game for them. Your new assignment is to create a maze game to help promote healthy eating in primary school children.

The maze game should have the following features.

- A start-up screen where the rules and controls of the game are shown using a list.
  The list disappears when the game player starts the game.
- The start screen should have instructions to Press SPACE BAR to start playing.

  Use the `wait` and `hide` code blocks to remove the list from the screen after a number of seconds.

- The user has only 60 seconds to complete the game.
- An animated sprite which you have created yourself.
- A start and home graphic to mark the start and end of the maze.
- A background image containing the maze image. The pathway should be a distinct colour from the rest of the maze. Make the pathway wide enough so that the game player's sprite can move around without touching the edges.

  Remember, the maze image is now part of your background. The pathway is a different colour from the rest of the stage. Try using the `touching colour` block with the `if` block to reset the gamer's sprite if they touch the edge of the maze pathway.

- Obstacles (unhealthy food choices) which appear randomly along the pathway. If the game player's sprite collides with an obstacle, the game player loses two points.
- Rewards (healthy food choices) for the main character to pick up and gain points (two points for each healthy food choice).

  Remember combining the `if` block and `touching` block on pages 98–99 to reset the skater when he touches the top or bottom of the screen. Think about how you could use this to increase or decrease points.

```
if  touching border1 ?  or  touching border2 ?  then
    set x to 0
    set y to 0
```

- If the game player's score goes below zero, they are sent back to the start of the game.
- If the main sprite touches the side of the maze, the player loses three points.

113

- Players can only play the game if their name is on a player list. If a player's name is on the player list, they will receive a welcome message after they type their name in. If their name is not on the list, they will be told they are unable to play.
- A sound (such as applause) should be played when the home graphic at the end of the maze has been reached (this is something you should try to figure out yourself).

Evaluation

- After you have created your game ask a friend to play the game.
  They should comment on:
  o how easy or difficult your game is for the target audience
  o the quality and appropriateness of your graphics, sounds, and so on
  o the accuracy of your scoring feature
  o whether your game met all of the requirements listed. And note the requirements that still need to be met
  o recommendations that they would make on how you could improve your game.
- Make improvements to your game based on the feedback from your friend. Test and play your game again. Are there any further improvements required?

Unit 7.5
Show and tell: Cloud based presentations

Working in the cloud

In this unit you will examine the features of a range of software applications which can be used to produce professional presentations, and combine data from a range of other applications.

An increasing number of organisations believe cloud based applications are the future for data processing, rather than using locally installed programs.

There are many reasons for this increase in the popularity of cloud based processing.
- **Cloud based applications** allow staff and customers to access data from any location with internet access.
- Staff can collaborate on tasks from anywhere in the world.
- Organisations can increase (or decrease) their storage and processing needs as required, simply by changing a subscription fee.

For smaller organisations, the responsibility and cost of data security becomes the responsibility of their service provider; the organisation no longer needs to employ a specialist to do the job.

> Note: Although this chapter uses the cloud based applications provided by Google, the tasks in this unit can also be completed using *Microsoft Office 365* tools. Both of these **application suites** provide the same tools and operate in a very similar manner.

We will look at how you can make use of *Google Docs* pages, sheets and slides applications to present data, firstly as individual applications, and then at how you can incorporate data from an **interactive multimedia application**.

Learning Outcomes

In this unit you will learn to:
- create and use a cloud based word processed document in *Google Docs* to
  - edit and format text in a document
  - refine and organise the layout of a document
  - use the internet to effectively locate images and insert images into a cloud based word processed document
- enter data into a cloud based spreadsheet application and use that tool to create charts
- produce a presentation to suit a specific set of needs
- add **hyperlinks** to a cloud based document and presentation

KEYWORDS

cloud based application: a software program which is accessed using a web browser and the internet but where processing is carried out on servers held in another location

application suites: a collection of computer programs with a similar user interface that can easily support the exchange of data between each program

interactive multimedia application: an application which incorporates a range of media, including text, images, animation, video and sound

cloud based application: Give an example of a cloud based application you use.

Application suites: Give an example of application suites you use.

Definition check: Close your book and make a list of as many terms you have learned in this unit as you can. Compare them with your partner's list. Together try to define as many of them as you can. Check your definitions against the definitions given in the key word boxes.

115

International Computing for Lower Secondary

> - combine data from a variety of cloud based applications to make a presentation which is fit for purpose
> - incorporate interactive quiz elements into a cloud based application
> - evaluate a completed cloud based presentation.

DID YOU KNOW?
Banks are one of the biggest users of cloud computing because of the increased use of internet banking and applications such as PayPal.

SCENARIO

As a new volunteer with an environmental group, Green Global, your first task is to produce an interactive presentation on the topic of climate change. The environmental group you are working with is attending a local science fair. It wants to use your presentation to help make young people more aware of environmental issues.

Your presentation is to be viewed as a **kiosk presentation**. Some examples of kiosk applications include:

- directory of information kiosks used in areas with a lot of people (for example, at a theme park or a shopping mall). Users are presented with a variety of options which they can select to find out more information about that particular area
- self-service checkouts found in some supermarkets and fast-food chains

kiosk presentation: Search the Internet to find an example of a kiosk presentation.

KEYWORD

kiosk presentation/application: a presentation which runs unattended by a speaker; it may contain hyperlinks to allow the person viewing it some element of control over its operation

116

Unit 7.5 Show and tell: Cloud based presentations

Your presentation will be controlled by navigation buttons and hyperlinks which can allow the user to move from one part of the presentation to the next page. It should also provide the user with links to other applications and websites to provide more detailed information.

At the end of your presentation, Green Global would like you to include a short self-assessment section so the user can check how much they learned from the presentation.

The climate change presentation will eventually form part of a larger application with a number of sections on environmental issues; each section will have its own self-assessment task at the end.

Your presentation must include:
- appropriate graphics
- links to external websites to allow the viewer to 'find out more'
- links between each of the pages of the presentation to allow the viewer to move from page to page
- a method for users to explore a topic further through linked, additional information
- up-to-date visual data, such as charts and graphs
- a self-assessment quiz containing multiple-choice questions
- hyperlinks to allow the user to control the presentation.

Do you remember?

Before starting this unit, you should be able to:
- ✔ access a *Google* online (or *Microsoft Office 365*) account (your school will help you with this)
- ✔ search the internet for suitable facts, images and supporting websites using appropriate key words
- ✔ accurately enter text and numbers into a range of applications such as a word processing application, a spreadsheet application and a presentation application.

International Computing for Lower Secondary

Going into the cloud

> **Learn**
>
> A cloud based application is one which is made available to users via the internet. The software used by the user is saved on a **server** in another location (a **remote server**). Users access the software via the internet. All processing is carried out on this server and the results are sent back to the user via the internet.
>
> Before we use any of the cloud based apps such as *Google*, it is important to consider why cloud based apps are becoming more popular with users today.
>
> The table below outlines some of the pros and cons of cloud based applications.
>
> | Cloud based applications ||
> |---|---|
> | **Pros** | **Cons** |
> | Users can work on projects together wherever they are. This can also help reduce an individual's impact on the environment (carbon footprint) as staff from all over the world can work collaboratively on tasks, without having to travel to a meeting place. | Users depend on their internet connection being reliable. |
> | It is no longer the user's responsibility to back up work. | Some users are concerned about the security of their data. Many users are worried about **cyberattacks**, **denial of service**, data theft and **insider threats**. |
> | You can increase and decrease your need for storage and processing at any time. | There is often a fee for cloud based applications. |

KEYWORDS

server: a computer in a network, which manages processing and access to resources for other users

remote server: a server which is accessed by users across the internet

cyberattacks: any attempt by **hackers** to cause damage to a computer system

hacker: anyone gaining unauthorised access to a computer system

denial of service: an attack on a computer system which stops authorised users from accessing it

insider threats: employees of an organisation misuse their authorised access to data in some way; for example, passing client data on to a competitor

Unit 7.5 Show and tell: Cloud based presentations

Practice

- Cloud based application users usually need a username and password to access the **cloud services** available to them. We will focus on tools made available by *Google Apps* but, as previously mentioned, these tasks can also be completed using *Microsoft Office 365*.
  Google Apps is a web based set of applications which contains tools for email, word processing, multimedia presentations, and spreadsheets among others.
  Your school should already have an account set up for you to use.
    - Open your web browser.
    - Access your account at
      https://accounts.google.com/signin
    - Log in to the account using the username and password provided by your teacher.
    - Click on the *Google Apps* icon to see the range of *Google Apps* you can use.
- Click on More and locate the icons for *Google Drive*, *Docs*, *Sheets* and *Slides*.

> **KEYWORD**
> **cloud services:** applications made available to a user using internet based technology and a web browser

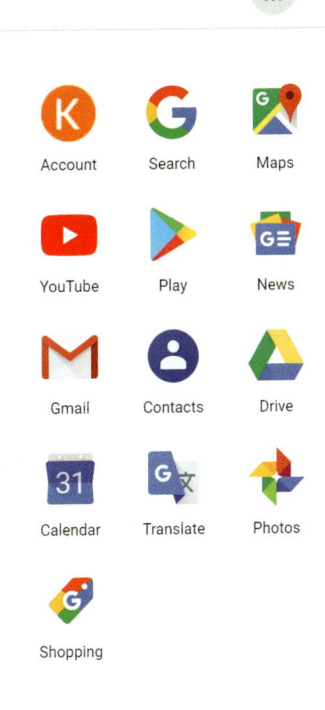

If you click on More, you will see a wide range of apps available to you. Scroll through them until you locate the ones you want.

Account | Search | Maps
YouTube | Play | News
Gmail | Contacts | Drive
Calendar | Translate | Photos
Shopping

More

Google Drive | Docs | Sheets | Slides

119

Get going with *Google Docs*

Learn

You can use *Google Docs* to create new word processed documents and share them with others. You can also import existing word processed documents from other applications and convert them to Doc format for editing.

One of the guest speakers at the science fair will give a brief talk about climate change. This will provide the basis of your presentation. He has recorded his speech using a voice dictation system and it is stored on an unformatted text file.

Your job is to convert the unformatted text file into a well-presented, professional booklet which can be accessed through the presentation if users would like more information. The target audience is 11–14 year olds. The aim of the document is to educate young people on what is meant by climate change and some of the main causes of climate change.

KEYWORDS

text file: a file which contains lines of plain text with no graphics or formatting

formatting: applying special features to a document to improve appearance, such as bold, italic, bullet points, and so on

Practice

- These next tasks involve Importing and opening files in *Google Docs*. Open the file **ClimateChange.txt** provided by your teacher. This is a basic **text file**. You will notice it has no **formatting** applied to it.
- This file will be used to create the information booklet at the science fair. Discuss with a partner how you could improve this document. The booklet will include a:
  - cover page
  - table of contents
  - page called 'What is climate change?'
  - page called 'What are the main causes of climate change?'
  - page called 'What effects will climate change have on the Earth'.

Unit 7.5 Show and tell: Cloud based presentations

- Make notes on your discussion, giving particular consideration to:
  - changes you might make to the document layout
  - how you might change the font, style, text size to improve the document
  - any other changes that might make the document look more professional.

> You may notice some spelling errors in the document. You can ignore those for the moment.

- Once you have completed your discussion, close the text file. You are now going to upload the text file provided by your teacher. It contains the text from the guest speaker's talk. Your task here is to format this text file so that it is presented professionally in a booklet style document.

> See page 119 for a reminder of what the *Google Drive* icon looks like

- Click on the icon for *Google Drive*.
- Click 'New' and then 'File Upload'.

> To create a new *Docs* file you can open *Google Docs* by clicking on the *Docs* icon in the list of available *Google Apps*. Then click the 'Blank' icon.

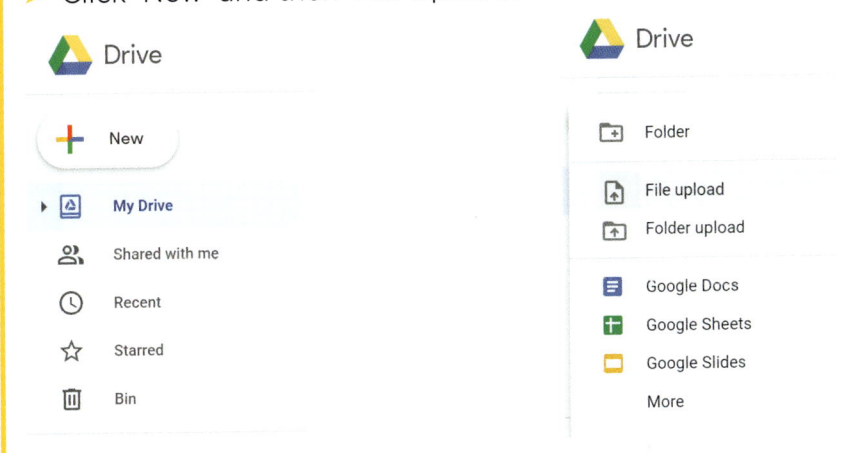

Drive
- New
- My Drive
- Shared with me
- Recent
- Starred
- Bin

Drive
- Folder
- File upload
- Folder upload
- Google Docs
- Google Sheets
- Google Slides
- More

- Locate the file called **ClimateChange.txt**.
- Your document will appear in 'My Drive'.

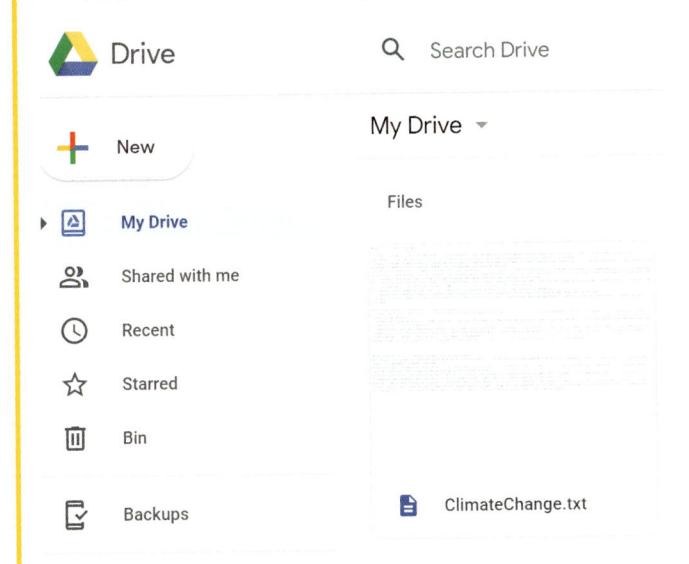

Drive
- New
- My Drive
- Shared with me
- Recent
- Starred
- Bin
- Backups

Search Drive

My Drive

Files

ClimateChange.txt

- Right click the icon for the file and select 'Open with' and then '*Google Docs*'.

121

International Computing for Lower Secondary

Page formatting and text layout

> **Learn**
>
> Basic text files such as **ClimateChange.txt** contain no formatting, which is why they are called text files.
>
> Documents which contain formatting which aids presentation and readability of a document are said to be in **rich text format (RTF)**.
>
> The image below shows a file presented in rich text format, compared to the same file in basic text file format.

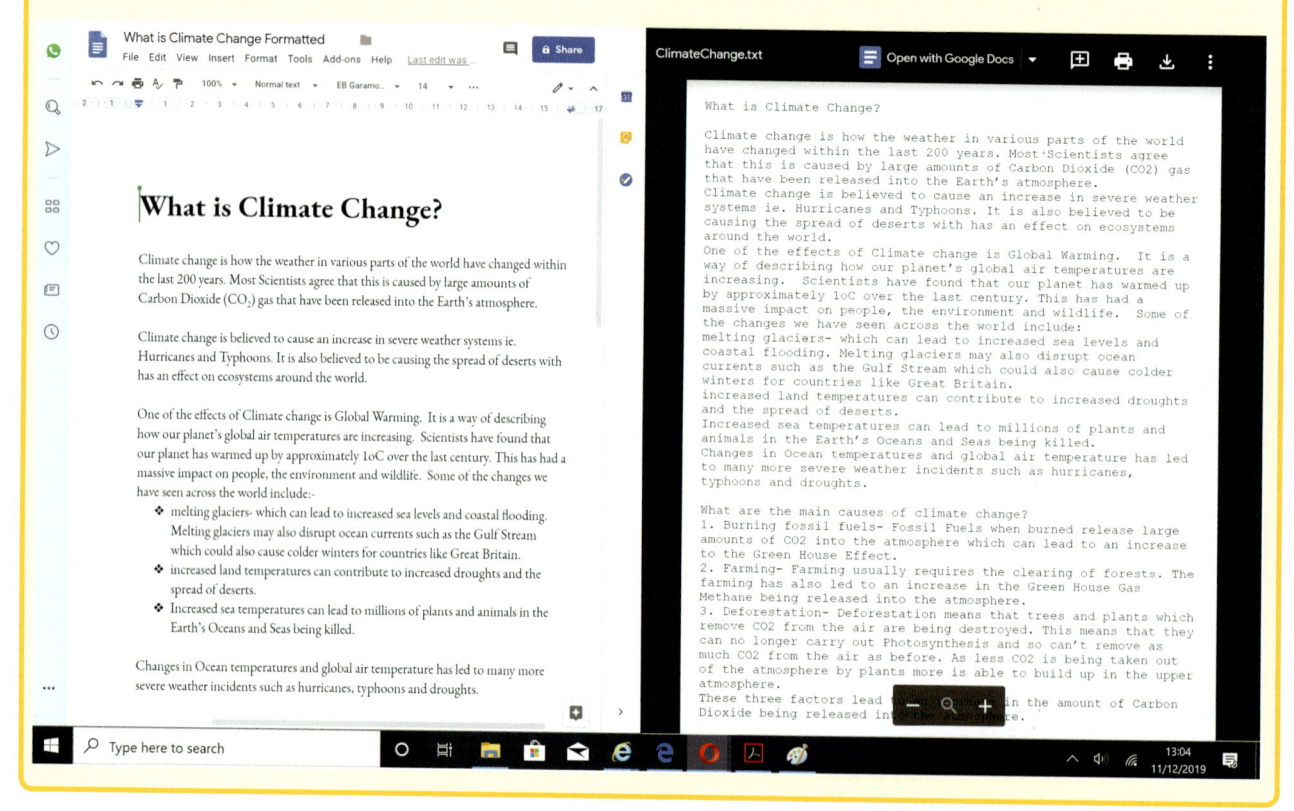

KEYWORDS

rich text format (RTF): documents which contain additional information about font style, size, images which allows the document to be shared **cross-platform**

cross-platform: allows a document or file or application to be opened using a variety of combinations of hardware and software

Cross-platform: Give an example of an app that is cross-platform.

DID YOU KNOW?
There are more than 3 000 000 possible fonts available in the world!

122

Unit 7.5 Show and tell: Cloud based presentations

Practice

Let us update the page set-up, font and style of the document to give it a more professional appearance.

▶ Open the text file **ClimateChange.txt**, previously uploaded on pages 120–121. Select 'File' and then 'Page setup'. Ensure your document is set up as an A4 document in portrait mode.

▶ Right click anywhere on the page and chose 'Select all matching text'. Since all text in the document is formatted the same, this will highlight all text in the document.

▶ Set the font to 'Arial' and the text size to '12'.

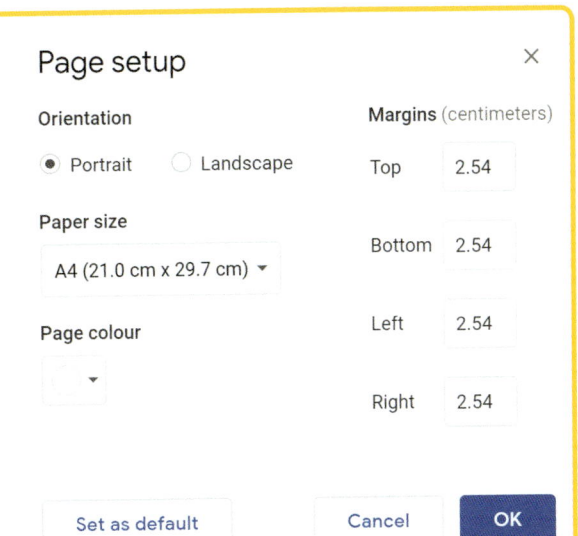

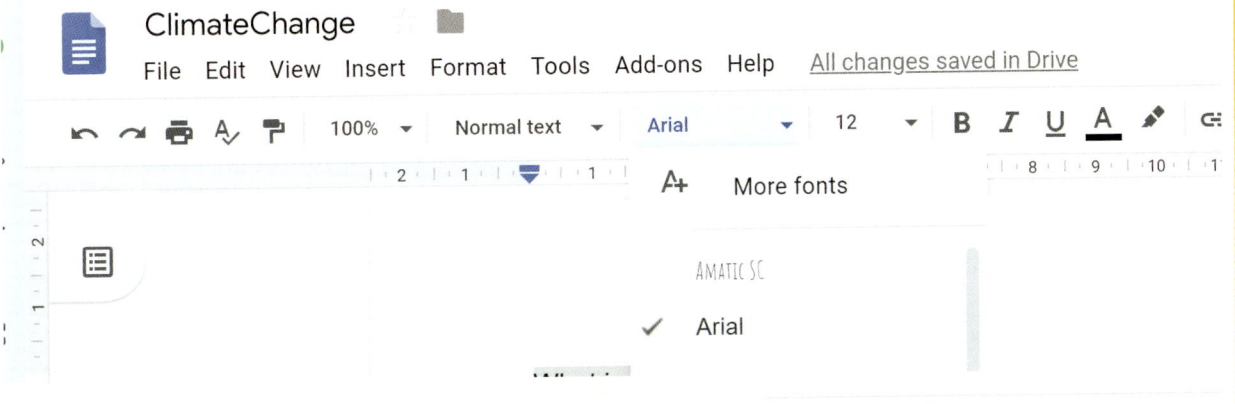

▶ The text in the document is divided into three sections of text each answering a question. Do the following:
  - Highlight the first question at the top of the page 'What is climate change?' and change the text style from 'Normal text' to 'Heading 1'.
  - Repeat this process with the next two questions:
    • What are the main causes of climate change?
    • What effects will climate change have on the Earth?

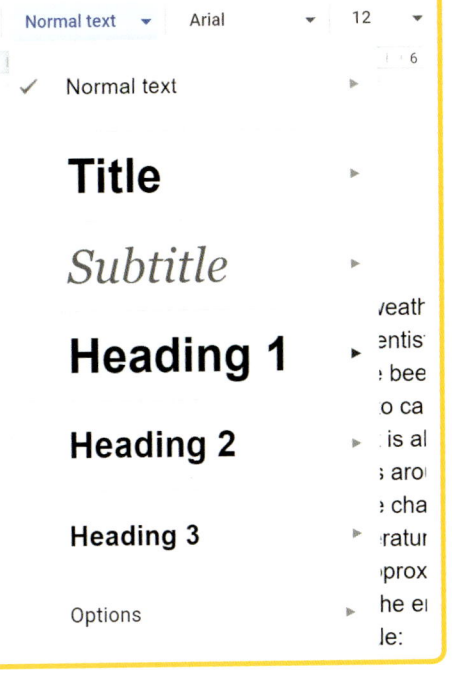

123

International Computing for Lower Secondary

Tools of the trade

Learn

Word processing applications provide users with many tools to help them improve the presentation of their document.

It looks unprofessional if organisations provide members of the public with documents that contain errors. One of the most important tools provided by word processing applications is the **spelling and grammar checker**.

Grammar checkers detect grammatical errors and suggest corrections.

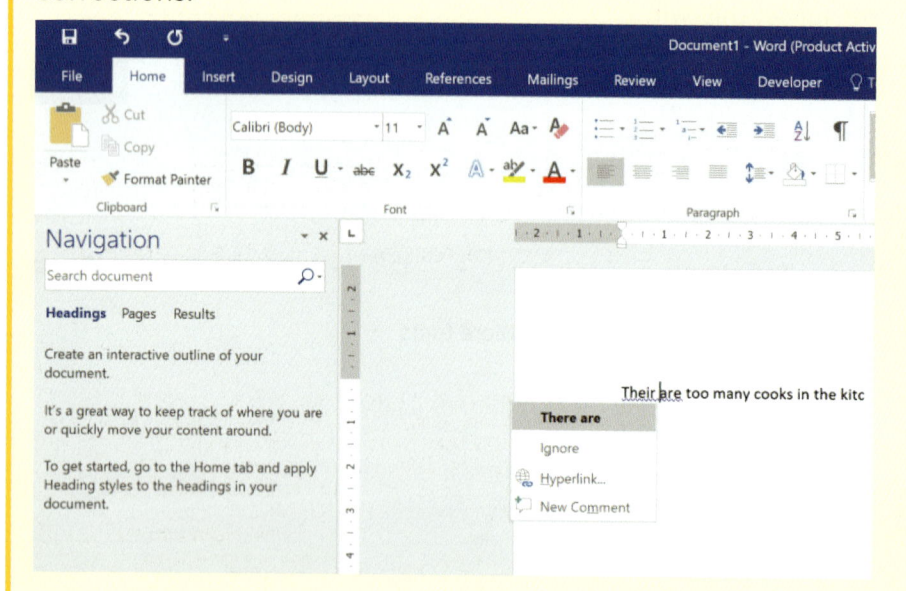

KEYWORD

spelling and grammar checker: a software tool which can be used to check the spelling and grammar in a word processed document; suggested corrections can be provided and users can build up a dictionary of specialised terms

Spell checks and grammar checks have become more intelligent in recent years due to the use of more advanced algorithms. Instead of just checking against a dictionary of words or looking for some sequences of words in a sentence, algorithms are used to search sentences from all over the world wide web to find best matches.

These have advanced further. For example, predictive text can suggest a word as you start typing, or even suggest a complete sentence or a number of sentences by matching the start of your sentences with many thousands across the world wide web.

Practice

The document you have uploaded contains a number of errors. Before formatting the document you must correct those errors. After importing the document from the previous task, you will have noticed that some of the words and phrases in the original document were underlined in blue and red. This shows where possible spelling and grammatical errors have occurred.

Unit 7.5 Show and tell: Cloud based presentations

- Correct the errors by right clicking on the underlined terms and selecting the correct term (word) from the suggested list.
- Some of the additional formatting tools available in *Google Docs* are shown below.
  In order to change the layout of a piece of text you must highlight the text first, before clicking on any of the formatting buttons, such as:
  o left or right align – places the selected text along the left- or right-hand side of the page
  o centre – places the selected text in the centre of the page
  o justify text – formats the selected text so that it has a straight edge along both the left- and right-hand side.

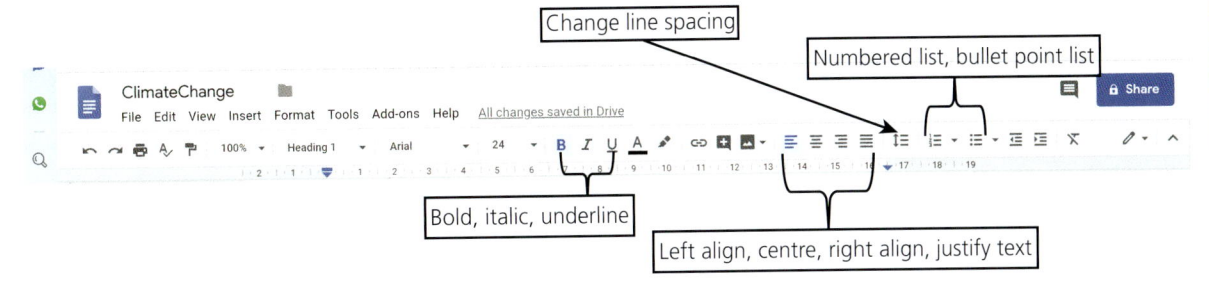

[Change line spacing]
[Numbered list, bullet point list]
[Bold, italic, underline]
[Left align, centre, right align, justify text]

- Highlight the last four paragraphs in the first section of text and apply the bullet point tool to this text.
- Repeat this process with the last three paragraphs of the document.
- Select and apply some of the other formatting tools to the *Google Docs* file until you are happy with how the document appears. For example:
  o change the font of the main text in each of the three paragraphs
  o justify the text in each of the paragraphs
  o bullet point the causes of climate change in the second paragraph instead of having a numbered list.

Remember to keep the font and text size consistent.

Climate change is how the weather in various parts of the world have changed within the last 200 years. Most Scientists agree that this is caused by large amounts of Carbon Dioxide (CO2) gas that have been released into the Earth's atmosphere.
Climate change is believed to cause an increase in severe weather systems ie. Hurricanes and Typhoons. It is also believed to be causing the spread of deserts with has an effect on ecosystems around the world.
One of the effects of Climate change is Global Warming. It is a way of describing how our planet's global air temperatures are increasing. Scientists have found that our planet has warmed up by approximately 1oC over the last century. This has had a massive impact on people, the environment and wildlife. Some of the changes we have seen across the world include:
Melting glaciers which can lead to increased sea levels and coastal flooding. Melting glaciers may also disrupt ocean currents such as the Gulf Stream which could also cause colder winters for countries like Great Britain.
increased land temperatures can contribute to increased droughts and the spread of deserts.
Increased sea temperatures can lead to millions of plants and animals in the Earth's Oceans and Seas being killed.
Changes in Ocean temperatures and global air temperature has led to many more severe weather incidents such as hurricanes, typhoons and droughts.

What are the main causes of climate change?

- Each question and its related text should be on a separate page.
  o Click at the start of the second question.
  o Click on 'Insert', 'Break', 'Page break' to place this text onto the next page.

125

International Computing for Lower Secondary

- o Do the same with the third question.
- o Your document should now have three pages.
- ➤ The 'Insert' toolbar contains a function which allows us to search for and include images from other internet web pages.
  - o Click in the middle of the first bullet point which starts 'Melting glaciers', underneath the question.
  - o Click on 'Insert', 'Image', 'Search the web'.
  - o A *Google* image search engine appears at the right hand side of the screen.
  - o Enter your key words for the search, in this case 'Melting glaciers' and press enter, a list of images matching those key words will appear below.
  - o Click the image you wish to use.
  - o Click 'Insert'.
  - o Click on the image on the page so that the resize handles appear on the outside of the image.
  - o Click and drag the image until it is an appropriate size for the page.
  - o Click on '**Wrap text**' so the writing on the page flows around the image.

Abstraction

The search method used in the previous section produces many results, some of which are not relevant to our booklet.

When searching for images to use, we can make use of abstraction. Instead of viewing every single image to do with 'burning fossil fuels' we can apply different layers of abstraction. This is where we can hide some of the results that are less likely to be useful.

These techniques could include abstracting the results by filtering to include images

- ✪ that are **free to share**
- ✪ that are a certain resolution or file size
- ✪ that contain a certain colour

KEYWORDS

wrap text: a formatting tool which allows text to scroll around the outside edges of an image on a word processed document

free to share: material presented electronically which is available for users to share freely with others

Free to share: Find some information, song, or image on the Internet that is free to share.

126

Unit 7.5 Show and tell: Cloud based presentations

Now try this:
- Open a new browser window and enter the URL:

    https://www.google.com/advanced_search

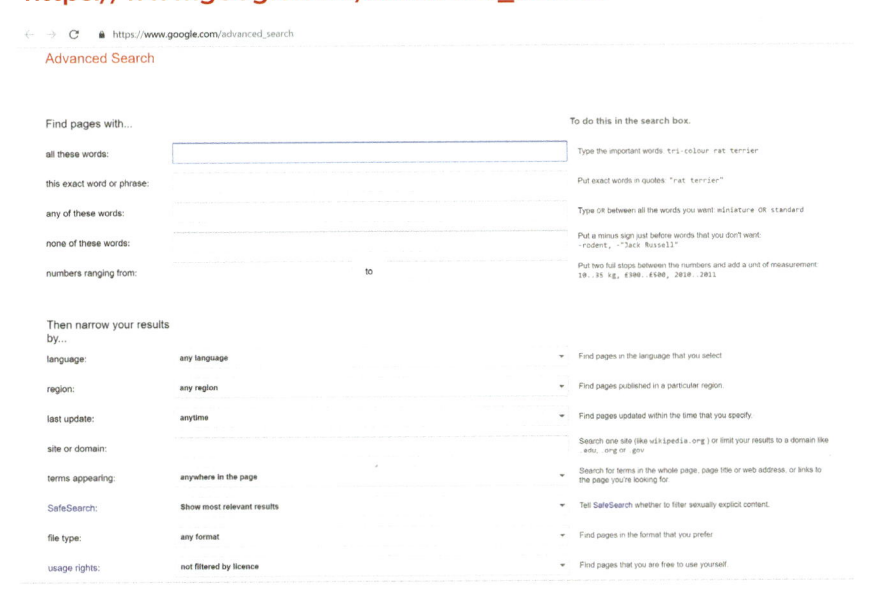

This allows us to narrow our search even further by, for example, stating 'this exact word or phrase' must appear on the page. Or we can select 'free to share, use or modify' under usage rights, so we know we are not breaking any **copyright laws** by using the information we find. This is important because, when individuals create a new product, design or piece of work, they are the owners of that product (in this case an image). If something is copyright protected, then its creator has the legal right to charge other people for using it.

- Use the advanced search to search for 'burning fossil fuels', by adding this term into the 'all these words' text box.
- Press enter to see your results; how many results did you obtain?
- Go back to the advanced search web page and enter 'burning fossil fuels' in 'all these words', and add 'climate change' beside 'exact word or phrase', then select 'free to share, use or modify'
- Press enter; how many results were returned this time? Discuss with a friend why this happened.
- Click on 'Images' to locate a suitable image for the section of your presentation on 'burning fossil fuels'.
- Once you have located a suitable image for your document, right click on the image and select 'Copy'.
- Now right click on your document where you would like to add your image, and select 'Paste' to add the image to your page.

KEYWORD

copyright laws: laws put in place which make it illegal to copy someone else's work without their permission

copyright laws: Explain to your partner what you know about copyright laws.

When using images created by others, it is important that you credit the source or provider of the image. Do this by including a comment saying, for example, 'image provided by [insert their name or web page]'.

International Computing for Lower Secondary

Finishing the booklet

Professional reports are often presented in a booklet format, with a cover page, table of contents, and a header and footer on the pages. Some documents contain specialised terms or calculations; for example, your climate change document contains the term CO_2, which is the chemical formula for carbon dioxide.

You can add all these features to your report using tools in *Google Docs*.

Practice

- Headers and footers are often used to tell the reader a little more about the document they are reading and their place in the document. For example, the header may contain the document title while the footer may tell them the page they are on, and the total number of pages in the document. Try adding a header and a footer to your Climate Change *Google Docs* file.
    o Click 'Insert', 'Header & page number' and then 'Header'.
    o Type the words 'Climate Change' in the header section which appears and format the text in a way that fits the remainder of your document's style.

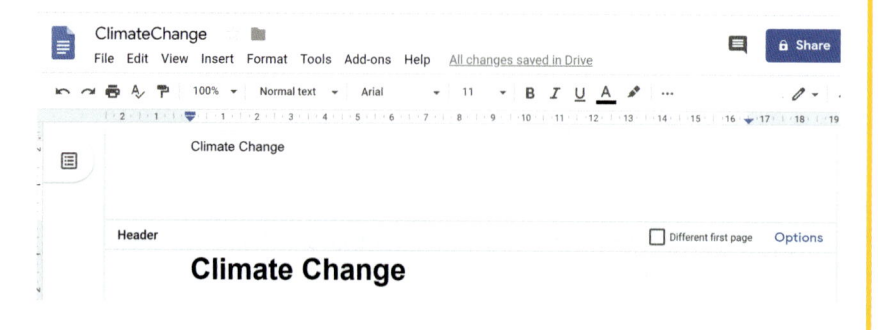

Unit 7.5 Show and tell: Cloud based presentations

- o Click 'Different first page' if you do not want the header to appear on the first page of the document.
- o Click 'Insert, 'Header & page number' and then 'Page number' and then select an appropriate location on the page for your page numbers to be placed.
- ➤ If we wish to add a cover page to our document we need to insert a new page at the beginning of the document.

Look back to page 125 to remind yourself how to add a page break.

- o Click 'Insert' and 'Image' and 'Search the web' to locate an appropriate image for your cover page. Click on the image and the 'Insert' to add it to your cover page.
- o Add the words 'Climate Change' above the graphic. Apply the 'Title' style to this piece of text.
- o Underneath the graphic enter 'Written by…' and add your name.
- ➤ You can edit the image by clicking on the image and selecting 'Image options'.
  - o A new tool panel will appear at the right hand side of the page. This will allow you to edit the image '**transparency**' or 'recolour' the image. Experiment with these options until you are happy with your cover page.
- ➤ Tables of contents are often useful in professional documents, especially larger documents.
  - o Once you are happy with your title page, insert another blank page between the title page and the first piece of text in your document.
  - o Click on 'Insert' and select 'Table of contents'.
  - o Select a table of contents with:
    - page numbers, or
    - blue links (this allows the reader to jump to a page by clicking on a blue hyperlink in the document).

Blue links in the table of contents might be useful to readers in long documents.

- ➤ Finally, to make sure you are presenting the scientific terms correctly, you need to make sure that you have formatted the chemical formula for carbon dioxide correctly wherever it appears in the document.

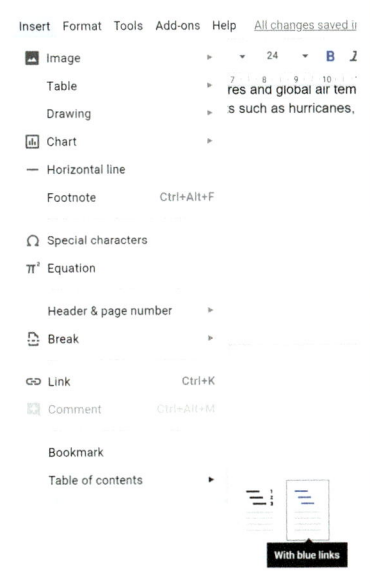

KEYWORD

transparency: a tool which edits the appearance of images in a digital document to allow the image to appear as though it is blending into the background

129

International Computing for Lower Secondary

- The first line of main text in the document contains the formula CO_2. We need to show the 2 as a **subscript** value (this makes it appear slightly below the main text line and a little smaller than the rest of the text).
- To do this, highlight the 2 in this formula and click on 'Insert', then 'Special characters'.
- Click on the 'Arrow' drop down, select 'Subscript' and then '2' from the list of characters available.

> **KEYWORD**
>
> **subscript:** a letter or figure which is written below a standard line of text (the opposite is superscript where a letter or figure is written above a standard line of text)

> **subscript:** Use a computer, tablet or phone to show your partner an example of subscript and superscript.

Introducing *Google Sheets*

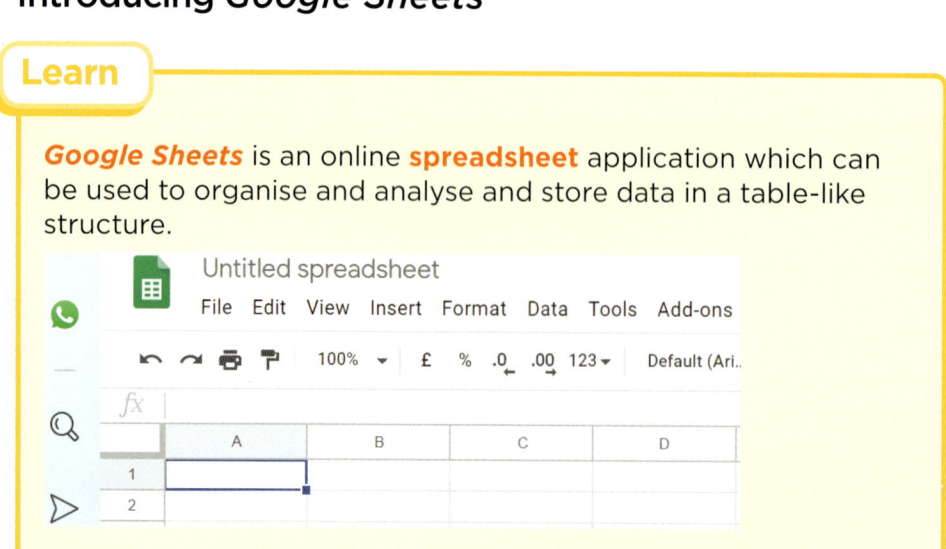

Learn

Google Sheets is an online **spreadsheet** application which can be used to organise and analyse and store data in a table-like structure.

> **KEYWORDS**
>
> **spreadsheet:** a software application which can be used to organise and store data and which allows analysis of data using formulas
>
> ***Google Sheets*:** a cloud based spreadsheet application

Unit 7.5 Show and tell: Cloud based presentations

Practice

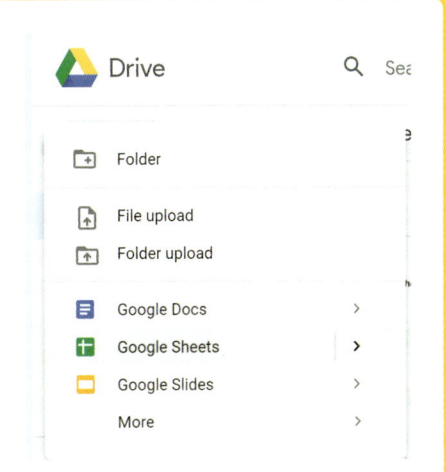

Data analysis can be carried out using formulas and other specialised features such as charts and **data filters**. We will focus our attention here on using *Google Sheets* to enter and store data and produce charts and graphs. You will use charts and graphs later, to illustrate facts in your multimedia presentation.

- From the *Google Drive* home screen select 'New', '*Google Sheets*'.
- Name this sheet **SeaAndLandTempChange From1970** and enter the data as shown below.

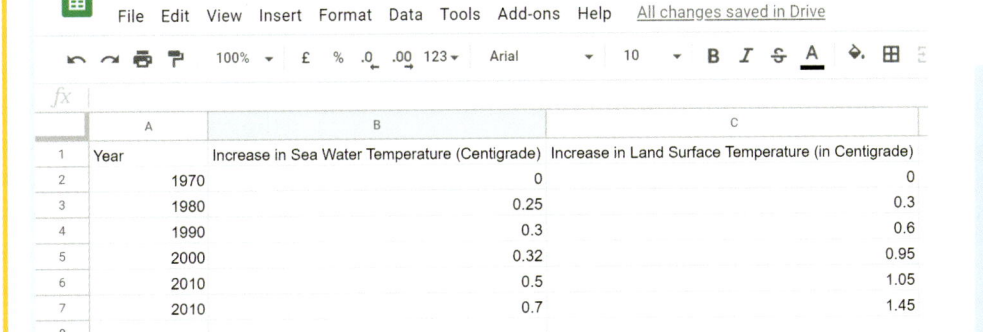

Year	Increase in Sea Water Temperature (Centigrade)	Increase in Land Surface Temperature (in Centigrade)
1970	0	0
1980	0.25	0.3
1990	0.3	0.6
2000	0.32	0.95
2010	0.5	1.05
2010	0.7	1.45

KEYWORDS

data analysis: the process of collecting, reviewing and applying calculations to data to help identify patterns and trends in the data

data filters: a tool used to remove unwanted data

- Highlight all of the data in the table from cell A:1 to cell C:7 and click 'Insert', 'Chart' and set the settings of the chart editor as shown in the panel below to create the line chart shown.

- Save your work and close *Google Sheets*, you will use this spreadsheet and chart later when you link it to the kiosk presentation we are creating for Green Global.

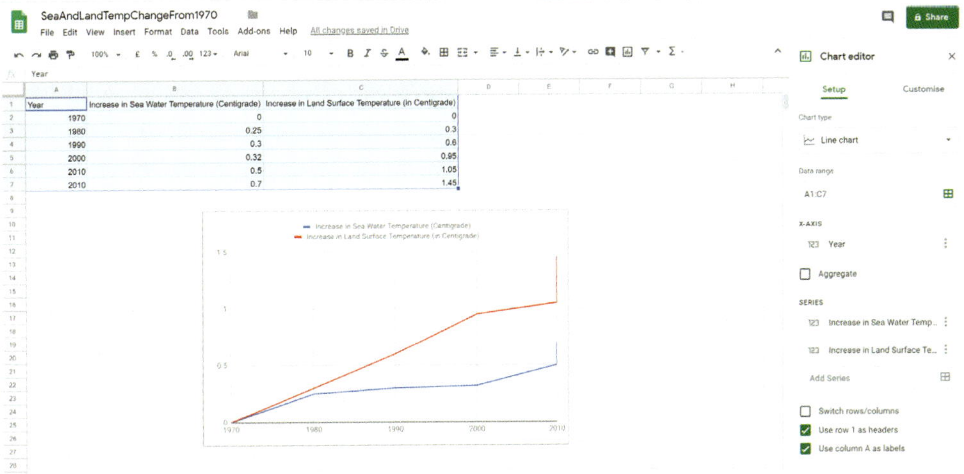

131

International Computing for Lower Secondary

Adding navigation to a multimedia application

Learn

Before developing a complex multimedia application it is important to plan your screen content. A detailed planning document will also consider animations, **page transitions** (the way the display changes when the user moves from one screen to the next) being used. Most importantly, it will consider the **navigation structure** of the multimedia application. Planners will often create a **logic flowchart** to illustrate navigation.

Navigation in software applications can be described as being linear, hierarchical, non-linear, or composite.

The user will go from one page to the next in a sequence, they cannot select their own pathway through the pages

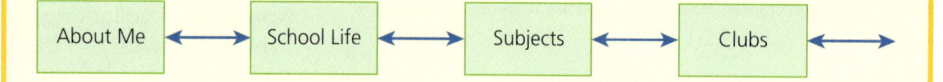

Linear

The user moves from one slide to the other in a line, moving from one slide to the next.

About Me ↔ School Life ↔ Subjects ↔ Clubs ↔

Hierarchical

The user navigates around the application one branch at a time, from top to bottom.

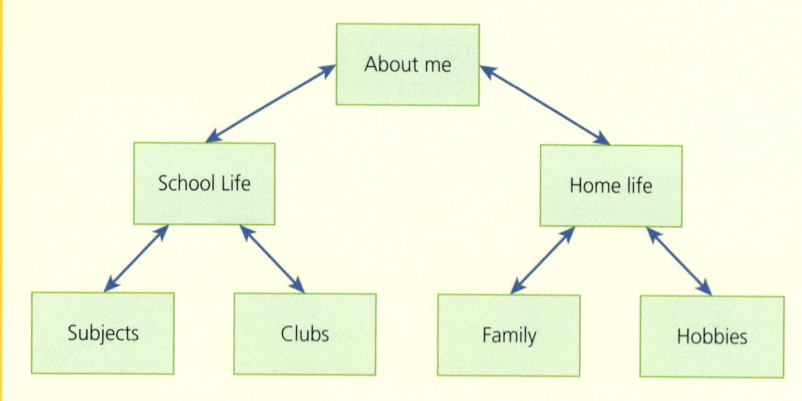

About me
├── School Life
│   ├── Subjects
│   └── Clubs
└── Home life
    ├── Family
    └── Hobbies

Non-linear

The users can move through the pages in any order they wish.

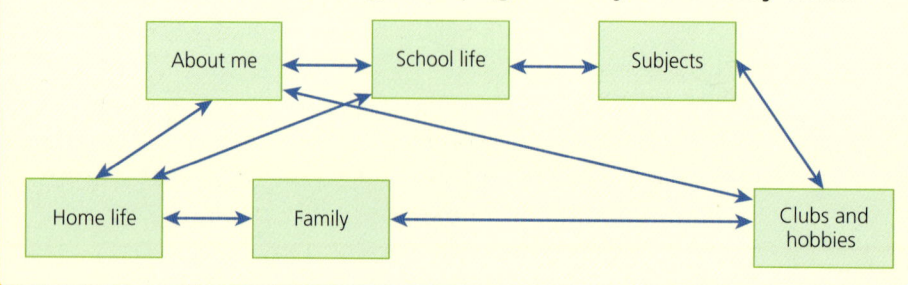

About me ↔ School life ↔ Subjects
Home life ↔ Family ↔ Clubs and hobbies
(with interconnecting arrows between all nodes)

KEYWORDS

page transition: a special effect which shows the change from one page in an application to another; for example, pages can *dissolve* into each other

navigation structure: the way individual pages or screens in an application are linked to allow the user to move through an application

logic flowchart: a diagram which shows the choices and pathways available to a user on each screen in an application

linear: a navigation structure which allows the user to view contents of a file or pages in a document one after another

hierarchical: a navigation structure which allows the user to move around the application one branch at a time, from top to bottom

non-linear: a navigation structure which allows the user to navigate a file visiting pages in any order

linear, hierarchical, non-linear: Close the book and draw a linear, hierarchical and non-linear diagram.

132

Unit 7.5 Show and tell: Cloud based presentations

Composite

A combination of the alternative navigational methods. In some parts of the presentation the user can select their own pathway, in others their movement between pages is more restricted.

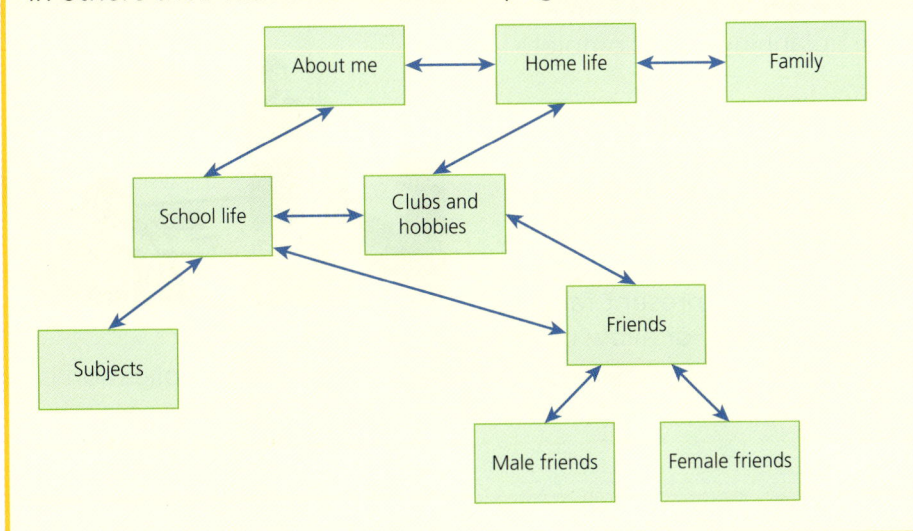

> **KEYWORD**
>
> **composite:** navigation structure which uses a combination of approaches

```
About me ↔ Home life ↔ Family
  ↕           ↕
School life ↔ Clubs and hobbies
  ↕         ↘
Subjects      Friends
            ↙      ↘
      Male friends  Female friends
```

Decomposition

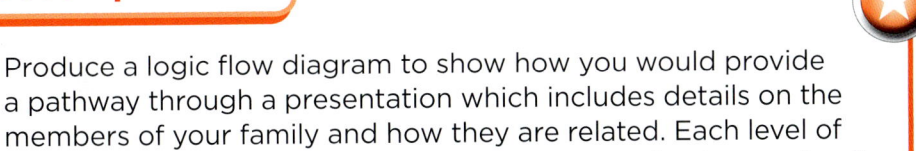

Produce a logic flow diagram to show how you would provide a pathway through a presentation which includes details on the members of your family and how they are related. Each level of the logic flow diagram could represent a generation in your family.

Practice

Look back to page 117 for a description of the main elements the climate change presentation must contain.

➤ Discuss, with a friend, the navigational structure you think will be most appropriate for your presentation.
  o Good navigation tools will make your application appealing to the user. Plan your navigation so you use
    - easy to understand images (icons)
    - navigation buttons which are consistent in size and location on screen
    - clearly divided content, so that all linked pages are related
    - a limited number of links on each page; too many links will confuse the user and make the screen appear cluttered
    - no more than five hyperlinks or clicks from the title screen or menu page to each page.
  o Think carefully about
    - when the user will take the quiz
    - if the user needs to view all of the content slides before taking the quiz
    - if the user is able to take the quiz questions in any order.

International Computing for Lower Secondary

Presenting with slides

Learn

Let us look more closely at the main features of *Google Slides* before you start planning your complete presentation.

The *Google Slides* app is a web based multimedia presentation tool. You can use it to combine information and data in a variety of formats, including text and video. They can be used to include links to other files and documents and external websites.

You can use multimedia applications to present facts to an audience when someone is speaking, or allow users to browse on their own. When users are browsing content on their own, the application is viewed as a kiosk application.

Practice

As the person responsible for producing the Climate Change presentation for the Science Fair, your task is to combine the facts from the *Google Docs* file with the statistics in the *Google Sheets* file to produce a multimedia presentation. You should also include a short movie in the presentation. To challenge the viewer, you should create a short interactive quiz to test their knowledge at the end.

➤ Return to the *Google Drive* home screen and select 'New', '*Google Slides*'.
  o A list of 'themes' or templates are available to choose from on the right hand side of the screen. Select a theme for your presentation.

> Page 119 shows you how to access the *Google Drive* applications.

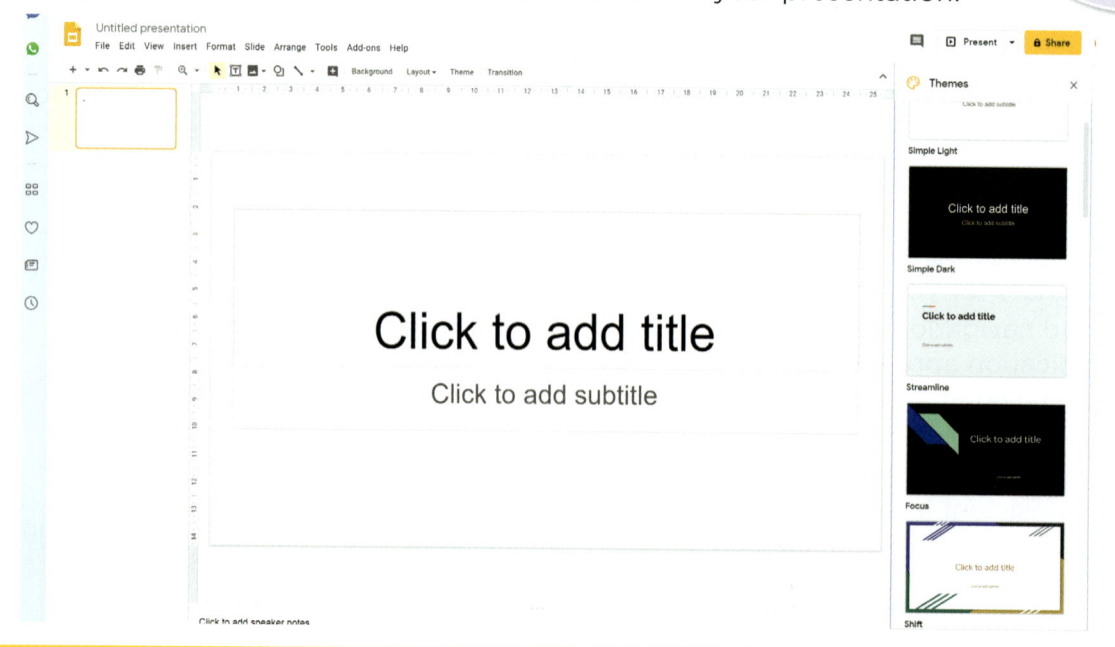

134

Unit 7.5 Show and tell: Cloud based presentations

- o Add the title 'Climate Change' to the first slide and add 'Created by (your name)' to the subtitle.
- o Click 'Slide', 'New slide' to insert a second slide into your presentation. 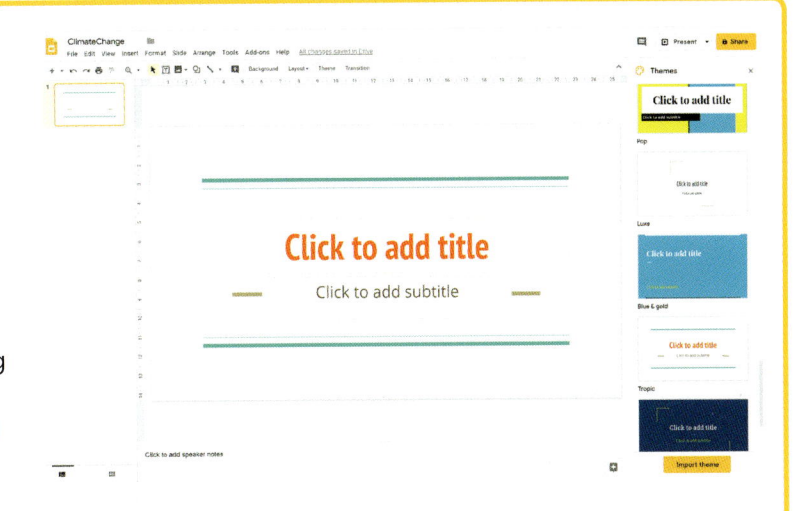
- ➤ Choose a suitable layout for your new slide by clicking on the Layout menu and selecting one of the options provided. In this case the 'Title and body' layout would be the most appropriate.

Using the methods used on pages 126–127, search for and insert an appropriate image to illustrate this slide.

- ➤ Add the title 'What is Climate Change?' to this slide.
- ➤ With a friend, examine the first section of your *Google Docs* booklet called Climate Change.

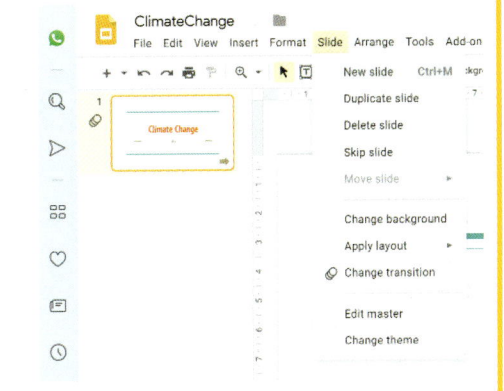

Summarise the first paragraph using three or four detailed bullet points to help explain 'What is climate change?

Add these bullets to this slide.

- ➤ Add a third slide called 'Impact of Climate Change' and add four bullet points to help summarise the next four sentences about melting glaciers, increased land temperature, increased sea temperature, and changes in ocean temperatures.

Use the bullet point or numbering tools and the bold, italic and underline tools where you need to add emphasis. See page 125 for a reminder about these (they operate the same way in all Google Apps).

- ➤ Use the chart you created earlier using *Google Slides* to illustrate facts about increased land and sea temperatures:
  - o Click 'Insert', 'Chart', 'From Sheets'.
  - o Click on your *Google Sheets* file called **SeaAndLandTempChangeFrom1970** and click 'Select'.
  - o Click on the chart you wish to import and ensure you have ticked 'Link to spreadsheet' before you click 'Import'.

135

International Computing for Lower Secondary

- Open your *Google Sheets* file and change the value in cell B:3 from 0.25 to 1. Notice how this updates the chart.
- Go back to your *Google Slides* presentation. Go to the slide containing the chart you have just imported.
- On the right hand panel you should now see a 'linked objects' panel; your *Google Sheets* file should be included there. Click on the refresh icon in this panel and notice how the chart has updated.

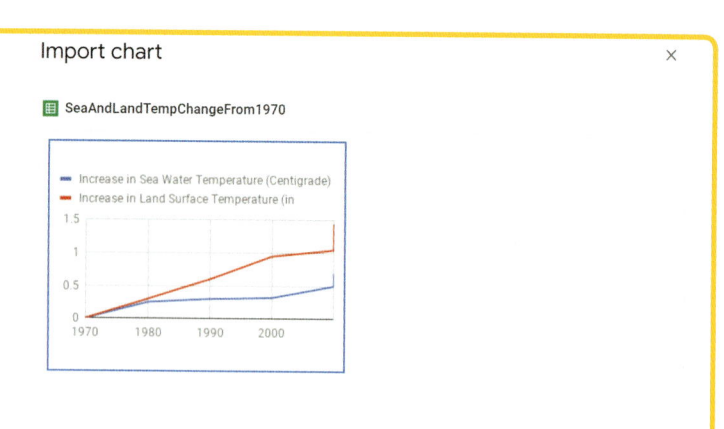

Remember to change the value back to 0.25 when you have finished testing the link between your Google Sheets and Google Slides documents; otherwise the chart in your presentation will be inaccurate!

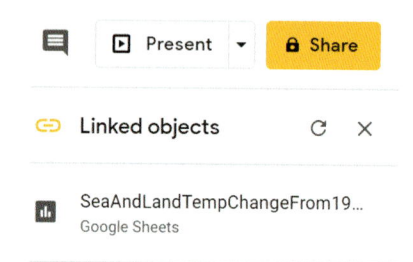

You have now successfully linked a chart from one app into another application. Changes made to the original table and chart will now also be shown on this presentation.

Abstraction

Use bullet points to summarise the content in the remaining two sections of the *Google Docs* file called Climate Change.

Create one slide per title in the document for the reader to view on the kiosk presentation.

This is an example of abstraction. When undertaking abstraction it is important that you provide the most relevant detail. Think about what key points should be abstracted from the text. For example, under the title 'What is climate change?' include

- a definition of climate change
- the problems caused by climate change.

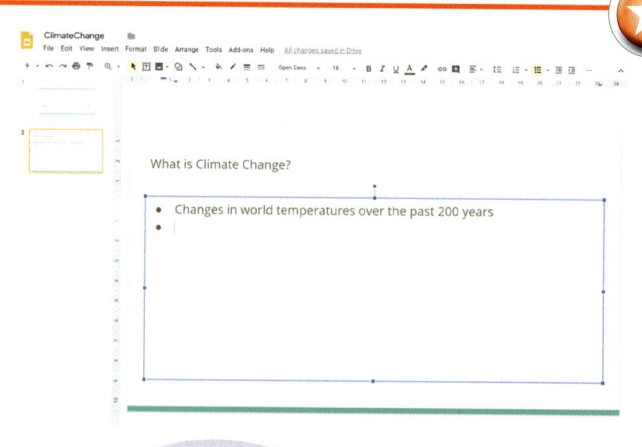

Consider how the content under each title can be reduced into two or three bullet points instead of long sentences.

Unit 7.5 Show and tell: Cloud based presentations

Navigational links

Learn

We will be adding hyperlinks between the slides in the next part of this unit. These can be used to allow the user to move from one slide in the application to another.

A logic flowchart for the *Google Slides* presentation you have created so far would look something like the one below.

> Check the direction of the arrow from the *Google Sheets* file called **SeaAndLandTempChangeFrom1970** to the third page of the presentation. This is because the data saved in this file is being imported and used in the slides application but it cannot be changed from inside the slides program.

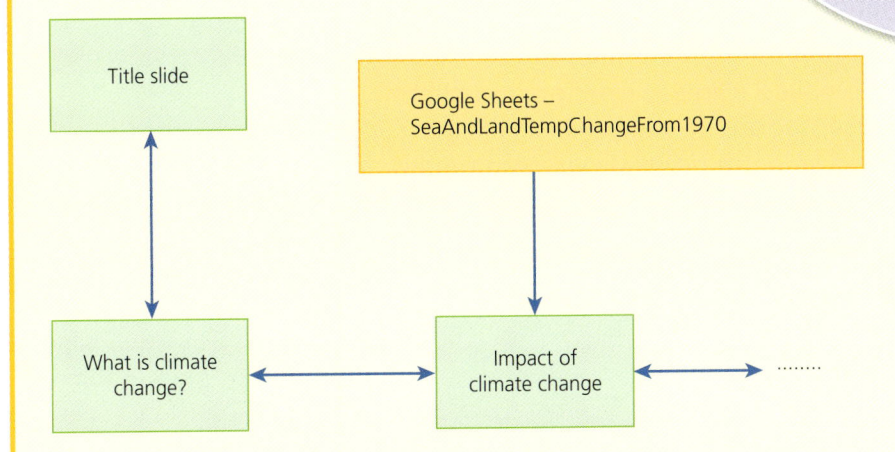

[Flowchart: Title slide ↕ What is climate change? ↔ Impact of climate change ↔ .... ; Google Sheets – SeaAndLandTempChangeFrom1970 ↓ Impact of climate change]

This shows that the user can move from the title slide through the next two slides in a fixed order, the arrows show that the user can move backwards and forwards through each of the slides and that data is imported into the third slide from a *Google Sheets* file.

Practice

- Open your Climate Change presentation and add suitable graphics to illustrate each slide.
- Expand the logic flowchart above to show the additional slides in your kiosk application.

> Remember adding images in pages 126 and 127.

International Computing for Lower Secondary

It's all in the links

Learn

You can use hyperlinks to help control how a user moves from one slide to another and to provide the user with links to external websites.

Practice

You are going to add navigation links to your Climate Change presentation.

➤ Open the *Google Slides* file called Climate Change and click on the first slide in the presentation.
  o Click 'Insert', 'Arrows' and select a right arrow from the list of shapes provided.

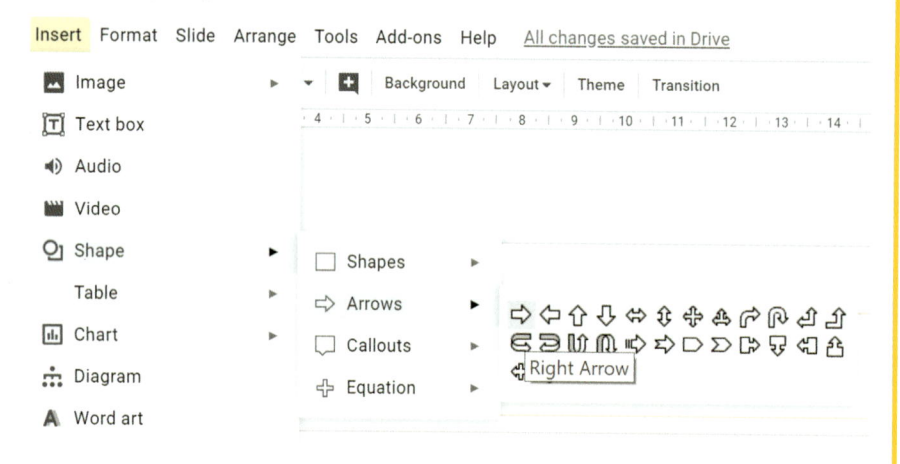

  o Use this tool to draw an arrow in the bottom right hand corner of the start screen of your presentation.
  o Right click on the arrow to add a link to the next slide, as shown below.

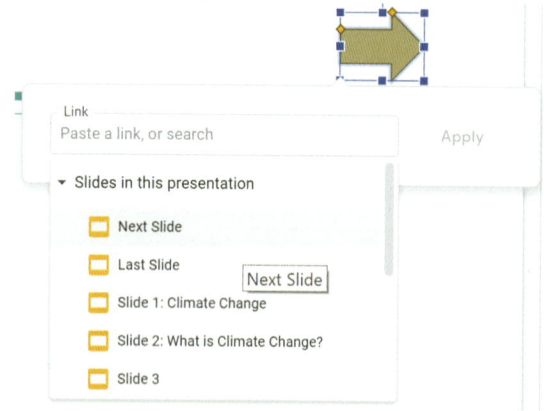

Unit 7.5 Show and tell: Cloud based presentations

- o Use the link and arrow tools to add hyperlinks in this way to each of your slides to allow the viewer to move between the slides at their own pace.

> Note how you can use this feature to add a link to any slide in the presentation.

- ► You could also use this feature to add a hyperlink to a suitable web page on Climate Change.
  - o Use an advanced internet search to locate a website which contains appropriate information on climate change.
  - o On your title slide include a line in the text which says 'Click here to see our web page on Climate Change'.
  - o Highlight the text and repeat the process used above.
  - o Paste the URL for the web page you wish to take the user to into the dialogue box were it says 'Paste a link, or search'.
- ► With a friend think about how you could use the hyperlink feature to create a link that opens the *Google Docs* file you created called Climate Change.
  - o Create a link to your document on Climate Change on the slide after the title slide.

> Remember all files created using *Google Apps* are web based and have a URL. Open the docs file and copy and paste the URL from the browser window.

- ► The insert tool is also useful if you wish to include video files to help illustrate a presentation.
  - o Click 'Insert', 'Video'.
  - o Using this feature you can Search for videos from YouTube to embed into your presentation, enter in the URL for a video if you already know it, browse to a video you have already stored in your *Google Drive*.
  - o Use 'Insert', 'Video' to insert an appropriate video into your presentation.
- ► Extend your logic flowchart from page 137 to include your new slides and hyperlinks.

Keeping it moving

Learn

Presentations should be designed to capture the interest of the person or people viewing them. For this reason, they may contain multimedia elements such as those already investigated, as well as animations and transitions. Transitions refer to the way a screen changes when an application moves between screen displays.

This is particularly important when creating presentations which will be viewed by individuals rather than controlled by someone giving a talk to an audience. When a presentation runs in this way, it is said to be running as a kiosk presentation.

When creating a multimedia presentation you should:

- ✔ be consistent in terms of colour scheme, font, text style and text size used throughout (templates will help with this)
- ✔ not overuse animations and **transitions** (which would be distracting); keep it simple!
- ✔ ensure that each slide should tell its own story; in our example we used one slide for 'What is climate change?' and another slide for 'The impact of climate change'
- ✔ ensure that each slide contains no more than five bullet points
- ✔ provide a balanced layout on each slide; for example, not too much **white space**, too much text, or cluttered text and images.

KEYWORDS

transitions: an effect used in an animation or a movie to help make the change from one scene or slide to another more subtle to the viewer; for example, dissolving between scenes

white space: unused space on screen or on a document, used to separate out parts of a document such as images, paragraphs, bullet points

white space: Show your partner an example of white space on this page.

Unit 7.5 Show and tell: Cloud based presentations

Practice

- Before adding animations and transitions to your presentation, open your *Google Slides* file called Climate Change. Review the slides you have created so far using the checklist in the Learn panel above. Make any changes needed to meet these guidelines.
- Open the title slide of your Climate Change presentation. Click on the title text and select 'Insert', 'Animation' to access the animation and transition panel. Chose the 'Fade in' animation style and select 'After previous' so the animation will run automatically.
- Apply another animation to the subtitle text which states who created the presentation.
    o Click on 'Transitions', select the 'Dissolve' transition and click on 'Apply to all slides'.
    o Work through the rest of your presentation applying transitions and animations to make your presentation more appealing to your audience.
- Once you are happy with your presentation you can make it available for others to view.
    o Click 'File' and select 'Publish to the web'. (Check with your teacher before you do this; remember that everything you post on the internet adds to your digital footprint.)
    o Select to Auto-advance slides 'every minute'.
    o Tick 'Start slideshow as soon as the player loads'.
    o Tick 'Restart the slideshow after the last slide'.
    o If you do not want to publish your work on the internet for everyone to see, click on the email icon to share the URL for the presentation to your teacher.
- To view the presentation in *Google Slides*, click on the 'Present' button at the top right of the screen.

> Use 'After previous' for all animations in this unit; this helps ensure the animation content plays automatically and does not require the person viewing the presentation to do anything to make the content appear.

> While animations and transitions are a good way of capturing the interest of the viewer, too many can be distracting. Try to get a balance!

> Ask yourself first: are you happy for other people to see your work?

Transitions ✕

Slide: Dissolve

Climat Fade in (After previous) ⊗

Fade in ▾

After previous ▾

☐ By paragraph

Slow — Medium — Fast

+ Select an object to animate

Play

141

International Computing for Lower Secondary

Go further

- We can use additional slides and hyperlink buttons to create a quiz at the end of the presentation. First, look at the logic flowchart for this new part of your presentation:

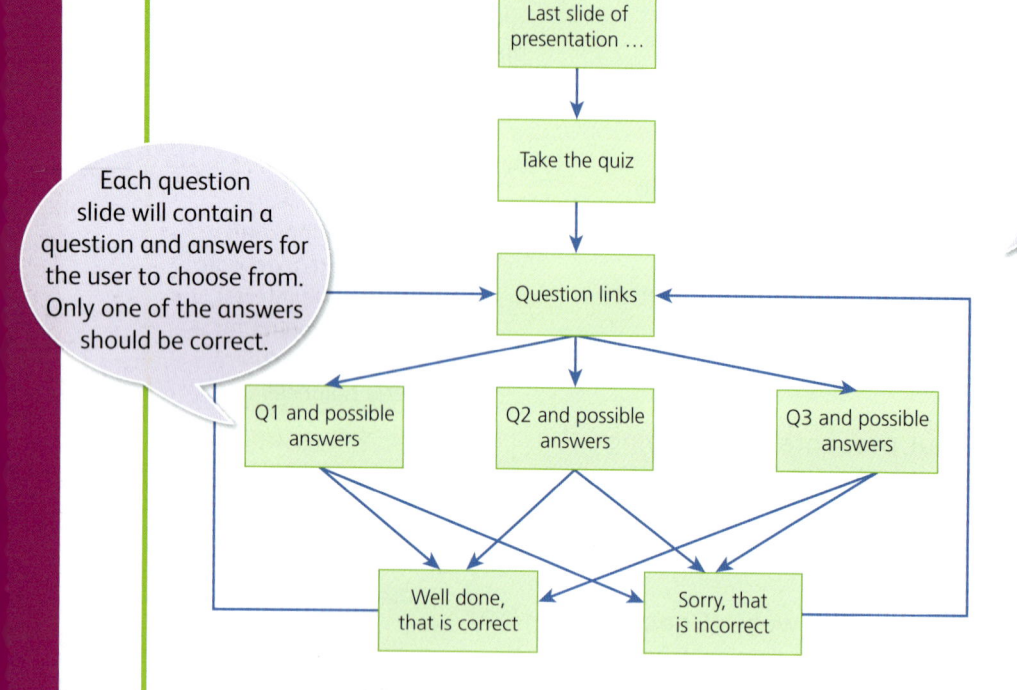

```
Last slide of presentation …
        ↓
    Take the quiz
        ↓
   Question links
   ↙    ↓    ↘
Q1 and  Q2 and  Q3 and
possible possible possible
answers answers answers
        ↓
Well done,    Sorry, that
that is correct   is incorrect
```

Each question slide will contain a question and answers for the user to choose from. Only one of the answers should be correct.

Remind yourself of the different navigational structures on pages 132 and 133

What hyperlinks should be included on the question links slide? Perhaps a text based hyperlink which says, "Click here for Q1"

- Discuss this logic flowchart with a friend.
    - What type of navigational structure is being used?
        - How can the user move from the 'Take the Quiz' slide, through each of the questions?
        - The user should be able to answer any question from the question links slide.
    - The presentation includes one slide with the message 'Well done, that is correct' and one which says 'Sorry, that is incorrect'. How will they be used to give the user feedback about their answers to the questions as part of the application?
- Add another new slide, select the 'Title only' layout for this slide.
- On the new slide with the 'Section header' layout add the title, 'Take the Quiz'. Below that, include hyperlinked text which reads 'Click here to take the quiz'.
- Add four new slides: two with the 'Title only' layout (these will be used for the Question list slide and Q1) and two with the 'blank' layout (these will be used for the feedback slides, which will say 'Well done, that is correct' and 'Sorry, that is incorrect').
    - **Slide 1** – Enter the title 'Question list'.
      Underneath the title text, use the 'Text box' tool four times to add the following four separate pieces of text.

142

Unit 7.5 Show and tell: Cloud based presentations

- ◆ Click on any of the links below to answer a question
- ◆ Question 1
- ◆ Question 2
- ◆ Question 3

❏ **Slide 2** – Enter the title 'Q1 Deforestation contributes to climate change (TRUE / FALSE)'.
Underneath the title, use the 'Text box' tool to add the text 'TRUE'.
Use the 'Text box' tool again to add the text 'FALSE'. These will be the two possible answers to the question.
Increase the text size of the question and the two possible answers to provide balance on the page.
Add one final piece of text saying 'Click here to return to the question list'.

❏ **Slide 3** – Use the 'Text tool' to add the following text to this slide.
'Well done, that is correct'
Use the 'Text tool' again, this time to add the following text to this slide.
'Return to Question list'

❏ **Slide 4** – Use the 'Text tool' to add the following text to this slide.
'Sorry, that is incorrect'
Use the 'Text tool' again, this time to add the following text to this slide.
'Return to Question list'

◆ Use your plan from your logic flowchart to guide you as you create an appropriate hyperlink between the question links slide, the Q1 slide and the correct and incorrect feedback slides.
  ❏ Link the Question 1 option on the question links page to the page containing the Q1 text and the two possible answers to the question, the TRUE and FALSE options.
  ❏ On the slide containing Q1 and the two possible answers:
    ◆ Create a hyperlink between the TRUE option and the slide which reads 'Well done, that is correct'.
    ◆ Create a second hyperlink between the FALSE option and the slide which reads 'Sorry, that is incorrect'.
◆ Add appropriate text and create a link on the two feedback slides which takes the user back to the 'Question list' slide.
◆ Create two additional questions using the steps shown above and using the logic flowchart to help you create the appropriate hyperlinks.
◆ Add a hyperlink to each slide to allow the user return to the start at any time.

> Each text box will be used to set up a hyperlink to different slides in the presentation.

> Bring the user to the 'Well done' slide or the 'Sorry' slide depending on their answer. The 'Well done' and 'Sorry' then link back to the questions slide so the user can select a new question.

> The practice task on page 138 will help you create hyperlinks.

> It is always a good idea to give the user the option of restarting the presentation at any time.

143

International Computing for Lower Secondary

Challenge yourself

Green Global is happy with your kiosk application. The company would now like you to incorporate it into a larger kiosk application which will have three additional topic areas:

1. Plastics in the environment
2. Recycling
3. Loss of animals habitats

One of the main advantages of working on cloud based applications is the ability to share documents with others so they can work on the project with you. Before developing the larger kiosk application with other team members, you have asked a partner to test your Climate Change application.

Before they can test your application, you must create a **test plan** for your partner to follow.

➤ Open a new *Google Docs* file and rename it **ClimateChangeTestPlan**. Your test plan will focus on the following three areas.

1. Have all objectives been met?

    Your partner should use your presentation and comment on each of the objectives on page 117 and give a number of examples of how your presentation meets each one.

2. **Usability** testing

    Usability means how easy it is to use. Ask your partner to complete a few simple tasks, such as
    - find the slide which contains the graph on land and sea temperature change
    - complete the quiz at the end of the presentation.

    At the end, ask them to comment on how easy it was to complete those tasks.

3. **Functionality** testing

    Functionality refers to the things the presentation is expected to do.

    In your test plan you should take each slide in turn and look at the functions you think each slide should provide; for example, the title should fly in from the right, the right arrow on the 'What is climate change?' slide should take you to a slide with the title 'Impacts of climate change', and so on.

    To help your partner test the functionality of your presentation, you should create a test plan similar to the one shown below.

KEYWORDS

test plan: a document which describes the areas of an application to be tested; includes details of the tests to be applied to each area of the application, including test data and expected results

usability: how easy to use an application is

functionality: how well an application completes the tasks it is expected to complete

Your friend will complete this column when they test your presentation.

Test Number	Area to be tested	Test	Expected outcome	Result of test	Corrective measures
1	For example, Title animation on first slide	Open presentation	Title should fly in from the right	Animation does not happen	
2	Next slide arrow on first slide	Click on arrow	Should open next slide on presentation	Next slide opens	

144

Unit 7.5 Show and tell: Cloud based presentations

- ➤ Complete the test plan by adding descriptions of additional tests you would like your friend to carry out on each slide on your presentation. Ensure you test that all
  - navigational links work correctly
  - linked documents open
  - multimedia elements operate as planned.
- ➤ Click the 'Share' button at the top right of your *Google Docs* file called **ClimateChangeTestPlan**.
- ➤ Enter the email address of the person you would like to share your document with and click 'Done'.
- ➤ Open your Climate Change presentation and click on the 'Share' option.
- ➤ Enter the email address of the person you would like to share your slides presentation with, and click 'Done'.
- ➤ Once your friend has also shared their test plan and slides presentation with you, you can access these on your own *Google Drive*.

To access the test plan and the presentation your partner has shared with you:
- go to *Google Drive*
- click on 'Shared with me'
- open up the *Google Docs* file and *Google Slides* file your friend shared with you
- carry out each of the tests they included on their testing table, using their shared *Google Slides* presentation
- complete the fifth column which tells them the result of the test.

- ➤ When all tests are completed, open your own *Google Docs* test plan and see the results of the tests carried out by your friend.
  - Did everything work as expected?
  - If not, record any changes you made to your presentation in the final column of the table.

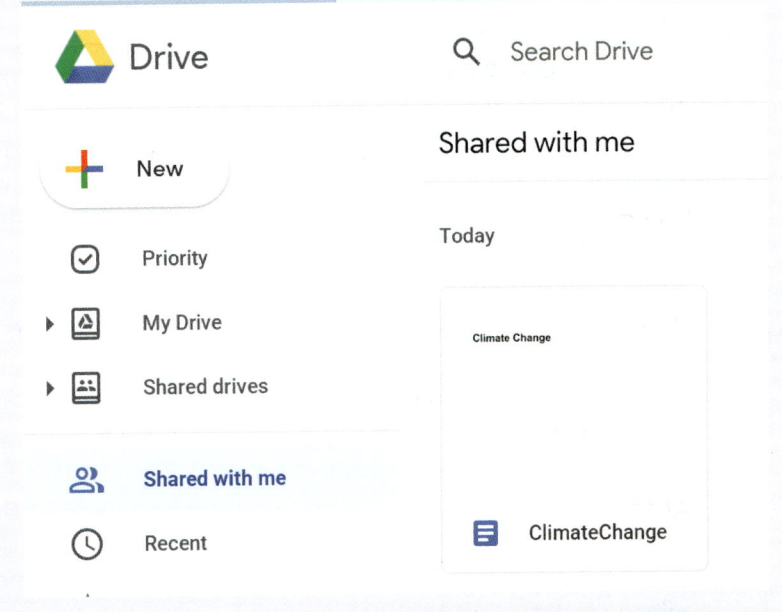

Final project

Green Global has asked you to be part of its team of developers. The team will create a larger kiosk application for the science fair.

The larger presentation will have three sections.

Climate change (you have already created this presentation) and two others from the topic areas:

1. Plastics in the environment
2. Recycling
3. Loss of animal habitats

Your group presentation should run as a kiosk presentation and should include:

- a generic title slide containing the text 'Green Global - Improving Environmental Awareness' plus the names of each group member, and a button which starts the presentation
- a slide that allows the user to select and view any of the new slide files contained in the application; this slide could be called the kiosk menu
- a range of animations, transitions and hyperlinks to allow the user to move through the presentation and visit the school website
- features from *Google Docs* and *Google Sheets*; for example, a hyperlink to a detailed *Google Docs* file which includes a cover page, a table of contents, and one or two pages of related text that you have found on the internet
- a simple quiz at the end of each section asking no more than four questions
- a video (located on the internet and embedded into the presentation) which is related to the presentation topic
- an option that allows the user to go back to the kiosk menu to select a hyperlink to one of the other two presentations.

> Create one slide with three options for the user to choose from. One group member can create this and include hyperlinks to everyone else's completed kiosk applications.

Before you start your presentation:

- produce a logic flowchart to show how the user will move from the title slide to the menu slide to each application; you can do this on paper or on computer
- decide which team members will work on which topic area
- decide how you will co-ordinate and organise your tasks
  - each team member should create their own separate application
  - one team member should create one shared title slide and a kiosk menu slide
  - all completed kiosk applications should be shared with this one team member
- add hyperlinks to the kiosk menu where users can access each of the completed applications.

Fully test your application before sharing. Do this by completing a test plan similar to the functional testing plan you created in the Challenge yourself task.

Unit 7.5 Show and tell: Cloud based presentations

Evaluation

➤ After you have created and tested your part of the group presentation ask a friend to work through the presentation for you.
When they have finished viewing the presentation, they should comment on:
- your title slide (does it include an appropriate title, appropriate graphics and your name?)
- how well the hyperlinks to the additional kiosk applications work (do the hyperlinks on the kiosk menu open the correct applications?)
- how easy it is to return to the kiosk menu from each individual kiosk
- how professional and consistent in presentation the application is (does it use the same theme throughout?)
- the use of appropriate graphics (including videos if available), animations and presentations
- the navigation; for example:
    - are there hyperlinks to allow for navigation between the slides in the presentation and to appropriate external websites?
    - is there a hyperlink to a *Google Docs* file containing more detail on the topic covered by that section of the kiosk?

➤ Your friend should write a report commenting on how effective your application was in meeting all of the user requirements outlined at the start of the final project panel.

➤ Make improvements to your application based on the feedback from your friend.

> Each kiosk application should include a link back to the kiosk menu which was shared with all members of the team.

Definition check: Close your book and make a list of as many terms you have learned in this unit as you can. Compare them with your partner's list. Together try to define as many of them as you can. Check your definitions against the definitions given in the key word boxes.

Unit 7.6 Data Mining: Using spreadsheets and databases

About spreadsheets

A spreadsheet is an electronic worksheet structured like a table with columns and rows. The columns are lettered (A, B, C …) and the rows are numbered (1, 2, 3 …). The point at which a column and a row intersect is called a **cell**. Each cell has its own cell reference. The cell shown below is cell A1. It is in column A, row 1. Data can be entered into cells.

Spreadsheets are used to record **data** and perform calculations on the data using **formulas**. Graphs and charts can be drawn using the data. Calculations are performed automatically and accurately and data can be sorted. Companies use spreadsheets to analyse data, create bills, predict how much money will be spent in the future, and much more. *Microsoft Excel* is a spreadsheet application which provides tools to organise, calculate and chart data.

Learning Outcomes

In this unit you will learn about:
- the structure of a spreadsheet
- **formatting** cells in a spreadsheet
- using simple formulas and functions in a spreadsheet
- using the chart feature to create visual information
- how to set values in a spreadsheet based on conditions
- password protect a spreadsheet to keep data safe
- using the chart feature to create visual information
- testing the spreadsheet to ensure it is operating correctly.

KEYWORDS

cell: an area where a row and column intersect and data can be entered

data: the words and values contained on the spreadsheet; these are raw facts and figures that, on their own, have no meaning; for example, the number 10 has no meaning on its own but if we say 10 cm it becomes a length

data type: the type of data to be stored; for example, number and text

format: the way in which data is displayed on the spreadsheet; for example, a number could be formatted as currency, where a $ symbol and two decimal places are added and then made bold – the number 45 would appear as **$45.00**

formula: used to perform calculations in cells; for example, A2 + A3 will add the contents of the cells A2 and A3

formula view: the spreadsheet shows the formula used in each cell rather than the data

chart feature: This feature allows the user to select data and automatically creates a chart or graph of the data

Unit 7.6 Data Mining: Using spreadsheets and databases

SCENARIO

CompiSue is a website which provides an online virtual fitness training game to help 11–14 year-old students stay fit and healthy.

Students are registered via their school. The CompiSue directors want to make the training games more enjoyable and increase the number of students accessing their website. When people use websites, they create a digital footprint containing data about themselves and the devices they are using.

As a member of CompiSue's **marketing** team, you have been challenged to collect and analyse the data, generated by the students, from the company website. You will need to provide information for the Marketing Manager, Lan, which will help her understand how students are using the website.

Your teacher will provide you with a set of **raw data** collected from the CompiSue website. During the data analysis you will edit, format and add to the data. This will help you to understand how spreadsheet features can be used to analyse data and create new information.

Graphs and charts are an important way of presenting information. You will be asked to create graphs and charts to help Lan understand the website data. At the end of the unit you will be asked to complete and test the spreadsheet using the skills you have developed.

> **marketing:** Give an example of marketing.

> **KEYWORDS**
> **marketing:** actions and activities taken by a company to gain customers, promote and sell products
> **raw data:** data collected from a source, such as the CompiSue website, which has not been processed or changed in any way

Do you remember?

Before starting this unit you should be able to carry out the following in *Microsoft Excel*:
- ✔ Open an existing spreadsheet document.
- ✔ Enter text and numbers into certain cells.
- ✔ Edit data in a cell to change its appearance.
- ✔ Add a row or column to a spreadsheet.
- ✔ Use simple formatting to change the way in which data is displayed.

149

International Computing for Lower Secondary

The structure of a spreadsheet

Learn

Spreadsheet software can provide many of the features you need to analyse the data for Lan. You can use formulas to quickly perform calculations on large quantities of data. Imagine calculating the sum of 1000 numbers using a calculator – it would take a long time. Spreadsheets do this almost instantly. Functions can also be used – these are built-in to the spreadsheet and can be used to perform more complex calculations.

As this task requires you to look at and use a lot of numerical data, spreadsheet software is ideal to help you provide the information that Lan needs.

A spreadsheet is made up of rows and columns of data. Each row is numbered starting at 1 and columns use letters starting at A.

The spreadsheet shows sample student data for CompiSue's website. Cell A1 (Username) is highlighted. A1 is an example of a **cell reference**.

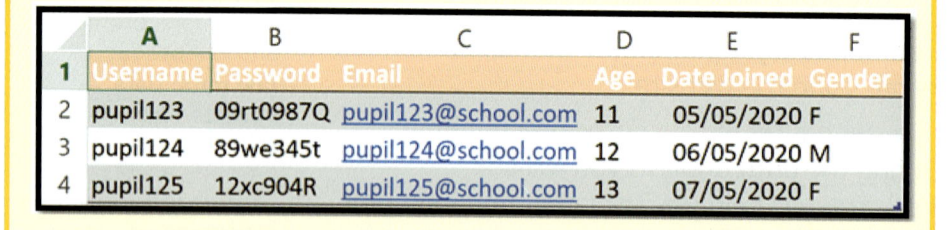

	A	B	C	D	E	F
1	Username	Password	Email	Age	Date Joined	Gender
2	pupil123	09rt0987Q	pupil123@school.com	11	05/05/2020	F
3	pupil124	89we345t	pupil124@school.com	12	06/05/2020	M
4	pupil125	12xc904R	pupil125@school.com	13	07/05/2020	F

KEYWORD

cell reference: made up of a letter and number representing the column and row of a cell

Practice

- Look again at the spreadsheet above. Can you identify the cell references for:
  o age
  o gender
  o password?
- There are different data types in the spreadsheet above.
  o Identify **three** cell references which contain text.
  o Identify **three** cell references which contain numbers.

Unit 7.6 Data Mining: Using spreadsheets and databases

Formatting cells in a spreadsheet

Learn

The appearance of cells can be changed using formatting options. Imagine looking at columns of numbers that were all the same colour. It would be difficult to pick out important data. So you could, for example, change the colour of certain columns, or make important values bold. This would make the data easier to read for Lan.

Simple changes can be made to the **font** and **alignment** of data. Numbers can be formatted as, for example, currency or percentages. Cells can be assigned a particular style.

Cell formatting can be accessed by selecting the HOME tab and using any of the Font, Alignment, Number or Styles sections shown below.

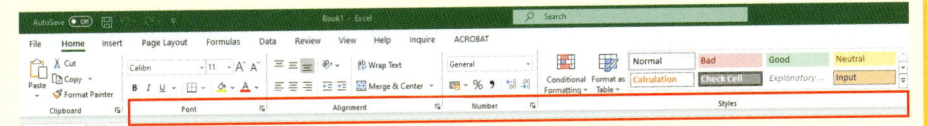

The spreadsheet cells shown below have been formatted by changing the colour of the values in cells A1, B1, C1, D1, E1, F1 and D2.

The data in cell E2 has been formatted as a 'long date'; this shows the date with the month in words rather than as a number. So, 05/05/2020 becomes 05 May 2020. The data in this cell has also had *italics* formatting applied.

	A	B	C	D	E	F
1	Username	Password	Email	Age	Date Joined	Gender
2	Pupil123	09RT980E	pupil123@school.com	11	05 May 2020	F

Game Data — Pupil Data

The spreadsheet below is made up of two **worksheets**. Each worksheet has a **tab** at the bottom of the screen. In this example, the Pupil Data tab is displayed. You could click on the Game Data tab to move to that worksheet. You can add more worksheets using the '+' icon:

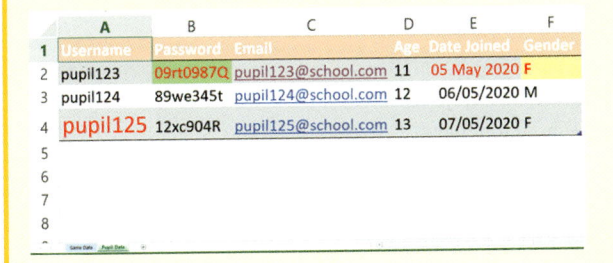

	A	B	C	D	E	F
1	Username	Password	Email	Age	Date Joined	Gender
2	pupil123	09rt0987Q	pupil123@school.com	11	05 May 2020	F
3	pupil124	89we345t	pupil124@school.com	12	06/05/2020	M
4	pupil125	12xc904R	pupil125@school.com	13	07/05/2020	F

KEYWORDS

font: the style and size of the text; this can be selected by the user

alignment: text alignment is a feature which enables users to place text horizontally on the page either to the left, right or centre

cell formatting: used to control the way in which data is displayed in a cell

worksheet: a single page in a spreadsheet file

tab: used to give a name to a worksheet

International Computing for Lower Secondary

> **Practice**

- Open the file called **CompiSue1.xls**, provided by your teacher.
  - Select the Game Data worksheet.
  - Review the data collected and discuss the formatting used with a friend.
    - Is the data easy to understand?
    - How could formatting help to improve the data for someone reading it?
    - Make a list of formatting that you would apply to the data to improve it for someone reading it.
  - Use cell formatting to improve the layout of the Game Data worksheet.
  - Think about:
    - making the column headings stand out
    - using colour to help the reader understand the data
    - using number formatting
    - changing the alignment of data
    - changing the font and size of the text and numbers.

  Make use of the Font, Alignment, Number and Styles section from the HOME tab to do this.

- Show your Game Data worksheet to a friend and explain why you have made the changes to the layout. Explain how you think the changes have made it easier to read.
- Add a new column to the spreadsheet, before column F (Time Taken Minutes). This will hold data about the percentage mark each pupil achieved in the different games. To do this you need to:
  - click on column F
  - right click and select Insert
  - select Entire column and click OK

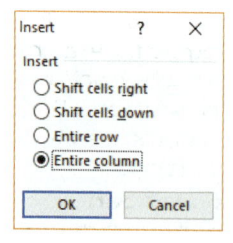

  - add a heading for the column; go to cell F1 and add the text Percentage Mark (you will add data to this column later in the project).
- Select the Pupil Data worksheet.
- Complete the password values for Pupil127–Pupil140, using the same format used for Pupil123–Pupil126 (two numbers, two letters, three numbers, one letter); for example, the password for Pupil123 is 09RT980E.
- Save this file as **myCompiSue1.xls**.

152

Unit 7.6 Data Mining: Using spreadsheets and databases

Using simple formulas and functions in a spreadsheet

Learn

The data that you have been given does not provide much information – it is just a list of words and numbers. You need to add formulas to the spreadsheet so you can identify patterns and make statements about the data. This will help Lan to write a good report.

A formula is used to perform calculations on a **cell range** within a spreadsheet. This is useful because, when a value in a cell changes, any formula which refers to that cell will automatically have its results updated. Spreadsheets also provide built-in **functions** which perform tasks.

> Commonly used functions are SUM (adds the contents of selected cells), AVERAGE (finds the average of selected cells), MIN (finds the smallest value in selected cells), and MAX (finds the largest value in selected cells).

Formulas can be entered into the spreadsheet on the **formula bar**.

For example, entering this formula into the formula bar will add up all of the numbers in the cells A1 to A3:

`= A1 + A2 + A3`

You could also use the **SUM** function, like this:

`= SUM (A1: A3)`

To enter a formula, start by moving to the cell that you want the results to appear in. Then type `=`. The formula bar will appear at the top of the spreadsheet.

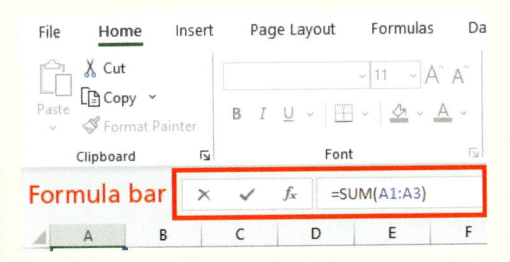

Formula bar — =SUM(A1:A3)

For example, to enter a formula in cell D5 which will add up the values in cells D2, D3 and D4:

▶ move to cell D5 using the arrow keys on the keyboard

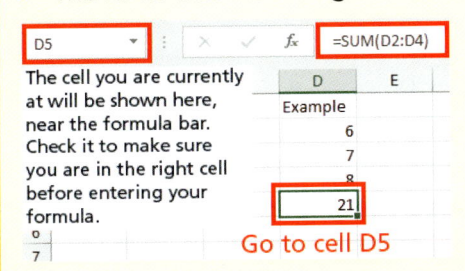

The cell you are currently at will be shown here, near the formula bar. Check it to make sure you are in the right cell before entering your formula.

=SUM(D2:D4)

D	E
Example	
6	
7	
8	
21	

Go to cell D5

You could also use =(D2+D3+D4)

KEYWORDS

cell range: a set of cells on a spreadsheet identified by specifying the first and last cells; for example, A1:A10 is a cell range identifying all the cells between cell A1 to cell A10

function: a routine that performs a set of operations and produces a single output; for example, the SUM function will add up all the numbers in a given cell range

formula bar: the location on the spreadsheet window where the formula is entered

SUM: a function which will add up all the numbers in a given cell range; for example, SUM(A1:A10) will add up all the values in cells A1 through to A10

153

International Computing for Lower Secondary

> ➤ check that the cell you are currently in is cell D5; you can do this by looking at the cell reference near the formula bar as shown in the screenshot
> ○ when you are sure you are in the correct cell, enter your formula.
>
> Some of the most common functions are listed in this table.
>
> | Function | What it does | Example |
> | --- | --- | --- |
> | AVERAGE | Finds the average value for a cell range. | To find the average age of the pupils, the following formula can be typed into the formula bar.

D21   ✗ ✓ fx   =AVERAGE(D2:D19)

This formula has been placed in cell D21 and it will find the average of the values in cells D2 to D19. The cell range is D2:D19. |
> | SUM | Finds the sum of the values in a cell range. | =SUM(G2:G55) will find the sum of all the values in the cell range G2:G55. |
> | MIN | Finds the minimum value in a cell range. | =MIN(G2:G55) will find the minimum value in the cell range G2:G55. |
> | MAX | Finds the maximum value in a cell range. | =MAX(G2:G55) will find the maximum value in the cell range G2:G55. |
> | COUNT | Counts all cells in a cell range that contain numbers. | =COUNT(G2:G55) will count the number of cells which contain numbers in the cell range G2:G55. |
> | COUNTIF | Counts values in a cell range based on a criterion. | =COUNTIF(H2:H55,"N") will count the number of pupils who did not complete the various games. |

Practice

> ➤ Open the file **CompiSue2.xls**, provided by your teacher.
> ○ Calculate the percentage marks for each of the pupils. To do this you will enter a formula in the first cell, F2.
>   Go to cell F2 and enter a formula which will calculate the Percentage Mark for the Score in E2 (the total marks available is 120). You do not need to multiply the formula in cell F2 by 100 because we will use percentage formatting in the next step. Percentage formatting will carry out the multiplication by 100 automatically and add the % symbol, making the data easier to read and understand.
>
> | | D | E | F |
> | --- | --- | --- | --- |
> | 1 | Date | Score | Percentage Mark |
> | 2 | 10/05/2020 | 112 | =E2/120 |
> | 3 | 10/05/2020 | 99 | |

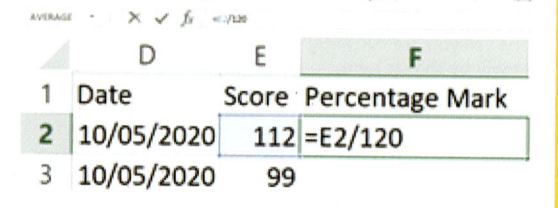

Unit 7.6 Data Mining: Using spreadsheets and databases

o You need a formula for Percentage Mark in every cell from cell F2 to cell F55. You could type the formula into every cell and change the cell reference. For example, the formula in cell F3 would be `=E3/120`. Note that you need to change the cell reference E2 to E3. The formula in F4 would use cell reference E4, and so on. However, this would take a long time. Luckily, spreadsheets allow you to copy a formula from one cell to another and change the cell reference at the same time. Copy the formula down to cells F3 to F55. Do this by dragging down the small square at the bottom of the cell.

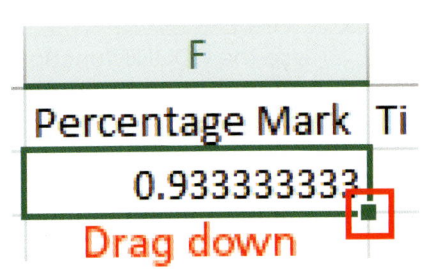

o The data is not displayed as a percentage so you need to correct this. To do this you need to format the contents of cells F2 to F55 as a percentage.

Select cells F2 to F55. Go to the Home tab, select the % symbol from the Number section.

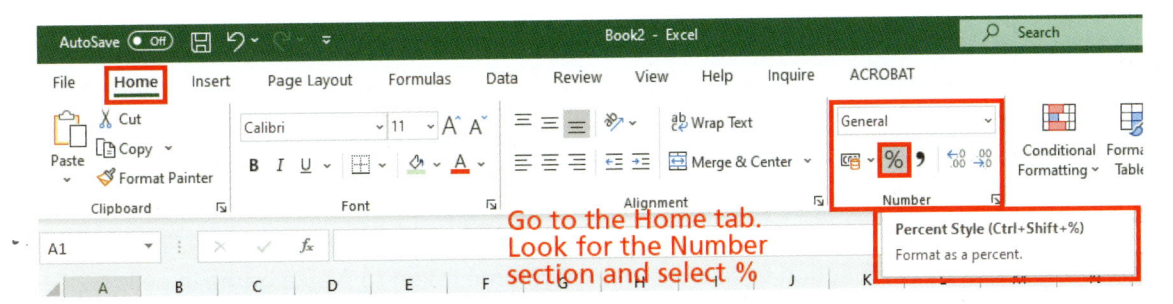

o Move to cell B60 and review the Summary Data section. This section will contain summarised information about the data that has been collected. The summary data will be used in Lan's report.

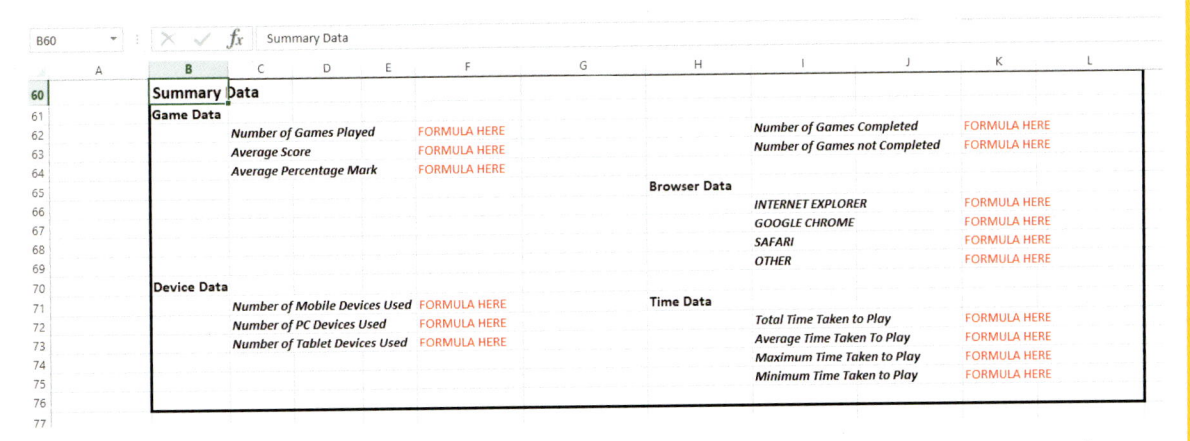

➤ Your challenge is to enter formulas into the cells where you see [FORMULA HERE] in the summary data. This will provide information about the games played and Lan will be able to make comparisons and he will get an overall picture of how the games are used. Refer back to the functions table on page 154 and use the information on the following table to help you create the formula.

155

International Computing for Lower Secondary

Cell	What functions do I use for each formula?
F62	Use the COUNT function to count the total number of entries in cells A2 to A55. This will give the total number of games played.
F63	Using the AVERAGE function, find the average of the data in cells E2 to E55.
F64	Using the AVERAGE function, find the average of the data in cells F2 to F55.
F71	Use the COUNTIF function to count the number of Mobile Devices used.
F72	Use the COUNTIF function to count the number of PC Devices used.
F73	Use the COUNTIF function to count the number of Tablet Devices used.
K62	Use the COUNTIF function to count the number of 'Y's in the cells H2 to H55. 'Y' tells us that the game has been completed by a student.
K63	Use the COUNTIF function to count the number of 'N's in the cells H2 to H55. 'N' tells us that the game has not been completed by a student.
K66	Use the COUNTIF function to count the number of 'INTERNET EXPLORER' users in the cells M2 to M55.
K67	Use the COUNTIF function to count the number of 'GOOGLE CHROME' users in the cells M2 to M55.
K68	Use the COUNTIF function to count the number of 'SAFARI' users in the cells M2 to M55.
K72	Use the SUM function to calculate the total time taken to play the games in cells G2:G55.
K73	Use the AVERAGE function to calculate the average time taken to play the games in cells G2:G55.
K74	Use the MAX function to find the maximum time taken to play a game in cells G2:G55.
K75	Use the MIN function to find the minimum time taken to play a game in cells G2:G55.

o Format the data in cell K73 to 2 decimal places. Do this by:
- selecting the HOME tab
- going to the Number section
- selecting the symbol to increase the decimal places as shown below.

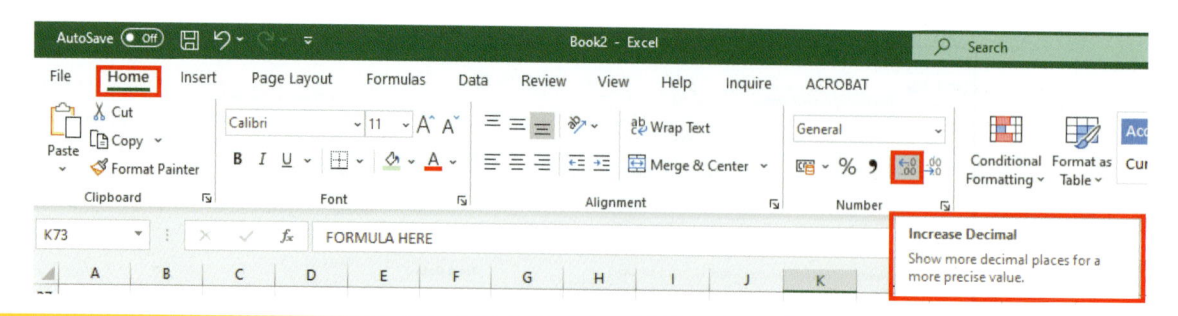

Unit 7.6 Data Mining: Using spreadsheets and databases

Decomposition and pattern recognition

You will need to break this problem up into smaller steps. The details in the table will help you to see what functions or formulas need to be used.

Look for a pattern in the use of functions. Which functions are used to count specific things?

Look at cell K69. With a friend, write down how you would calculate the number of people who use other browsers. Remember that you have already calculated the number of people who use *Internet Explorer*, *Google Chrome* and *Safari*. How can this data be used to help you?

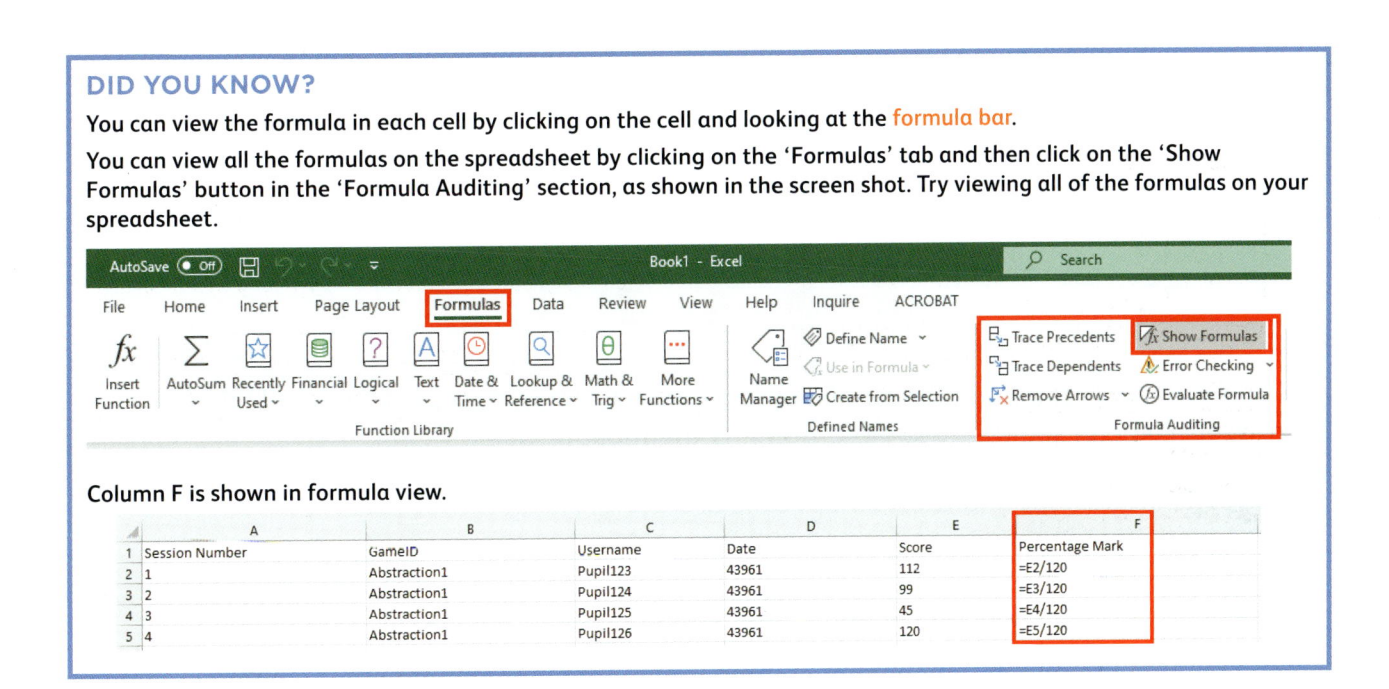

DID YOU KNOW?

You can view the formula in each cell by clicking on the cell and looking at the **formula bar**.

You can view all the formulas on the spreadsheet by clicking on the 'Formulas' tab and then click on the 'Show Formulas' button in the 'Formula Auditing' section, as shown in the screen shot. Try viewing all of the formulas on your spreadsheet.

Column F is shown in formula view.

	A	B	C	D	E	F
1	Session Number	GameID	Username	Date	Score	Percentage Mark
2	1	Abstraction1	Pupil123	43961	112	=E2/120
3	2	Abstraction1	Pupil124	43961	99	=E3/120
4	3	Abstraction1	Pupil125	43961	45	=E4/120
5	4	Abstraction1	Pupil126	43961	120	=E5/120

International Computing for Lower Secondary

Using the chart feature to create visual information

Learn

Charts and graphs can be used to present information visually, so that you can see trends and patterns in data much more easily. There are different types of charts, such as pie-charts, bar-charts and line charts. Lan wants to include charts so that the report will be much easier to read and understand.

To create a chart, you must select the data first. For example, to draw a graph that shows the number of users who use the different browsers, select the data and click on 'Insert'. Use the Charts section to select a chart type.

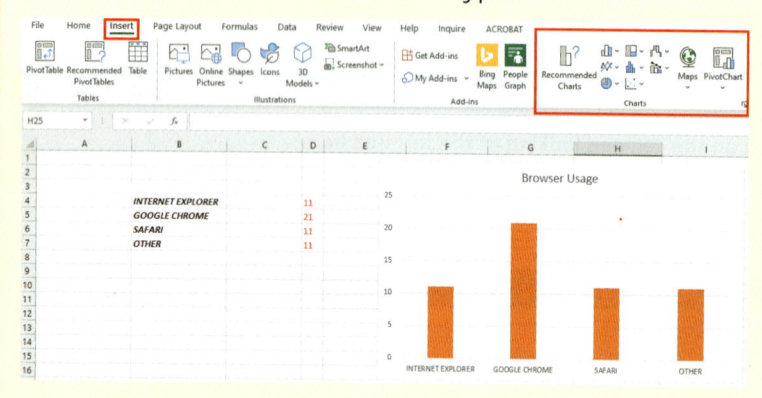

This chart shows the number of pupils that use each different browser. You can see that *Google Chrome* is the most popular, simply by looking at the graph. This information helps Lan to analyse what devices and browsers people are using. He can then target the most popular devices and browsers when the website is being developed.

When you create a chart, the words 'Chart Title' appear at the top of the chart in a text box. To change the Chart Title, click on this text box and enter a new title: The title in the chart above has been changed to 'Browser Usage'. You need to pick a title that explains what the chart is about.

The chart below has two axes: the vertical (*y*-axis) and the horizontal (*x*-axis). These can be given titles to help the reader understand what data the chart is about. To change the Axis Titles on either axis, click on the 'Axis Title' textbox and type the new text. Adding information to the chart improves the presentation and readability of the graph.

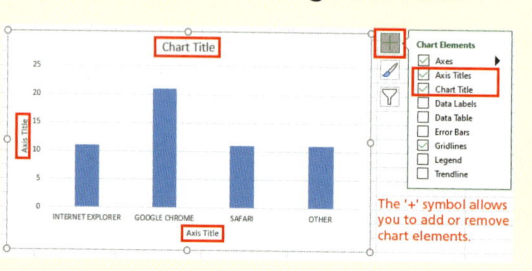

KEYWORD

chart: a graphical representation of the data

chart: Go onto Excel and look at the various types of available charts. Find an example of a hierarchical chart.

Unit 7.6 Data Mining: Using spreadsheets and databases

DID YOU KNOW?

Charts can be customised using the Chart options which appear to the side of the chart. You can see these in the screenshot below. For example, the style and colour of a chart can be changed. The chart below shows some of the things that can be changed to make the information clearer to the reader.

KEYWORD

customised: modified to suit individual preferences or needs

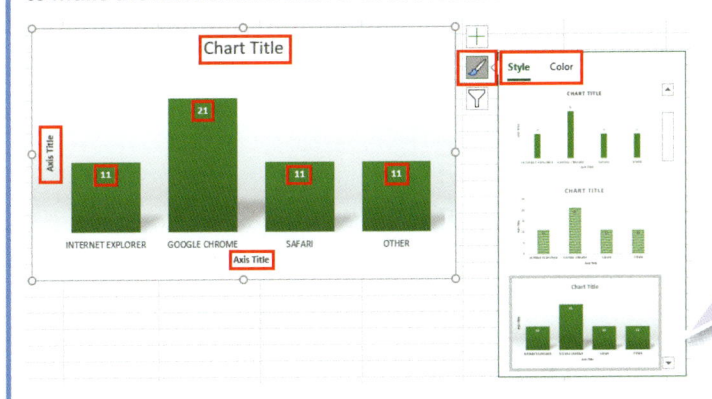

This chart has been customised by changing the colour and style. The data value for each bar has been placed at the top. So, you can clearly see that 11 people use *Internet Explorer*. This makes it easier for users to read and understand the data. You will need to customise any charts for Lan so that he can present the information in a way that the managers can understand.

Practice

Summary data is very useful for completing data analysis: it allows you to compare sections of the data with each other. You are going to make use of the summary data to draw graphs and charts for Lan's report. This will enable you to make comparisons and provide an analysis.

- Open the file called **CompiSue3.xls** which shows the results of the summary data after the formulas have been completed.
  o Review the summary data in cells B60 to K75. Ensure you understand what each value means and the formulas used to get the value. You are going to copy this data to another worksheet and create well-designed charts for Lan.
  o Add a new worksheet to the spreadsheet. Revisit page 151 to remind yourself how.
  o Name the worksheet 'Summary Data Charts'.
  o Copy the Summary Data to the new sheet called 'Summary Data Charts'.
    • Move to the Game Data worksheet.
    • Select cells B50 to K75 and right click to copy these cells.
    • Move to cell A1 of the Summary Data Charts worksheet.
    • Right click and paste the **values** onto the worksheet.
    • Select the paste values option shown below. This will copy only the values that are in the cells and not the formulas. You do not need the formulas to create the charts, only the values.

KEYWORD

values: data or numbers used in the spreadsheet

159

International Computing for Lower Secondary

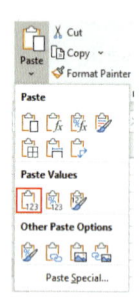

> Increase the width of columns B and H so that all the text inside each cell is visible. Do this by moving the mouse in between the column header until a double arrow is shown. Then, click and drag the mouse to the left or right to decrease or increase the size of the column.

	A	B	C
4		Average Score	103
5		Average Percentage Mark	86%
6			

> You should now see that there are blank columns in the spreadsheet: C, D and I. Delete these columns from the Summary Data Charts by selecting the column, right clicking and selecting delete. When you do this, your spreadsheet should look like this:

> During copying, some of the formatting is been lost. Format the values Average Percentage Mark and Average Time Taken to Play again.

> Create a chart for the Device Data. Customise the chart so that the information is clear and easy to understand. Remember you can add a Chart Title, Axes Titles and you can change the colour and style.

> Create a chart for the Browser Data. Customise the chart so that the information is clear and easy to understand. You can do this by changing the Axes Titles and the Chart Title so that they show what the data in the chart is about. Look at page 158 to remind yourself about how a chart can be improved.

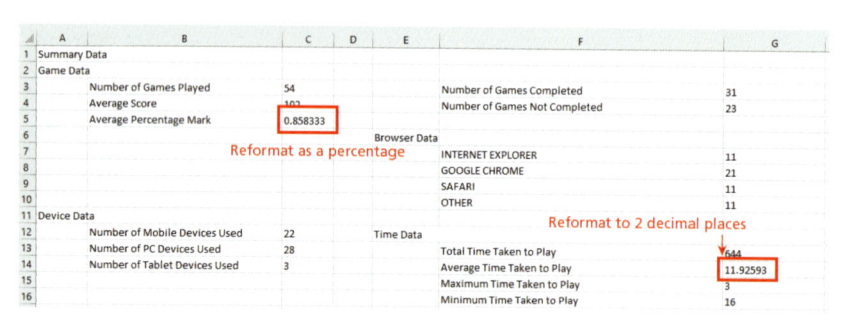

Unit 7.6 Data Mining: Using spreadsheets and databases

DID YOU KNOW?

Cell formatting can be lost when values are copied and pasted. You can protect the contents of cells and worksheets to prevent editing. Select the Review tab. Click the Protect Sheet button in the changes section.

You will be prompted to enter a password. You can also select what users of the worksheet can do when they unlock the spreadsheet.

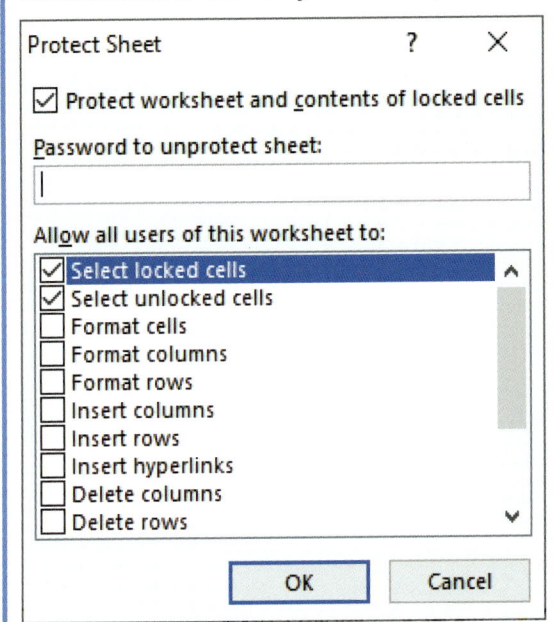

Selecting a good password is important so that the data is well protected. A good password should not be easy to guess. So do not use the name of your pet or your favourite sports team.

A good password should:
- be made up of numbers and letters
- use a mix of upper and lower case letters
- be at least eight characters long
- be changed regularly.

Try protecting the data in the Summary Data Charts worksheet.

Do not forget your chosen password so that you can unprotect the data if changes are required.

KEYWORDS

review: a tab on the spreadsheet software which contains editing features and the protect sheet feature; these features make it easy to keep data secure

protect sheet: the cells on a spreadsheet can be protected to prevent other users from accidentally or deliberately changing, moving, or deleting data using a password; users need to enter this password if they want to make changes to the worksheet

How to set values in a spreadsheet based on conditions

Learn

In certain situations you may want to check one cell value before setting values in other cells. For example, if a student achieves a mark of 120 then they have completed the game otherwise they have not. Move to the Game Data Worksheet. The formula for the data in the Game Completed column (H) uses an `IF` **statement**.

For example, in cell H2 the formula is:

`=IF(E2=120, "Y", "N")`

An `IF` statement checks to see if a condition is true or false and then does one of two things. It controls which statement is executed. There are two branches that can be followed.

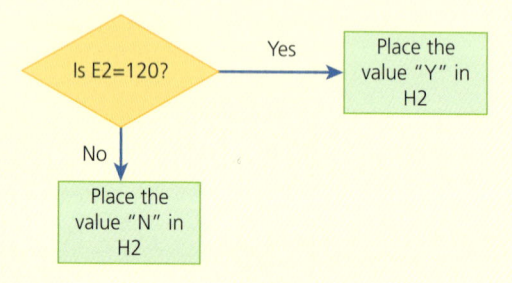

Is E2=120?
- Yes → Place the value "Y" in H2
- No → Place the value "N" in H2

Only one of the two statements will be executed.

Algorithmic thinking

Using a selection statement such as an if statement enables the program to provide two different routes and to provide one of two outputs, in this case Y and N.

`E2=120` is a **condition**. It asks a question: is the contents of the cell E2 equal to 120?

A condition contains a **comparison operator**. The comparison operator combines the parts of a condition together. The comparison operator is the `=` symbol in the example above.

The condition can evaluate to true or false.

For example, if the contents of cell `E2=119`, then the condition `E2=120` will return a value of false because E2 is 119. In the Game Data worksheet, if `E2=120`, this means that the student in row 2 has completed the game.

KEYWORDS

IF statement: perform an action on the spreadsheet based on a condition

comparison operator: operators that compare values and return true or false. The operators include: >, <, >=, <=

Unit 7.6 Data Mining: Using spreadsheets and databases

Other comparison operators are:

Less than	<
Greater than	>
Less than or equal to	<=
Greater than or equal to	>=

These operators can be used in conditions.

Look at the table below; we assume E2 has been set to 120. Answering each of the questions (or evaluating each of the conditions) will give the outcomes shown.

Condition	Outcome after evaluating the condition
E2<120?	False
E2<=120?	True
E2>120?	False
E2 >=120?	True

A Rating is to be added for each student. This will show how close the student is to completing the game.

The rating is given based on the value of their Percentage Mark. The table below shows the required Percentage Mark for each Rating.

Percentage Mark	Rating
0–44	None
44–70	3 Star
70–90	4 Star
90–100	5 Star

Practice

- Open **CompiSu4.xls** provided by your teacher.
- You are going to assign a level to each student based on their Score. If the student's Score (in column E), is greater than 110, the Level Assigned is 'EXPERT' otherwise the Level Assigned is 'NOVICE'.
  Create a flowchart which will solve this problem.
  From the flowchart, create an `IF` statement formula which will solve the problem.
  Remember the format of an `IF` statement:
  `=IF` (condition, value if true, value if false)
  Insert the `IF` statement in cell I2.
  - Copy the formula to cells I3:I55. This will save you typing an individual formula for each cell.
  - Review the Rating column and ensure the Rating assigned to each student is correct by checking at least four of the Scores together with their Level Assigned.
  - Save the file.

International Computing for Lower Secondary

Go further

The company have decided to collect more data about the pupils to make the exercise programs more individual.

Review the table of formulas and functions on page 154 and use this to help with the following tasks:

- Open the file **CompiSue6.xls** provided by your teacher and select the **Pupil Data** worksheet.
- Add the text 'Height cm' to cell G1.
- Enter the values for each pupil's height into cells G2 to G19. These values should be between 149 and 164.
- Enter the text 'Hobby' into cell H1.
- Enter the values for each pupil's hobby into cells H2 to H19.
  Pupil126, Pupil130, Pupil136, Pupil140 like Dancing
  Pupil124, Pupil128, Pupil129, Pupil132, Pupil138 like Football
  Pupil123, Pupil127, Pupil134, Pupil135 like Reading
  Pupil125, Pupil131, Pupil133, Pupil137, Pupil139 like Swimming
- Enter a formula into cell D21 which will calculate the average Age of the pupils. Use the AVERAGE function to find the average value in the cells D2 to D19.
- Enter a formula into cell D22 which will find the Maximum age of the pupils. Use the MAX function to find the maximum value in the cells D2 to D19.
- Enter a formula into cell D23 which will find the Minimum age of the pupils. Use the MIN function to find the minimum value in the cells D2 to D19.
- Enter a formula into cell F21 which will count the number of male pupils. Use the COUNTIF function to count the number of cells containing 'M' in cells F2 to F19.
- Enter a formula into cell F22 which will count the number of female pupils. Use the COUNTIF function to count the number of cells containing 'F' in cells F2 to F19.
- Format the data so that it is clear and easy to understand. Ensure that you include text which helps explain the calculations. For example, place the words 'Average Height' beside the result of the calculation for average height. This helps people understand the data.
- Save the file as **MyCompiSue.xls**.
- Discuss with a friend what mistakes have been made when creating and editing the document and how you corrected them. You might think about mistakes in formulas or improvements made to charts.
- Edit the document so that the layout and organisation of the information is easy to understand for the Marketing Manager, Lan. You can use different fonts, colour, cell shading and alignment to improve the readability of your data. You can also create and customise charts so that the data can be summarised and patterns and trends can be identified easily.
- Show your edited document to a friend. Explain what you have changed about the document in terms of layout, font, colour, alignment and the inclusion of charts. How will these changes help the target audience understand the data. Will they see the patterns and trends immediately? Will they identify the most important data?

Unit 7.6 Data Mining: Using spreadsheets and databases

Challenge yourself

Lan wants to be able to change the way that data is presented. He wants to sort the data so that he can rank marks to find the best performing pupils. He also wants to be able to select specific data in the spreadsheet. For example, he may want to look at the data for male students only. He can sort data using the sort feature. He can select data by using the filter feature.

▶ To add filters or sort data:
  • select the Home tab
  • select Sort and Filter from the Editing section.
▶ Select Filter.
  • Each column will now have an arrow to the right of the column heading. These can be used to select the data you want to show. For example, to show all female pupils click on the Gender filter and check the 'F' box shown in the menu.

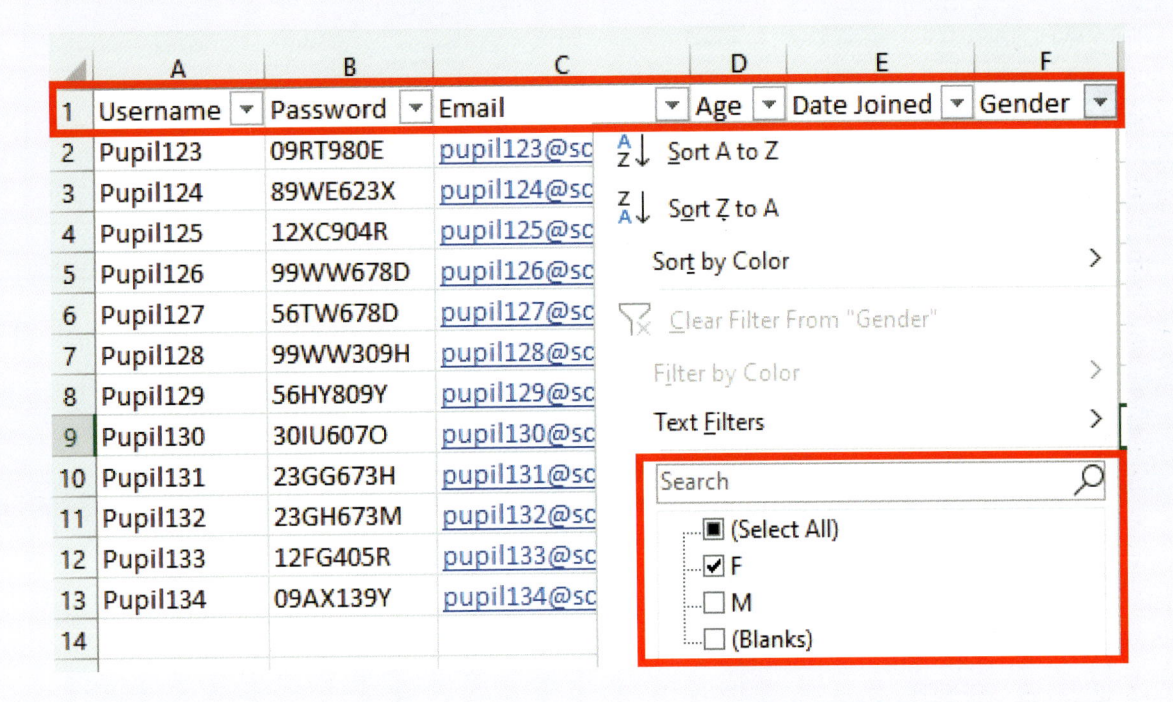

  • To clear the filter and display all the data again, tick the Select All box.
▶ To sort data, select a cell in the column you want to sort. Then you can use A to Z or Z to A or Custom Sort to change the order in which the data is displayed.
▶ Continue using **CompiSue6.xls** and select cells A1 to I19 and apply filters to the data.
  • Sort the data in order of Age.
  • Sort the data in order of Gender.
  • Sort the data in order of Hobby.

With a partner, discuss how the data could be used by Lan to improve the website for the students.

International Computing for Lower Secondary

Final project

So far, the company has only done analysis on the Game Data worksheet. Now Lan wants to know more about the students who are using the website: how many males and females use the website, and what are their hobbies? This will help Lan to target advertising on the website. He will present this information to a large audience showing patterns and trends. But first, you need to carry out further data analysis on the Pupil Data worksheet.

➤ Using the file called **myCompiSue.xls**, identify an area on the Pupil Data Worksheet where you will place summary data. This will be called your summary data area.

This screenshot shows how you might lay out your summary data area.

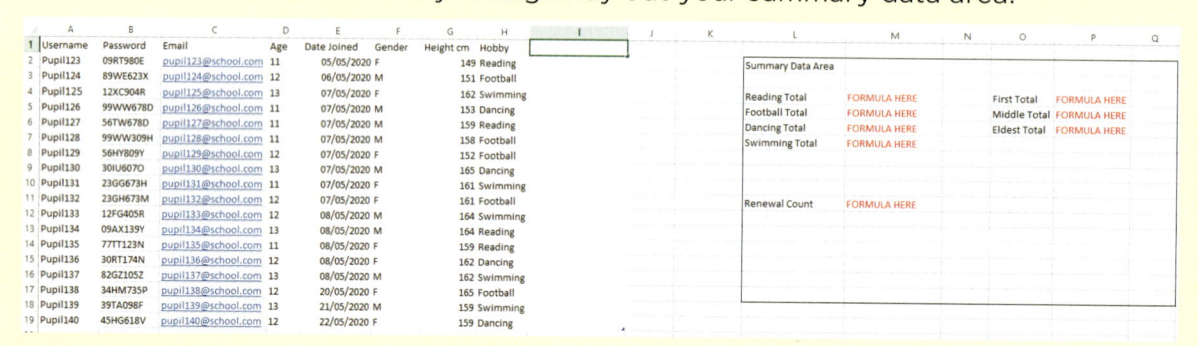

- In your summary data area: Add formulas to count the number of pupils in each hobby category.
- Create a chart of the hobby information.
- Format the chart so that it is easy to understand.
- Enter the text 'Age Group Category' into cell I1. Assign an Age Group Category to each pupil based on the data in the following table. You can simply type this information in. For example, Pupil123's Age Category is 'First'.

Remember to think about using colour, style, editing the chart title and axes titles.

Age	AgeGroupCategory
Age=11	First
Age=12	Middle
Age=13	Eldest

- Add formulas to count the number of students in each Age Group Category.

➤ The company wants to find out which students need to renew their membership:
- Enter the text 'Renewal Due' into cell J1.
- Add an `IF` Statement formula to cell J2. The formula should place the word 'Yes' into cell J2 if the DateJoined is before 12/05/2020; otherwise, the formula should place 'No' into cell J2. Use the following formula =IF(E2<DATEVALUE("12/05/2020"),"Y","N").
Using the DATEVALUE function makes sure that "12/05/2020" is understood as a date.
- Copy the formula so that each student has a value in column J.
- In your summary data area, add formulas to count the number students who need to renew their membership.

166

- ➤ Review the spreadsheet:
  - Check that you have used formatting and colour well.
  - Ensure that the summary data and Age Group Category data are correct and that the formulas work correctly.

Evaluation

- ➤ After you have completed your data analysis ask a friend to look at your summary data area. They should comment on:
  - the accuracy of your summary results
  - the layout and organisation of your summary data area in terms of its readability
  - how well you used formatting to present and emphasise data
  - how easy your chart is to understand and the Chart Title and Axes Titles you have chosen to help with this
  - any recommendations they would make to improve the spreadsheet.
- ➤ Make improvements to your data analysis based on the feedback from your friend. Review your spreadsheet again. Are there any further improvements required?

About databases

A database is a collection of information organised so that it can be searched easily. Your school will have a database of pupil information. The database will include information such as your name and address.

Databases make it easy to quickly retrieve large amounts of information, and make quick decisions when needed. Companies, for example, could search through a database of customers to find all those who live in a particular country or area.

International Computing for Lower Secondary

You will learn to:
- manage tables in a database
- use data types and primary keys
- use **data validation** and conditions to ensure that data in the table is acceptable
- create validation rules to support data validation
- create **queries** to analyse data.

SCENARIO

CompiSue would like to produce more information about the students and their online activities. The company has decided to use database software to present information in organised reports, and to search and select information using the query feature. Lan wants to be able to produce neatly presented, up-to-date daily reports. The database software will help him to do this.

You will be provided with a set of raw data collected from the CompiSue website. The data shows information about the students and their game data. You need to edit, format and add to the raw data and present information in the form of reports.

DID YOU KNOW?

The Library of Congress in US is one of the largest physical databases in the world. It spreads over a massive 530 miles of shelf space. It's said to be the ideal place to find information that is not found on the internet.

Facebook has got the world's largest database 30 petabytes in size – that's 3000 times the size of the Library of Congress!

KEYWORDS

field: a single piece of data about one person or one thing

field names: users can select names for fields; for example, Username is a field name used in the Pupil Data table. It tells us what the pupil's username is for logging on to the website

data validation: an automatic check to ensure the data input is acceptable

length check: checks that the data input contains a particular number of characters

presence check: checks to ensure that a field has not been left blank; that is, that there is data entered for a particular field

input masks: controls the layout or format of data entered; characters and numbers will have a set order

Unit 7.6 Data Mining: Using spreadsheets and databases

Managing tables in a database

Learn

A database stores data in **tables**. Tables are given a name. Here is a table of data called PUPIL DATA. This data shows the information that is currently collected by CompiSue about pupils who use the website. You will have seen this data in the section about spreadsheets.

Each table is made up of **records**. In the PUPIL DATA table, one record has been circled.

A record is made up of fields. In the PUPIL DATA table, one field (Password) has been shaded.

There are six fields (Username, Password, Email, Age, DateJoined, Gender) and three records shown.

PUPIL DATA					
Username	**Password**	**Email**	**Age**	**DateJoined**	**Gender**
Pupil123	09RT980E	pupil123@school.com	11	05/05/2020	F
Pupil124	89WE623X	pupil124@school.com	12	06/05/2020	M
Pupil125	12XC904R	pupil125@school.com	13	07/05/2020	F

Use **datasheet view** to look at data in a table. To do this, you simply click on the name of the table to open it up. A datasheet view from the Pupil Data table is shown below.

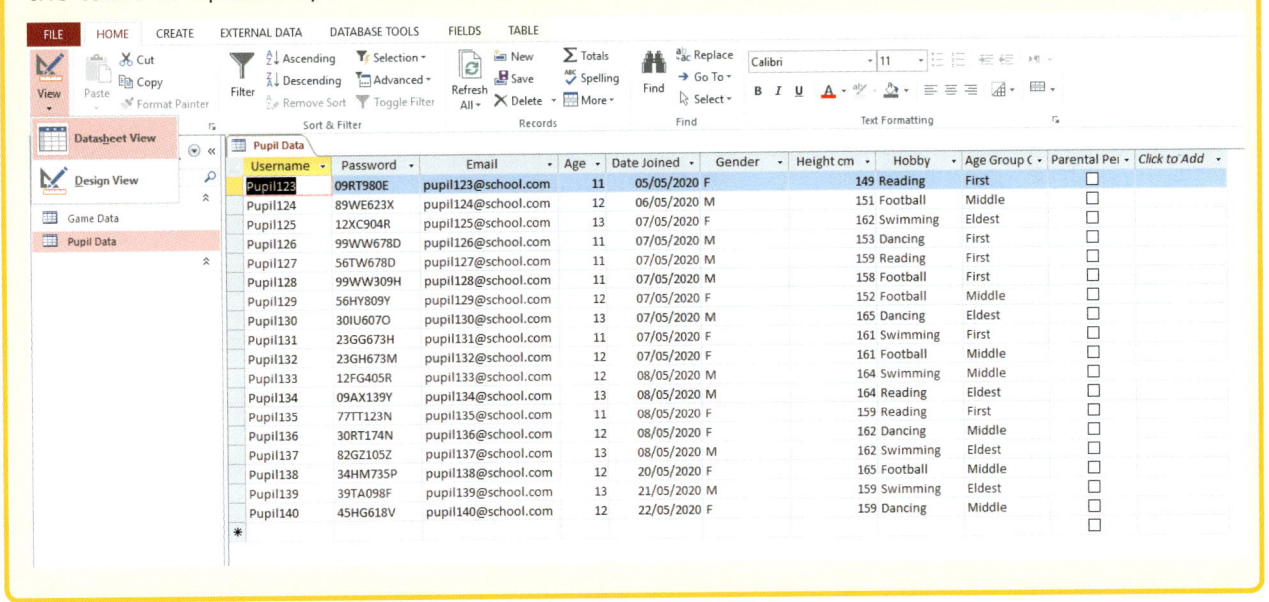

Username	Password	Email	Age	Date Joined	Gender	Height cm	Hobby	Age Group
Pupil123	09RT980E	pupil123@school.com	11	05/05/2020	F	149	Reading	First
Pupil124	89WE623X	pupil124@school.com	12	06/05/2020	M	151	Football	Middle
Pupil125	12XC904R	pupil125@school.com	13	07/05/2020	F	162	Swimming	Eldest
Pupil126	99WW678D	pupil126@school.com	11	07/05/2020	M	153	Dancing	First
Pupil127	56TW678D	pupil127@school.com	11	07/05/2020	M	159	Reading	First
Pupil128	99WW309H	pupil128@school.com	11	07/05/2020	M	158	Football	First
Pupil129	56HY809Y	pupil129@school.com	12	07/05/2020	F	152	Football	Middle
Pupil130	30IU607O	pupil130@school.com	13	07/05/2020	M	165	Dancing	Eldest
Pupil131	23GG673H	pupil131@school.com	11	07/05/2020	F	161	Swimming	First
Pupil132	23GH673M	pupil132@school.com	12	07/05/2020	F	161	Football	Middle
Pupil133	12FG405R	pupil133@school.com	12	08/05/2020	M	164	Swimming	Middle
Pupil134	09AX139Y	pupil134@school.com	13	08/05/2020	M	164	Reading	Eldest
Pupil135	77TT123N	pupil135@school.com	11	08/05/2020	F	159	Reading	First
Pupil136	30RT174N	pupil136@school.com	12	08/05/2020	F	162	Dancing	Middle
Pupil137	82GZ105Z	pupil137@school.com	13	08/05/2020	M	162	Swimming	Eldest
Pupil138	34HM735P	pupil138@school.com	12	20/05/2020	F	165	Football	Middle
Pupil139	39TA098F	pupil139@school.com	13	21/05/2020	M	159	Swimming	Eldest
Pupil140	45HG618V	pupil140@school.com	12	22/05/2020	F	159	Dancing	Middle

KEYWORDS

table: a collection of related records; for example, the table PUPIL contains records about individual pupils

record: a collection of related fields; for example, one record in the table PUPIL contains information about one pupil

datasheet view: a feature of a database which allows the user to view all of the data in the form of a table

International Computing for Lower Secondary

> **Practice**
>
> - Open the file **CompiSue.accdb** provided by your teacher. The database contains two tables, 'Pupil Data' and 'Game Data', which show each pupil's details and the games that they have already taken online.
> - Open the Pupil Data table in datasheet view.
>   o How many records are in the Pupil Data table?
>   o How many fields are in the Pupil Data table?
> - Open the Game Data table in datasheet view.
>   o How many records are in the Game Data table?
>   o How many fields are in the Game Data table?

KEYWORDS

data type (more information): each field has a data type, such as currency (which stores money values) or Yes/No (sometimes called Boolean, which can only take on one of two values such as a Yes or No question)

primary key: a field that uniquely identifies a record

design view: a feature of the database which allows you to view the field names and data type of the fields in the table; validation rules and validation text can be inserted in this view

Data types and primary keys

> **Learn**
>
> In a database table, each field can be assigned a **data type**. The data type shows what kind of data the field can store. For example, numbers or text. Here is a list of data types used in the Pupil Data table.
>
> | Field name | Data Type |
> |---|---|
> | Username | Text (made up of numbers and letters) |
> | Password | Text |
> | Email | Text |
> | Age | Number (whole numbers only; these are called integers) |
> | DateJoined | Date/Time (a date or time value) |
> | Gender | Text |
>
> *Do you remember the spreadsheet Data Types on page 150? There were numbers and text data in the spreadsheet. Databases support these data types too.*
>
> You need to be able to identify records individually in a table. So, we need a field which contains a unique value for each record. For example, in a table that contains data about cars, the registration number would identify a car individually. We could use the registration number as a **primary key**. That is, it uniquely identifies each car.
>
> Every table should have a primary key. In the PUPIL DATA table on page 169 this is the Username. This field contains data that is unique for each person. No two people have the same Username. So, we can search for a pupil in the table using their Username.
>
> The structure of a table can be changed. You can change the data type or name of a field or add new fields. This is done in **design view**. Design view shows the fields in the table and their data type.

Unit 7.6 Data Mining: Using spreadsheets and databases

To set the primary key for a table:
1. open the table in design view by right clicking on the table name
2. click on the field you want to set as the primary key

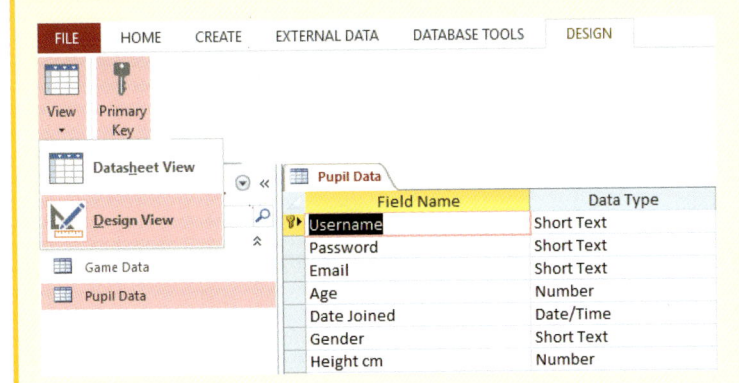

3. click on the primary key icon; when you do this, a key symbol will appear beside the Username field to indicate that this is now set as the primary key.

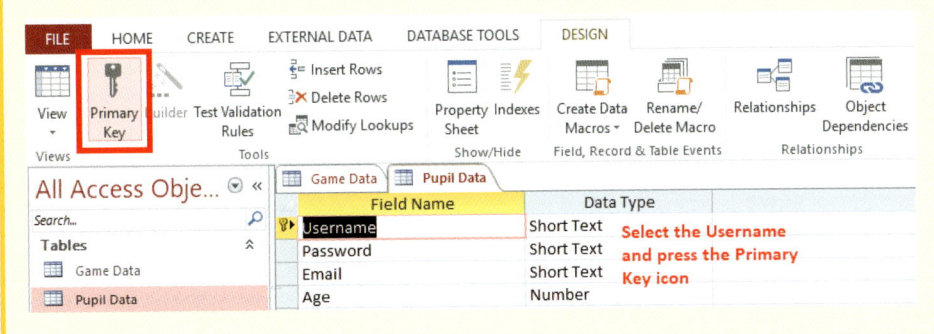

Select the Username and press the Primary Key icon

Practice

- Open the file **CompiSue.accdb** provided by your teacher
- You are going to add a new field to the Pupil Data table. This field will allow CompiSue to ensure that all pupils using the website have got parental permission.
  - Open the 'Pupil Data' table in design view by right clicking on the table name. You can see how to do this above.
  - Add a new field called Parental Permission to the Pupil Data table. To do this:
    - go to the first empty row in the Field Name column
    - enter the text 'Parental Permission'
    - go to the Data Type column and set the data type to Yes/No.

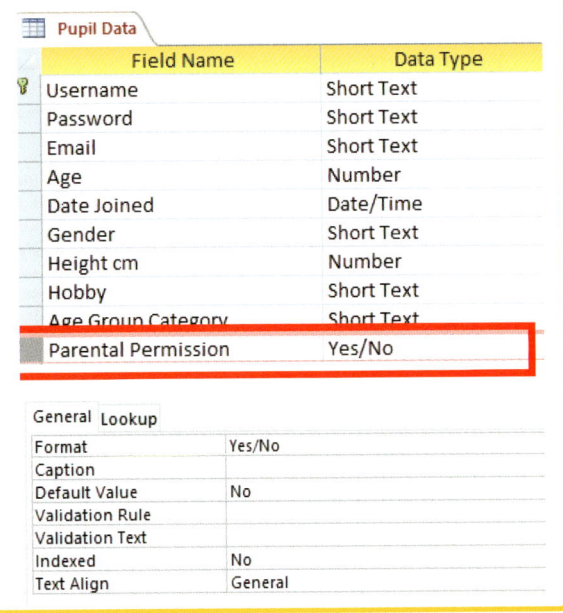

171

International Computing for Lower Secondary

- Close design view as shown.

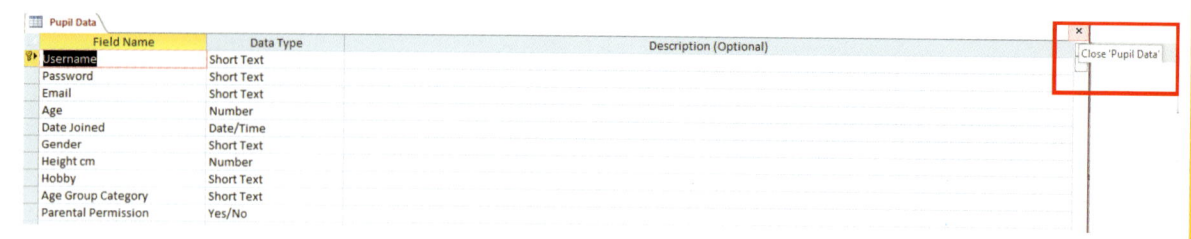

Field Name	Data Type
Username	Short Text
Password	Short Text
Email	Short Text
Age	Number
Date Joined	Date/Time
Gender	Short Text
Height cm	Number
Hobby	Short Text
Age Group Category	Short Text
Parental Permission	Yes/No

- Open datasheet view for the 'Pupil Data' table, by clicking on the table name. Datasheet view is shown on page 169.
- To show that each individual pupil has permission to use the website, you must place a tick in 'Parental Permission' box for everybody as shown.
- Lan has discovered that some pupils have not received permission from their parents; so, you must uncheck the boxes for the following pupils.
  Pupil123, Pupil128, Pupil130, Pupil131, Pupil132, Pupil133, Pupil135, Pupil137, Pupil138, Pupil140
- Close the table and save the changes.

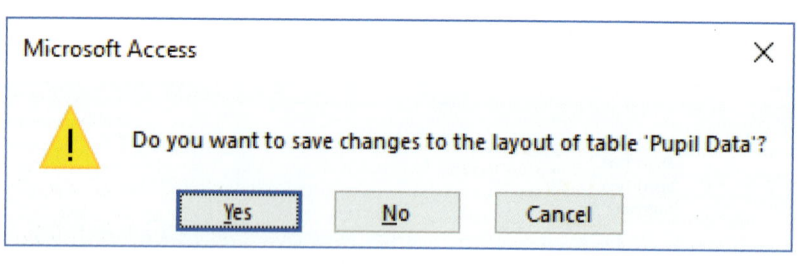

> Microsoft Access: Do you want to save changes to the layout of table 'Pupil Data'? [Yes] [No] [Cancel]

▶ Now you are going to select a primary key for the Game Data table so that Lan can pick out the individual games that have been completed by pupils.

A primary key should uniquely identify a record. No two records should have the same value as a primary key.

  - Open the Game Data table in datasheet view.
  - Look at the data and, with a partner, think about which field you would select as a primary key. You should think about the reason for having a primary key in a table.
  - Look at the session number field. Every time a pupil plays a game, a new record is added to the table and the record is given a session number. The session number is used to show the individual game that has been played by a pupil. Each game played has a unique session number. Discuss with your partner why session number would be a good primary key.
  - Open the Game Data table in design view and select the session number as the primary key.

▶ Save and close the table.

Unit 7.6 Data Mining: Using spreadsheets and databases

Data validation and using conditions in a table

Learn

It is easy to make a mistake when entering data. Database software allows the user to set rules for checking the data being entered. The data entered is checked against the rules and, if it breaks the rules, it will not be allowed. This type of checking is called data **validation**. It helps to ensure that the data is valid. There are a number of different checks that can be applied to data.

Validation check	Purpose
Length check	Ensures the data entered has up to a certain amount of characters.
Presence check	Ensures that data is entered into a field.
Look up lists	Makes use of a drop down list of values to enter data into a field. The user can select the value from the list on screen and no typing is required.
Input mask	Ensures that data is entered in a certain format. Look at the password for Pupil123, it is 09RT980E. The password has the same format for each pupil. That is two numbers, two letters, three numbers and one letter, in that order.

KEYWORDS

validation: ensures that data entered into the table meets certain criteria; it cannot ensure that the data is accurate; for example, an age between 11 and 13 may be entered but that age may not be correct for the pupil

characters: individual letters or numbers such as A, B, 1, or @

look up lists: a set of data contained in a list; the user selects the value from the list provided on screen

Decomposition and algorithmic thinking

In order to search through the database you need to select data based on conditions. For example, to list all the girls in the Pupil Data table you will need to select all those where `Gender='F'`. The condition in this case is `Gender='F'`.

Conditions can be combined using **logical operators**. Two of the most common logical operators are:

- AND
- OR

These can be used to combine conditions.

For example, in the Pupil Data table, Gender can only take on the values 'F' or 'M'.

That means that users should not be able to enter any other values. We should check the data when it is being entered to ensure that only 'F' or 'M' is entered. This is called **validation**. Conditions can be combined to create validation rules.

How could we combine conditions to create a validation rule for the Gender field, in the Pupil Data table? We need two conditions:

Condition 1: `Gender='F'`

Condition 2: `Gender='M'`

Do you remember conditions in your spreadsheet on page 162. A condition is checked to see if it is true or false.

173

International Computing for Lower Secondary

Imagine the Gender values in the table below were entered into the Pupil Data table, for checking using the conditions shown.

Condition used when data was entered into the Pupil Data table	Gender entered into the Pupil Data table	Was the data accepted into the Pupil Data table?	Should the data have been accepted into the Pupil Data table?	Was the decision right or wrong?
`Gender='F'`	'M'	No	Yes as 'M' is a valid gender	wrong
`Gender='F'`	'H'	No	No as 'H' is not a valid gender	right
`Gender='F'`	'F'	Yes	Yes as 'F' is a valid gender	right
`Gender='M'`	'F'	No	Yes as 'F' is a valid gender	wrong
`Gender='M'`	'R'	No	No as 'R' is not a valid gender	right
`Gender='M'`	'M'	Yes	Yes as 'M' is a valid gender	right

You can see above that valid data is not accepted if the two conditions are used separately.

If we combine the two conditions the decisions made will be different.

We can combine them using the `OR` operator as either 'M' or 'F' is acceptable.

When conditions are combined using `OR`, only one of the conditions must be true to give an overall true, this allows the data to be accepted. The correct condition is:

`Gender='F' OR Gender='M'`

> When using text values in a condition you must place quotation marks around them. For example, Gender is a text field and so the values are 'M' or 'F'. Also, the Hobby field contains text data and so if we are using these in a condition we write them using quotation marks. For example, 'Reading' or 'Swimming' or 'Dancing' or 'Football'.

Now, using the table below with the correct condition, check to see which data is accepted.

Condition used when data was entered into the Pupil Data table	Gender entered into the Pupil Data table	Was the data accepted into the Pupil Data table?	Should the data have been accepted into the Pupil Data table?	Was the decision right or wrong?
`Gender='F' OR Gender='M'`	'M'			
`Gender='F' OR Gender='M'`	'H'			
`Gender='F' OR Gender='M'`	'F'			
`Gender='F' OR Gender='M'`	'F'			
`Gender='F' OR Gender='M'`	'R'			
`Gender='F' OR Gender='M'`	'M'			

The pupils who use the CompiSue website must be aged 11–13. Therefore, the Age field in the Pupil Data table can only contain values between 11 and 13.

How could we combine conditions to create a validation rule for this field?

We need two conditions:

Condition 1 : `>=11`

Condition 2 : `<=13`

Imagine the ages in the table below are entered for checking. If each condition is used individually, will only valid data be accepted? Look at the table below.

Condition used when data was entered into the Pupil Data table	Age entered into the Pupil Data table	Was the data accepted into the Pupil Data table?	Should the data have been accepted into the Pupil Data table?	Was the decision right or wrong?
>=11	10	No	No	right
>=11	55	Yes	No	wrong
>=11	12	Yes	Yes	right
<=13	13	Yes	Yes	right
<=13	5	Yes	No	wrong
<=13	18	No	No	right

From the completed table, you can see that invalid data is accepted if the conditions are used separately. They must be combined using AND.

When conditions are combined using AND, both of the conditions must be true to give an overall true, this allows only valid data to be accepted. The correct condition is:

`Age >=11 AND Age <=13`. This means that only ages 11, 12 and 13 will be accepted.

Practice

➤ Complete the table below which contains the correct condition for Age and check to see if the data from the original table is accepted.

Condition used when data was entered into the Pupil Data table	Age entered into the Pupil Data table	Was the data accepted into the Pupil Data table?	Should the data have been accepted into the Pupil Data table?	Was the decision right or wrong?
>=11 AND <=13	10			
>=11 AND <=13	55			
>=11 AND <=13	12			
>=11 AND <=13	13			
>=11 AND <=13	5			
>=11 AND <=13	18			

International Computing for Lower Secondary

Algorithmic thinking

Conditions are statements that can be true or false.

AND and OR can be used to combine a number of conditions.

Boolean logic is used to compare the statements in the condition and a **Boolean value** of true or false is returned after every comparison.

Discuss with a partner the difference between using AND in a condition and OR in a condition.

For example, what if Lan needs to identify:

- all of the pupils who are aged 12 AND whose hobby is Reading; there is one pupil

Username	Age	Hobby
Pupil141	12	Reading

- all of the pupils who are aged 12 OR whose hobby is Reading; there are five pupils

Username	Age	Hobby
Pupil123	11	Reading
Pupil127	11	Reading
Pupil134	13	Reading
Pupil135	11	Reading
Pupil141	12	Reading

> **KEYWORDS**
> **Boolean logic:** a form of algebra where all values are reduced to either true or false
> **Boolean value:** a data type which has one of two possible values, true or false

Together, complete the two tables below.

Condition 1: Age=12

Condition 2: Hobby='Reading'

Condition 1 is …	AND	Condition 2 is …	Overall
true	AND	true	true
true	AND	false	
false	AND	true	
false	AND	false	false

Condition 1 is …	OR	Condition 2 is …	Overall
true	OR	true	true
true	OR	false	
false	OR	true	
false	OR	false	false

Create a rule for AND conditions and a rule for OR conditions.

Using the AND operator we will get an overall outcome of true if both condition 1 and condition 2 are true, otherwise we will get an overall outcome of false.

Using the OR operator we will get an outcome of true if _____.

Unit 7.6 Data Mining: Using spreadsheets and databases

Creating validation rules

Learn

A **validation rule** is made up of conditions which can be entered into the database. This is done by selecting the field and typing the condition into the validation rule section, as shown below.

You can also enter validation text which will be displayed if an invalid value is entered. This text will help the user understand what is wrong with the value they have entered. It is a type of error message.

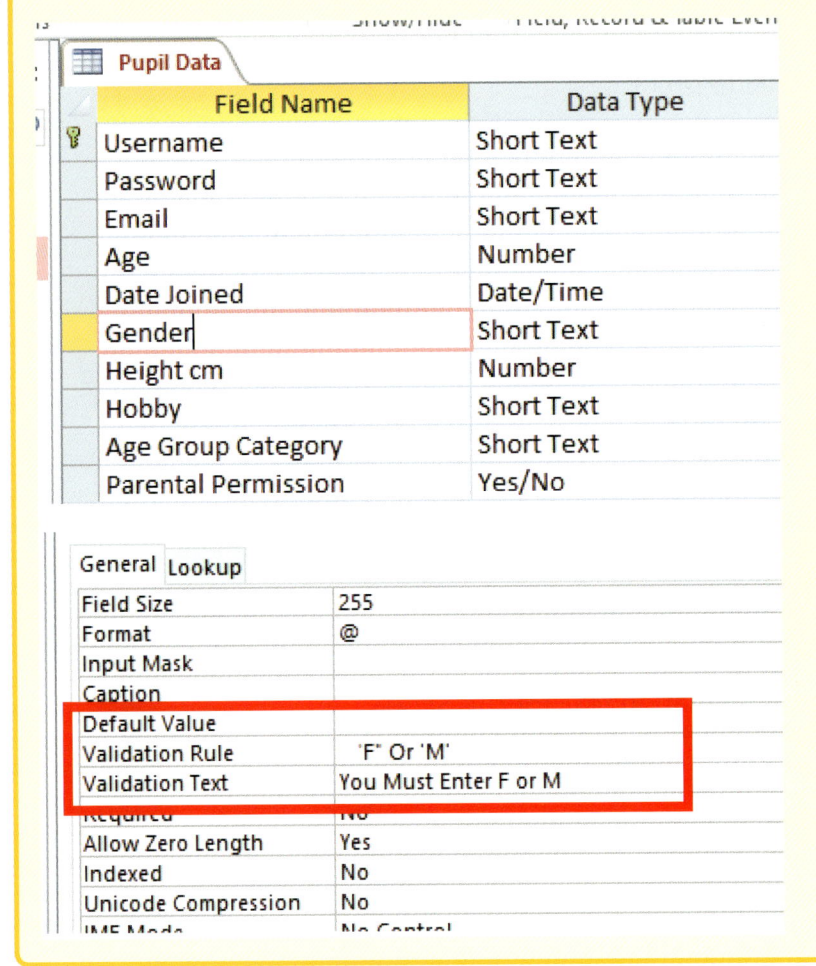

Field Name	Data Type
Username	Short Text
Password	Short Text
Email	Short Text
Age	Number
Date Joined	Date/Time
Gender	Short Text
Height cm	Number
Hobby	Short Text
Age Group Category	Short Text
Parental Permission	Yes/No

General | Lookup

Field Size	255
Format	@
Input Mask	
Caption	
Default Value	
Validation Rule	'F' Or 'M'
Validation Text	You Must Enter F or M
Required	No
Allow Zero Length	Yes
Indexed	No
Unicode Compression	No
IME Mode	No Control

KEYWORDS

validation rule: a rule which specifies the values that a data item can store

Len function: a function which will count the number of characters entered

DID YOU KNOW?

In the CompiSue website, all usernames must start with the word Pupil and have a number following this. For example, Pupil1 or Pupil123. So, the minimum length for a username is six characters. To carry out a Length check use the **Len function**. To check that the Username has more than 6 characters the validation rule would be:

`Len([Username])>6`

Note that there are square brackets [] around the field name.

A length check will ensure that the data entered is made up of a certain number of characters.

177

International Computing for Lower Secondary

Practice

- Open the database **CompiSue1.accdb**.
- Open the Pupil Data table in design view.
- Select the Gender field by clicking on it.
- Add the validation rule and validation text shown on page 177 to the Gender field so that only the values 'F' or 'M' can be entered.
- Select the Hobby field by clicking on it.
- Add a validation rule and validation text, in the general section below, to ensure that the Hobby field only contains valid values.
- Select the Username field by clicking on it.
- Add a validation rule and validation text, in the general section below, to check that the Username contains more than six characters.
- Select the Age field by clicking on it.
- Add a validation rule and suitable validation text, in the general section below, for the Age field so that only values between 11 and 13 can be entered.
- Close the Pupil Data table and save the changes.
- Open the Game Data table in design view.
- Select the Level Assigned field by clicking on it.
- Add a validation rule and validation text for the Level Assigned field so that only the values 'EXPERT' or 'NOVICE' can be entered.
- Select the Score field by clicking on it.
- Add a validation rule and suitable validation text for the Score field so that only values between 0 and 120 can be entered.
- Close the Pupil Data table and save the changes.

> A range check can be created using the key word BETWEEN or using inequalities. For example `Between 11 AND 13` or `>=11 AND <=13` will have the same effect.

Unit 7.6 Data Mining: Using spreadsheets and databases

Creating queries to analyse data

Learn

Queries are used to search through the database and select data based on criteria. **Criteria** are simply conditions.

Queries allow data to be extracted from the database and presented separately. They can provide summary data like totals and averages. Queries are a powerful feature of a database which will help Lan to select data for analysis. Examples of queries might be:

Query	Table used in query	Fields used in query	Criteria
List the Username, Email and DateJoined for all of the pupils aged 12	Pupil Data	Username DateJoined Age	Age = 12
List the Username and Age for all of the female pupils	Pupil Data	Username Age Gender	Gender='F'
List the Username and Age for all of the female pupils who like reading	Pupil Data	Username Age Gender Hobby	Gender='F' and Hobby='Reading'

KEYWORDS

queries: a feature of a database which allows the user to retrieve information from the tables based on criteria; the user can specify what fields are to be included in the results of the query

criteria: the values or rules used to compare and select data

Abstraction

When you query a database you are using abstraction because fields can be selected or omitted. We can hide data that we do not wish to see for the purpose of the query.

How could we design a query to list the Age, Username and Hobby of the pupils who are aged 12 AND whose hobby is Reading.

What fields should be included?

What conditions are needed?

What logical operator is needed? Refer back to page 173 to remind yourself.

Practice

- Lan wants to look at the data about female pupils who use the website. You are going to create a query which will list all of the female pupils in the table.
- Open the file **CompiSue1.accdb**.
  - Select the CREATE tab.

179

International Computing for Lower Secondary

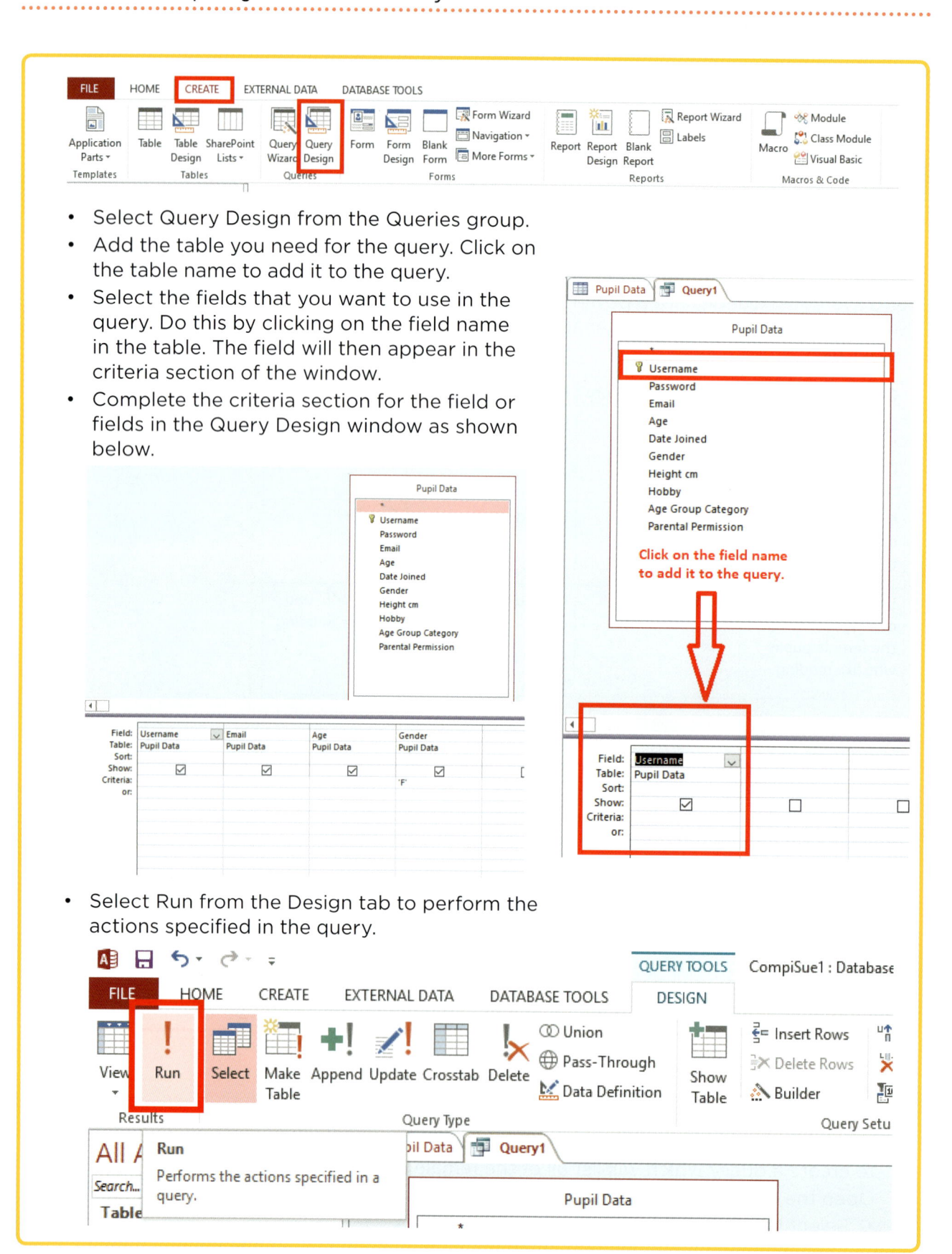

- Select Query Design from the Queries group.
- Add the table you need for the query. Click on the table name to add it to the query.
- Select the fields that you want to use in the query. Do this by clicking on the field name in the table. The field will then appear in the criteria section of the window.
- Complete the criteria section for the field or fields in the Query Design window as shown below.

Click on the field name to add it to the query.

- Select Run from the Design tab to perform the actions specified in the query.

Run — Performs the actions specified in a query.

Unit 7.6 Data Mining: Using spreadsheets and databases

- The records which meet the criteria will be shown as a datasheet.

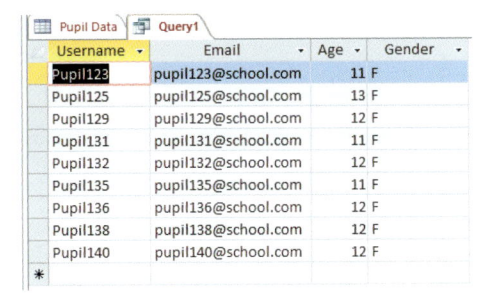

Username	Email	Age	Gender
Pupil123	pupil123@school.com	11	F
Pupil125	pupil125@school.com	13	F
Pupil129	pupil129@school.com	12	F
Pupil131	pupil131@school.com	11	F
Pupil132	pupil132@school.com	12	F
Pupil135	pupil135@school.com	11	F
Pupil136	pupil136@school.com	12	F
Pupil138	pupil138@school.com	12	F
Pupil140	pupil140@school.com	12	F

To save the query click on the icon to close the query and you will be prompted to save it

Abstraction

You will use abstraction to select data to be included in the results of the query and remove data which is not necessary. The results of queries can be used to help make decisions about changes to the website and to better understand what games and activities are most popular.

- Open your version of **CompiSue1.accdb**
- Open the PUPIL DATA table.
    - Create a query to list the Username, Email and DateJoined for all of the pupils over 12 years of age.
    - Run the query and review the results.
    - Save the query as Over12.

    Refer to page 180 to remind yourself about how to create a query.

- Create a query to list the Username and Age for all of the female pupils.
    - Run the query and review the results.
    - Save the query as FemaleData.
- Create a query to list the Username and Age for all of the female pupils who like reading.
    - Run the query and review the results.
    - Save the query as FemaleData2.
- Now use the GAME DATA table.
    - Create a query which will list the Username, Level Assigned and Rating for all of the pupils who have a score over 100 in the game called 'Abstraction2'.
    - Run the query and review the results.
    - Save the query as Over100.
- Create a query which will list the Session Number and the Device Type used for all games that have been completed using *Internet Explorer*.
    - Run the query and review the results.
    - Save the query as IEUsers.
- Create a query which will list the Username, the Date Taken and the Time Taken for all students who completed the game called 'Abstraction3'.
    - Run the query and review the results.
    - Save the query as AbstractTime.

International Computing for Lower Secondary

Go further

Creating queries which produce lists of information can be helpful. However, information which is well presented in a report layout is much more useful for Lan. You are going to create reports which Lan can use immediately and pass to other people in the team.

The data to be used for the reports will come from queries.

- Use the file **CompiSueRel.accdb**, provided by your teacher.
  - Open the Game Data table and select the Time Taken Minutes field.
  - Add a validation rule that will ensure that the number of minutes entered is between 1 and 59.
  - Add suitable validation text for the validation rule. The text should let the user know that the number of minutes should be between 1 and 59.
  - Create a query that will list the Username and Age Group Category for all pupils who do not have Parental Permission. In this case the criterion for the Parental Permission field should be set to No.
  - Save the query as NOPERMISSION.
  - Create a report using the data from the FemaleData query created earlier.
    - Select Report Wizard from the Reports group.
    - Add the table or query you need for the report. In this case FemaleData.
    - Add a grouping level if required. Grouping levels are not required for reports that use a simple query like FemaleData.
    - Select a sort order for the records. You can sort on any of the selected fields.
    - The wizard allows you to select layout options.
    - What layout would you like for your report? Select Tabular layout.
    - Change the orientation to landscape.
    - What title do you want for your report? Leave the title as FemaleData.
    - Do you want to preview the report or modify the report's design? Select Preview the report.
    - A report will be created.

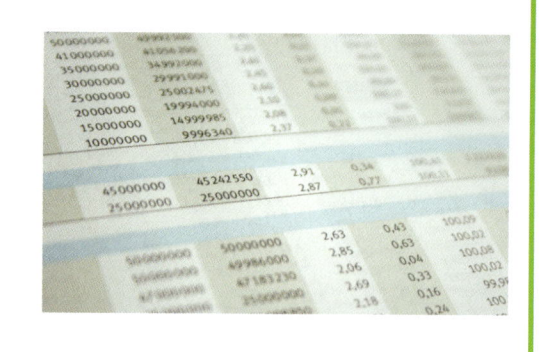

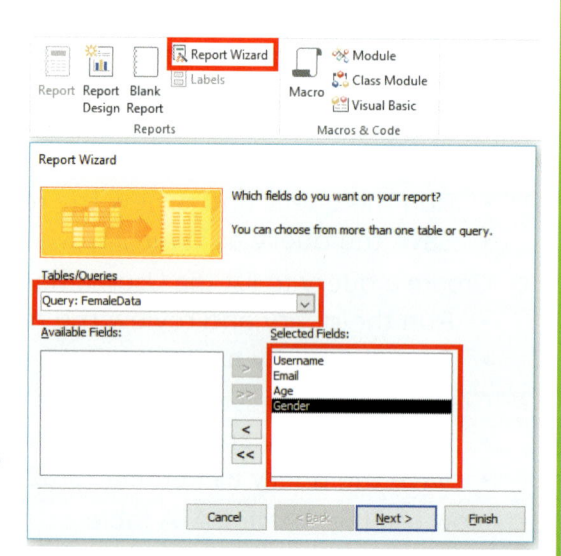

> The report design can be modified by selecting design view or layout view. Formatting and colour options can be used. There are special report features that allow data to be summarised.

Unit 7.6 Data Mining: Using spreadsheets and databases

- Create a report using the NOPERMISSION query to show Lan which pupils should not be using the website.
  Select the CREATE tab.
  Select Report from the Reports group as shown.
  Select the NOPERMISSION query as input to the report.
  Follow all the steps in the wizard

> The report design can be modified by selecting design view or layout view. Formatting and colour options can be used. There are special report features that allow data to be summarised.

- Show your report to a friend and discuss how the changes you have made to the layout make the report easier to read. Think about layout, orientation, title font and colour.

International Computing for Lower Secondary

> **Challenge yourself**
>
> You have learnt how to use tables, reports, queries and forms. You will now learn how to use input masks to ensure data is entered in the correct format. An input mask will check to ensure that data conforms to a set pattern when it is entered.
>
> There is a set of **input mask definition characters**. For now we only need to know two:
>
> 0 means that the user MUST enter a number in that position.
>
> L means that the user MUST enter a letter in that position.
>
> - Open **CompiSueRel.accdb**
> - Open the Pupil Data Table in datasheet view
> - Look at the password for a pupil and write down a 0 when you see a number and an L when you see a letter.
>
> > [Password for Pupil123 is 09RT980E = 00LL000L. You have worked out the input mask for the Password!]
>
> The '>' symbol will make sure that any letters input are changed to capitals. This means that all of the letters will be converted to capital letters even if the user enters them as small letters. This ensures that the data in the Password field will be in the same format for every pupil.
>
> - Open the Pupil Data table in design view and select the Password field. In the input mask section of the properties, enter the following code `>00LL000L`
>
>   **KEYWORD**
>
>   **input mask definition characters:** placeholder characters used in input masks; for example, 0 is the placeholder for a number

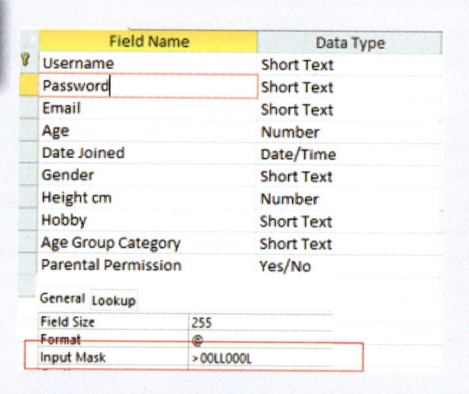

Unit 7.6 Data Mining: Using spreadsheets and databases

Final project

CompiSue is delighted with the work your company has completed for Lan. It is going to employ coaches for the online activities and it wants to hold the data about the coaches in the database. A table called Coach Data has been created for you by a work colleague. However, you are required to edit that table and create queries using the data in the table.

➤ Open the database file called **CompiSueCoach.accdb**, provided by your teacher.
➤ Lan wants to ensure that the data in the table is valid and correct. So you must add validation rules.
  - Create a validation rule for the YearsExperience field so that all values entered are between 0 and 4.
  - Add suitable validation text for the YearsExperience field.
  - Create a validation rule for the Surname field so that all values entered have a length of at least seven characters. Use the Len function.
  - Add suitable validation text for the Surname field.
  - Create a validation rule for the Gender field so that only 'F' or 'M' will be accepted.
  - Add suitable validation text for the Gender field.
  - Test your validation rules by adding 3 new records to the table.
➤ Analysing the Coach Data is important so Lan has asked you to create the following queries.
  - Create a query which will list the names and Date of Birth of all the coaches who have more than one year experience. Call the query CoachExperience.
  - Create a query which will list all the male coaches who have more than two years experience. Call the query MaleCoach.
  - Add a new field to the table called FitnessChecked. This field will tell Lan whether or not the coach has undertaken a fitness check.
  - Check the FitnessChecked field for any three of the coaches.
  - Create a query which will list the names and email addresses of all the male coaches who have had a fitness check. Call the query FitnessCheck.

Evaluation

➤ Discuss with your partner two other queries that could be created using the data in the Coach Data table. Write down:
  o what data (fields) would be included in the queries
  o what information would be provided by the queries.
➤ After you have made the changes to the tables and created the queries ask a friend to test the validation rules and queries. They should comment on:
  o how well the validation rule works
  o how informative the validation text is
  o the accuracy of your results when running queries
  o what recommendations they would make to improve your database.

Definition check: Close your book and make a list of as many terms you have learned in this unit as you can. Compare them with your partner's list. Together try to define as many of them as you can. Check your definitions against the definitions given in the key word boxes.

Glossary

Key Term Definition

abstraction focusing on important details only and ignoring irrelevant detail which does not help produce a solution

accessibility providing features which will assist those who have impairments or disabilities

actuator a part of a system that is responsible for moving; for example, a robotic arm

algorithm a computer program used to find patterns in the data accessed by a user to make predictions about similar articles/websites they might be interested in viewing; uses an element of machine learning and artificial intelligence

algorithm step-by-step instructions, which when followed will solve a problem

alignment text alignment is a feature which enables users to place text horizontally on the page either to the left, right or centre

app short for application; referring to software applications often available on portable digital devices such as mobile phones

application a computer program designed for an end user; for example, child, teenager, adult

application suites a collection of computer programs with a similar user interface that can easily support the exchange of data between each program

array another term for a list

artificial intelligence (AI) an area of computing which focuses on creating intelligent computers which can mimic the way humans think and make decisions; a computer system able to perform tasks normally done using human intelligence, such as understanding speech

assignment the process of assigning a data value to a variable name

big data extremely large amounts of data that are analysed to show patterns in things such as human behaviour and use of technology

bit the smallest amount of data a computer can store, represented as either 0 or 1

bitmap graphics graphics produced using a rectangular grid of pixels

Boolean expression a statement or expression which, when tested, produces a result of only either TRUE or FALSE

Boolean logic a form of algebra where all values are reduced to either true or false

Boolean value a data type which has one of two possible values, true or false

carbon monoxide a poisonous gas which is odourless and flammable

Cascading Style Sheets (CSS) a language used to describe how the content of a HTML document will be presented

cell an area where a row and column intersect and data can be entered

cell formatting used to control the way in which data is displayed in a cell

cell range a set of cells on a spreadsheet identified by specifying the first and last cells; for example, A1:A10 is a cell range identifying all the cells between cell A1 to cell A10

cell reference made up of a letter and number representing the column and row of a cell

characters individual letters or numbers such as A, B, 1, or @

chart a graphical representation of the data

chart feature this feature allows the user to select data and automatically creates a chart or graph of the data

click bait a headline that may not be entirely true or truly reflect the contents of the article it leads to, but which is designed to encourage a reader to access that link

client the person or organisation who requested the app and who will pay for it

closed user group a method of restricting access to a network or communication group by providing only those authorised with a username and password

cloud a network of remote servers on the internet used to store and process data transmitted from IoT devices

cloud based application a software program which is accessed using a web browser and the internet but where processing is carried out on servers held in another location

Glossary

cloud services applications made available to a user using internet based technology and a web browser

cloud storage a network of remote servers on the internet used to store and process data transmitted from IoT devices

colour depth a measure of the number of bits used to represent colour in individual pixels in an image

command line interface (CLI) a user interface which requires the user to enter commands at a prompt to operate it

comparison operator operators that compare values and return true or false. The operators include: >, <, >=, <=

complex problem a problem which is made up of many smaller problems

composite navigation structure which uses a combination of approaches

compound conditional the use of logical operators to combine conditions before deciding if a block of code needs to be executed

compression the removal of some unnecessary data to help reduce the amount of storage taken up by a file

condition a statement which evaluates to true or false; for example, x<10 is an example of a condition; if x is equal to 11, the condition will evaluate to false

conditional statements used to make decisions about running lines of code; the decision is based upon testing a condition. If the condition is true the lines of code within the 'if statement' will be carried out. But if the condition is false the lines of code are not carried out

content resizing a feature which allows the user to select the size of the text or images on the screen

copyright laws laws put in place which make it illegal to copy someone else's work without their permission

criteria the values or rules used to compare and select data

cross-platform allows a document or file or application to be opened using a variety of combinations of hardware and software

customised modified to suit individual preferences or needs

cyberattacks any attempt by hackers to cause damage to a computer system

data the words and values contained on the spreadsheet; these are raw facts and figures that, on their own, have no meaning; for example, the number 10 has no meaning on its own but if we say 10 cm it becomes a length

data analysis the process of collecting, reviewing and applying calculations to data to help identify patterns and trends in the data

data filters a tool used to remove unwanted data

data item information processed or stored by a computer

data type the type of data to be stored; for example, number and text

data type (more information) each field has a data type, such as currency (which stores money values) or Yes/No (sometimes called Boolean, which can only take on one of two values such as a Yes or No question)

data validation an automatic check to ensure the data input is acceptable

datasheet view a feature of a database which allows the user to view all of the data in the form of a table

debug the process of identifying and removing errors from a computer program

denial of service an attack on a computer system which stops authorised users from accessing it

design view a feature of the database which allows you to view the field names and data type of the fields in the table; validation rules and validation text can be inserted in this view

digital assets any digital resources used to create an application; it is any text or multimedia files saved in binary format

digital data computers can only understand digital data; any data to be processed has to be turned into digital data so that the device can understand it; this data can be one of two values, '1' or '0'

digital footprint the data that exist about you as a result of online interactions and activities

digital solution a digital artefact made from instructions for a computer to solve a problem

download speed the speed at which data is downloaded from the internet usually measured in bits per second

embed the process of inserting a file created with one application into a file created by another application

ethernet cable high speed cable used to connect devices on a network over short distances

ethically acting in an honest and principled way

executed when code is translated to be run by the computer's processor

external aerials receive information about the car's current location so that routes can be followed

external hyperlinks hyperlinks which when clicked on take the user to a resource on another website

feedback a message or information about an action or event; for example, increased score in a game

International Computing for Lower Secondary

fibre optic cable cable which consists of one or more strands of glass used to transmit data using pulses of light along long distances

field a single piece of data about one person or one thing

field names users can select names for fields; for example, Username is a field name used in the Pupil Data table. It tells us what the pupil's username is for logging on to the website

filter bubble often generated because of artificial intelligence (AI) algorithms which predict the sites/articles a user would be interested in based on those previously accessed; can limit the formation of broad opinions and ideas

flash memory cards a storage device that uses non-volatile electronic memory to store data; cameras, for example, use these devices

flowchart a graphical representation of a solution to a problem which uses special symbols

font the style and size of the text; this can be selected by the user

forever block an indefinite loop where tasks repeat until the end of the game

format the way in which data is displayed on the spreadsheet; for example, a number could be formatted as currency, where a $ symbol and two decimal places are added and then made bold – the number 45 would appear as **$45.00**

formatting applying special features to a document to improve appearance, such as bold, italic, bullet points and so on

formula used to perform calculations in cells; for example, A2 + A3 will add the contents of the cells A2 and A3

formula bar the location on the spreadsheet window where the formula is entered

formula view the spreadsheet shows the formula used in each cell rather than the data

free to share material presented electronically which is available for users to share freely with others

function a routine that performs a set of operations and produces a single output; for example, the SUM function will add up all the numbers in a given cell range

functionality how well an application completes the tasks it is expected to complete

gateway a physical device or software program that is the connection for the cloud, sensors and intelligent devices

General Data Protection Regulation (GDPR) a law which protects the personal data and privacy of citizens

gestures actions on a touch screen which allow people to interact with smart phones; for example, swipe down

global positioning system (GPS) a satellite based navigation system that provides location details

Google Sheets a cloud based spreadsheet application

GPS receivers a device which works to locate four or more satellites and then uses a process called trilateration to calculate the distance to each; it uses this information to calculate its own location

graphical user interface (GUI) a user interface which makes use of windows, icons, menus and pointers on a screen; it is suitable for inexperienced users

hacker anyone gaining unauthorised access to a computer system

hard disk drive (HDD) a form of external memory which permanently stores data

hierarchical a navigation structure which allows the user to move around the application one branch at a time, from top to bottom

home page the first page to be launched when a website is loaded by a web browser

humidity the amount of water vapour present in air

hyperlink a word, phrase or image that once clicked on will take the user to another location, page, website, or open a document linked to the current file

HyperText Markup Language (HTML) the language used to create documents which can be published on the world wide web

IF statement perform an action on the spreadsheet based on a condition

image optimisation reducing file size without losing image quality

infographic a visual representation of information or data

informed consent permission given when the individual knows exactly how the data will be used

input data which is entered into a computer using a device such a keyboard, mouse, touch screen, joystick, and so on

input mask definition characters placeholder characters used in input masks; for example, 0 is the placeholder for a number

Glossary

input masks controls the layout or format of data entered; characters and numbers will have a set order

insider threats employees of an organisation misuse their authorised access to data in some way; for example, passing client data on to a competitor

interactive allowing two way flow of information between the device and the user; an application which accepts input from the user

interactive multimedia application an application which incorporates a range of media, including text, images, animation, video and sound

internal hyperlinks hyperlinks which when clicked on take the user to a resource on the same website

internet an interconnected network or networks with a global reach

Internet of Things (IoT) a network of smart devices connected to the internet

internet router a hardware device that can connect a local network to the internet

internet service provider (ISP) a company which provides services to support internet access, for example companies which provide broadband access, mobile phone and 4G or 5G services

intranet a private network used mainly by the members of an organisation

iteration a code construct that repeats code many times in a loop

kiosk presentation/application a presentation which runs unattended by a speaker; it may contain hyperlinks to allow the person viewing it some element of control over its operation

latency the delay between a request being sent and the request being processed

Len function a function which will count the number of characters entered

length check checks that the data input contains a particular number of characters

LiDAR works on the same principle as radar but uses lasers instead

linear a navigation structure which allows the user to view contents of a file or pages in a document one after another

list a data structure that allows us to store more than one variable

live streams using the internet to provide live video or audio from an event as it is happening

load times a measure of the time taken to download and display the entire contents of a web page

logic flowchart a diagram which shows the choices and pathways available to a user on each screen in an application

logical operator words such as AND and OR which are used to combine two or more conditions

look up lists a set of data contained in a list; the user selects the value from the list provided on screen

loop a feature of a programming language that allows for sections of code to be repeated

lossless compression a method of reducing file size of a graphic which does not result in loss of image quality

lossy compression a method of reducing file size of a graphic which results in some loss of image quality

machine learning software that enables artificial intelligence (AI) systems to automatically learn and improve from past experiences without being programmed to do so; the computer programs access data and then use it to learn things for themselves

mapping services a feature on the web which allows you to develop an online map

marketing actions and activities taken by a company to gain customers, promote and sell products

Mbps megabits per second; a unit of measurement for transmitting data

megapixel one megapixel is one million pixels

metadata data about data

motion sensor a device that detects moving objects

navigation links hyperlinks which allow users to move from one web page to another

navigation structure the way individual pages or screens in an application are linked to allow the user to move through an application

non-linear a navigation structure which allows the user to navigate a file visiting pages in any order

non-volatile data in memory is retained when the computer is switched off

output data which is produced by a computer program and made available to the user via a device such as a screen, speaker, printer, and so on

page transition a special effect which shows the change from one page in an application to another; for example, pages can dissolve into each other

parameter a special kind of variable used to pass data between procedures

phone-led where access to something is led by your phone (or apps you access on your phone) rather than decisions you have made

pick up game a game which requires the user to navigate around a screen and collect objects in order to score points

pixel short for picture element; refers to the individual dots used to make up an image or display on a computer screen

predictive maintenance continuously monitoring equipment to ensure that it is repaired before it breaks down

presence check checks to ensure that a field has not been left blank; that is, that there is data entered for a particular field

primary key a field that uniquely identifies a record

privacy policies a legal document that explains how an organisation collects and uses an individual's data

procedure a set of coded instructions used to tell a computer how to carry out a process; sometimes called function or sub program

profile a collection of in-depth information collected about an individual online

protect sheet the cells on a spreadsheet can be protected to prevent other users from accidentally or deliberately changing, moving, or deleting data using a password; users need to enter this password if they want to make changes to the worksheet

protocol a set of rules which govern the way in which data is transferred around a network

push notifications a message which appears on an app to let you know something new has occurred

queries a feature of a database which allows the user to retrieve information from the tables based on criteria; the user can specify what fields are to be included in the results of the query

radar sensor a system which uses radio waves to determine range or distance

random access memory (RAM) a volatile storage medium; loses any information it is holding when the power is turned off

range the distance within which a device must be to send and receive data

raw data data collected from a source, such as the CompiSue website, which has not been processed or changed in any way

reach the number of people who visit a web page

read only memory (ROM) a non-volatile storage medium; does not require a constant source of power to retain the information stored on it

real-time data data which is processed immediately after collecting

record a collection of related fields; for example, one record in the table PUPIL contains information about one pupil

remote server a server which is accessed by users across the internet

repetition repeating a section of a program or app a number of times or until a particular criterion is met; it allows for looping in an app

resistive (touch screen) is made of two transparent layers of glass or plastic; when pressure is applied the top layer bends and touches the bottom layer and a current flows between the layers

resolution a measure of the quality of an image (or the amount of detail a camera can capture); relates to the number of pixels used to create an image – the greater the number of pixels, the better the quality of the image

review a tab on the spreadsheet software which contains editing features and the protect sheet feature; these features make it easy to keep data secure

rich text format (RTF) documents which contain additional information about font style, size, images which allows the document to be shared cross-platform

satellites an object which orbits the earth which can transmit communication signals across the globe

school network computers linked together through a main computer using cables or Wi-Fi; computers can share printers and the main computer will store users' data

script lines of code which determine how objects, such as sprites, move and interact with each other on screen

search engine a program which can be used to access information on the world wide web by taking key words entered by the user and searching for websites containing those key words

search engine optimisation (SEO) steps taken by organisations to help increase the number of visitors to their website

selection a programming construct with more than one possible pathway; a condition is tested (using a question or criterion) before deciding which pathway to follow (which parts of the program or app will be executed next)

sensor a device which detects and measures a physical property, for example, the temperature in a room, sound intensity or motion activity

sequencing lines of code often carried out one after another

Glossary

server a computer in a network, which manages processing and access to resources for other users

smart devices an electronic device that is able to connect, communicate and share data with other devices via a network

social media websites and apps where users can create and share their own multimedia content

social media harvesting collecting data from social media sites to help identify trends in news stories, often done using algorithms

social media influencer an individual with a large following on social media whose online posts can influence opinions or decisions

solid state drive (SSD) a form of permanent storage which has no moving parts and operates much faster than a traditional hard drive

sound bites short extracts from a longer piece of audio recording

spelling and grammar checker a software tool which can be used to check the spelling and grammar in a word processed document; suggested corrections can be provided and users can build up a dictionary of specialised terms

spreadsheet a software application which can be used to organise and store data and which allows analysis of data using formulas

sprite an image in a Scratch project that can be changed or moved (such as a skateboard image)

stage area on a Scratch project where the game is created and displayed

subscript a letter or figure which is written below a standard line of text (the opposite is superscript where a letter or figure is written above a standard line of text)

SUM a function which will add up all the numbers in a given cell range; for example, SUM(A1:A10) will add up all the values in cells A1 through to A10

surf (the internet) the process of navigating through content on the world wide web by following hyperlinks on web pages

switch a device that can take many signals from lots of devices and organise them so they can travel down one single communication line

tab used to give a name to a worksheet

table a collection of related records; for example, the table PUPIL contains records about individual pupils

tags hidden key words in a web page which tell the browser how to display the content on the page

target audience the group of people at which the app or program is aimed

terabytes 1000 gigabytes

test plan a document which describes the areas of an application to be tested; includes details of the tests to be applied to each area of the application, including test data and expected results

text file a file which contains lines of plain text with no graphics or formatting

touch target size the size of the area on the screen which is set aside for tapping an item

transitions an effect used in an animation or a movie to help make the change from one scene or slide to another more subtle to the viewer; for example, dissolving between scenes

transparency a tool which edits the appearance of images in a digital document to allow the image to appear as though it is blending into the background

trending a topic which is currently popular online

ultrasonic sensor a device that can measure the distance to an object by using sound waves

uniform resource locator (URL) an address which tells browsers where to locate individual resources on the world wide web

universal serial bus (USB) a technology for connecting peripherals to a computer

usability how easy to use an application is

user interactions describes how a user can provide instructions to a program and receive information from a program

user interface sometimes called the UI; it is every part of the system with which the user can interact

user requirements a list of tasks and features that the software must provide, and that a user would expect the software to do; it is created in agreement with the client who is paying for the development of the app

user stories a description of what the app will do from the user's point of view

validation ensures that data entered into the table meets certain criteria; it cannot ensure that the data is accurate; for example, an age between 11 and 13 may be entered but that age may not be correct for the pupil

validation rule a rule which specifies the values that a data item can store

values data or numbers used in the spreadsheet

variable a stored value which can change during the execution of a program

variable declaration the process of creating a variable by giving it a name and in some programming languages a data type

vector graphics graphics made up from a series of objects placed on a computer screen

video cameras keep track of the vehicles and look out for pedestrians and obstacles on the road; they are also used to detect traffic lights

visual feedback output from the system which allows the user to see what is happening and to react accordingly

voice recognition software software which can process voice commands and execute them on a device or computer

volatile data in memory is lost when the computer is switched off

walled garden virtual fence put in place, often by an internet service provider (ISP), to make it difficult to access material which displays a certain opinion or set of facts

web browser a software application which allows users to locate, access and display information on the world wide web; interprets HTML code and displays the web page content

web server a computer which manages resources on a network and acts as a central storage place for resources on a network

web space the amount of space on a computer's hard disk used to store your web pages and multimedia content which makes up your web space

website source code the HTML code which is used to control the layout of any online web page

website traffic the number of web users who visit a site

white space unused space on screen or on a document, used to separate out parts of a document such as images, paragraphs, bullet points

Wi-Fi a wireless networking technology which transmits data using radio signals

wireframes a drawing or graphic which displays the design of a screen in an app or program

worksheet a single page in a spreadsheet file

wrap text a formatting tool which allows text to scroll around the outside edges of an image on a word processed document

Index

Numbers
4G 12
5G 13

A
abstraction 6, 15, 36, 74, 92, 136
accessibility 52
actuators 22, 23
algorithmic development 6, 36, 94
algorithms 44, 61, 62
analytics 15
animation 90–2
app development 35–7
  accessibility 52
  data collection 40–1
  evaluation 55
  feedback collection 47
  interactivity and gestures 51–3
  selection 48–50, 54
  structure charts 42–4
  target audience 37–8
  user interfaces 40, 44–5
  user requirements 42
  user stories 38–9
  wireframes 46–7
applications (apps) 34, 87
application suites 115
arrays 111, 112
artificial intelligence (AI) 4, 8
assignment 100
audio files 74

B
Berners-Lee, Tim 66
big data 4
bitmap graphics 71–2, 73, 74–5
Bluetooth 12
Boole, George 98
Boolean expressions 97–9
Boolean logic 176

C
capacitive touch screens 17
Cascading Style Sheets (CSS) 56
  see also style, HTML

cell formatting 151–2
cell ranges 153
cell references 150
cells 148
central heating control systems 22
charts 158–9
click bait 63
clients 42
closed user groups 68
cloud based applications 115–16
  pros and cons 118
cloud services 119
cloud storage 9, 14, 21
colour depth 71–2
colours, HTML 75, 80
command line interfaces (CLIs) 44–5
comments 92
comparison operators 162–3, 166
complex problems 34
composite navigation 133
compound conditional statements 98–9
compression 73
computational thinking 6, 34
computer science 4
conditional statements 97–9
  spreadsheets 162–3, 166
conditions 97
  Boolean logic 176
  validation rules 173–5
content resizing 52
copyright laws 127
criteria 179
cross-platform apps 122
cyberattacks 118

D
data 148
data analysis 131
databases 167–8
  evaluation 185
  input masks 184
  queries 179–82, 185
  reports 182–4
  tables 169–78

data collection   40–1
data filters   131
data storage   20–1
data types   148, 170
data validation   168
debugging   87, 91–2
decomposition   6, 26, 36, 43, 83, 101
denial of service   118
digital assets   56
digital cameras   18, 19
digital data   8
digital footprints   10
digital literacy   4
digital solutions   87
document creation   120–30
download speeds   12, 13
driverless cars   27, 28

E

embedding   75
ethernet cables   68
ethical actions   41
evaluation   6, 33, 36
external hyperlinks   75

F

fake news   57–9, 65
feedback   87
   collection   47
   sound   52
   visual   51
fibre optic cables   68
field names   168
fields   168
filter bubbles   61
filters   165
flash memory cards   20
flowcharts   48–50, 54, 94, 103
fonts   123
forever blocks   90
format of data   148
formatting cells   151–2
formatting documents   120–6
formula bar   153, 157
formulas   129–30, 148
   spreadsheets   153–7
free to share material   126

functionality testing   144
functions   153

G

game development
   Scratch   87–8, 90–114
   user requirements and target audiences   89
gateways   14
General Data Protection Regulation (GDPR)   40
generalisation   6, 36
gestures   51–2
global positioning system (GPS)   31
Google Apps   119
Google Docs   120–30
Google Sheets   130–1
Google Slides   134–6
grammar checks   124
graphical user interfaces (GUIs)   45
graphs   158–9

H

hackers   118
hard disk drives (HDDs)   20
headers and footers   128–9
hierarchical navigation   132
home pages   79
home security   23
hyperlinks   58, 75, 137–9
HyperText Markup Language (HTML)   56, 75–9
   multimedia files   81–2
   style   80–1

I

'if' statements *see* conditional statements
image editing   129
image optimisation   73
infographics   10
information technology   4
informed consent   40
input   87
input masks   168, 173, 184
'insert' toolbar   126, 129
insider threats   118
interactive multimedia applications   115
interactivity   51–2
internal hyperlinks   75
internet   8, 68, 69
Internet of Things (IoT)   8–10

Index

commercial uses 25–6
functions of IoT devices 16–17
hardware 18–19
home uses 22–3
how it connects devices 12–14
transport 27–30
internet routers 68
internet service providers (ISPs) 61
intranets 68–9
iteration (loops) 49–50, 90

J

journalism, social media influence 63
    see also news sites

K

keyboards 16
kiosk presentations/applications 116–17, 140

L

latency 13
Len function 177
length checks 168, 173
Library of Congress 168
linear navigation 132
lists 111–12
live streams 58
load times 73
logical operators 98, 173
logic flowcharts 132–3
look up lists 173
loops (iteration) 49–50, 90
lossy and lossless compression 73

M

machine learning 4
mapping services 13
marketing 149
Mbps (megabits per second) 13
megapixels 19
memory 20
metadata 76
mobile technology 12
motion gaming 13
motion sensors 22, 23
movement management, Scratch 93–6, 101–3
multimedia files 71–4
    on web pages 81–2

N

navigational links 137–9
navigation structure 132–3
Near-Field Communication (NFC) 12
news algorithm 62
news sites 57–60
    associated problems 61
    fake news 65
    social media influence 63
non-linear navigation 132

O

output 106

P

page transitions 132
parameters 108
passwords 161
pattern recognition 6, 15, 74, 96
phone-led access 59
pick up games 88
pixels 19, 71–2
predictive maintenance 25–6
predictive text 124
presence checks 168, 173
presentations 116–17, 140–1
    adding a quiz 142–3
    document creation 120–30
    evaluation 147
    navigational links 137–9
    navigation structure 132–3
    slide presentations 134–6
    spreadsheets 130–1
    test plans 144–5
primary keys 170–1
privacy policies 40
procedures 87, 108–9
profiles 41
protocols 14
pseudocode 99, 101
push notifications 59

Q

queries 179–82, 185
quizzes 142–3

R

Radio Frequency Identification (RFID) 12
random access memory (RAM) 20
range 12, 13
raw data 149
reach 56
read only memory (ROM) 20
real-time data 27, 28
records 169
remote servers 118
repetition 49–50
reports 182–4
resistive touch screens 17
resolution 19
rich text format (RTF) documents 122–3
robotic arms 23–4

S

satellites 68
school networks 9
score keeping 104–5
Scratch 87–8
   animation 90–2
   conditional statements 98–9
   keeping score 104–5
   lists 111–12
   movement management 93–6, 101–3
   procedures 108–9
   user input 106–7
   variables 101–3
scripts 90
search engine optimisation (SEO) 67
search engines 57
searches 126–7
selection 48–50, 54
sensors 12, 13, 14
   user interfaces 16–17, 40, 44–5
sequencing 90
servers 118
slide presentations 134–6
   navigational links 137–9
smart cities 27, 29–30
smart devices 8, 10
   see also Internet of Things
smart phones 10, 17, 19, 22
smart shelves 26

social media, impact on journalism 63
social media harvesting 63
social media influencers 63
solid state drives (SSDs) 20
sorting data 165
sound bites 58
spell checks 124
spreadsheets 130–1, 148, 150
   charts 158–9
   comparison operators 162–3, 166
   evaluation 167
   formatting cells 151–2
   formulas and functions 153–7, 164
   protect sheet 161
   sorting and filters 165
   summary data 159–60, 166
sprites 88, 90
stages 93
style, HTML 80–1
subscripts 130
SUM function 153
summary data 159–60, 166
surfing the internet 58
switches 68

T

tables 169–73
   data validation 173–5
   validation rules 177–8, 185
tables of contents 129
tags 75
target audience 37–8, 89
terabytes 20
test plans 144–5
text files 120–1
touch screens 16, 17
touch target size 52
traffic management 27
transitions 140
transparencies 129
trending topics 63

U

uniform resource locators (URLs) 66–8
universal series bus (USB) 20
usability testing 144
user input 106–7

Index

user interactions 87
user interfaces (UIs) 16, 40, 44–5
user requirements 42, 89
user stories 38–9

V

validation 173–5
validation rules 177–8, 185
variable declarations 100, 102
variables 100–3
vector graphics 72–3
video files 73–4
visual feedback 51
voice recognition software 16
volatile and non-volatile data 20

W

walled gardens 61
wearable technologies 23, 24
web browsers 57
web servers 66
website development 75–86
website source code 56
website traffic 67
web space 73
white space 140
Wi-Fi 12, 68
wireframes 34, 46–7
wireless technologies 12
worksheets 151
wrap text 126